D0843379

INTERNATIONAL POLITICAL ECONOMY SERIES

General Editor: Timothy M. Shaw, Professor of Political Science and International Development Studies, and Director of the Centre for Foreign Policy Studies, Dalhousie University, Nova Scotia, Canada

Recent titles include:

Manuel R. Agosin and Diana Tussie (*editors*)
TRADE AND GROWTH: NEW DILEMMAS IN TRADE POLICY

Mahvash Alerassool
FREEZING ASSETS: THE USA AND THE MOST EFFECTIVE ECONOMIC SANCTION

Robert Boardman
POST-SOCIALIST WORLD ORDERS: RUSSIA, CHINA AND THE UN SYSTEM

Richard P. C. Brown
PUBLIC DEBT AND PRIVATE WEALTH

Jerker Carlsson, Gunnar Köhlin and Anders Ekbom
THE POLITICAL ECONOMY OF EVALUATION

Edward A. Comor (*editor*)
THE GLOBAL POLITICAL ECONOMY OF COMMUNICATION

O. P. Dwivedi
DEVELOPMENT ADMINISTRATION: FROM UNDERDEVELOPMENT TO SUSTAINABLE DEVELOPMENT

Steen Folke, Niels Fold and Thyge Enevoldsen
SOUTH–SOUTH TRADE AND DEVELOPMENT

Anthony Tuo-Kofi Gadzey
THE POLITICAL ECONOMY OF POWER

Betty J. Harris
THE POLITICAL ECONOMY OF THE SOUTHERN AFRICAN PERIPHERY

Jacques Hersh
THE USA AND THE RISE OF EAST ASIA SINCE 1945

Bahgat Korany, Paul Noble and Rex Brynen (*editors*)
THE MANY FACES OF NATIONAL SECURITY IN THE ARAB WORLD

Howard P. Lehman
INDEBTED DEVELOPMENT

Matthew Martin
THE CRUMBLING FAÇADE OF AFRICAN DEBT NEGOTIATIONS

Paul Mosley (*editor*)
DEVELOPMENT FINANCE AND POLICY REFORM

Tony Porter
STATES, MARKETS AND REGIMES IN GLOBAL FINANCE

Stephen P. Riley (*editor*)
THE POLITICS OF GLOBAL DEBT

Alfredo C. Robles, Jr
FRENCH THEORIES OF REGULATION AND CONCEPTIONS OF
  THE INTERNATIONAL DIVISION OF LABOUR

Ann Seidman and Robert B. Seidman
STATE AND LAW IN THE DEVELOPMENT PROCESS

Timothy M. Shaw and Julius Emeka Okolo (*editors*)
THE POLITICAL ECONOMY OF FOREIGN POLICY IN ECOWAS

Frederick Stapenhurst
POLITICAL RISK ANALYSIS AROUND THE NORTH ATLANTIC

Deborah Stienstra
WOMEN'S MOVEMENTS AND INTERNATIONAL ORGANIZATIONS

Larry A. Swatuk and Timothy M. Shaw (*editors*)
THE SOUTH AT THE END OF THE TWENTIETH CENTURY

Arno Tausch (with Fred Prager)
TOWARDS A SOCIO-LIBERAL THEORY OF WORLD DEVELOPMENT

Nancy Thede and Pierre Beaudet (*editors*)
A POST-APARTHEID SOUTHERN AFRICA?

Peter Utting
ECONOMIC REFORM AND THIRD-WORLD SOCIALISM

Sandra Whitworth
FEMINISM AND INTERNATIONAL RELATIONS

Asian Industrialization and Africa

Studies in Policy Alternatives to Structural Adjustment

Edited by

Howard Stein
Associate Professor of Economics
Roosevelt University, Chicago

St. Martin's Press

First published in Great Britain 1995 by
MACMILLAN PRESS LTD
Houndmills, Basingstoke, Hampshire RG21 2XS
and London
Companies and representatives
throughout the world

A catalogue record for this book is available
from the British Library.

ISBN 0–333–59147–X

10   9   8   7   6   5   4   3   2   1
04   03   02   01   00   99   98   97   96   95

Printed in Great Britain by
Ipswich Book Co Ltd, Ipswich, Suffolk

First published in the United States of America 1995 by
Scholarly and Reference Division,
ST. MARTIN'S PRESS, INC.,
175 Fifth Avenue,
New York, N.Y. 10010

ISBN 0–312–12433–3

Library of Congress Cataloging-in-Publication Data
Asian industrialization and Africa : studies in policy alternatives to
structural adjustment / edited by Howard Stein.
p.   cm.
Includes bibliographical references.
ISBN 0–312–12433–3
1. Industrial promotion—Asia, Southeastern.   2. Industrial
policy—Asia, Southeastern.   3. Industrial promotion—East Asia.
4. Industrial policy—East Asia.   5. Industrial policy—Africa.
6. Africa—Economic policy.   7. Africa—Economic conditions—1960–
I. Stein, Howard, 1952–
HC441.Z9I533   1995
338.95—dc20   94–31707
                                                        CIP

To Alisa and Joshua

Contents

List of Tables and Figures

Tables

Figures

Notes on the Contributors

Deborah Brautigam is Associate Professor in the School of International and Public Affairs at Columbia University in New York. Her research has focused on Taiwan and China as well as West Africa. She has published widely in journals such as *World Development, the Journal of Developing Areas* and *the Journal of Modern African Studies.*

Chris Edwards is Senior Lecturer in the School of Development Studies at the University of East Anglia. His research has concentrated on Southeast Asia. He is the author of a number of books including *The Fragmented World: Competing Perspectives on Trade, Money and the Crisis,* 1985.

Kwan S. Kim is Professor of Economics at the University of Notre Dame. Professor Kim's is one of the rare development economists to have undertaken extensive research in Asia, Africa and Latin America. He is the author of numerous publications. His latest book is a co-edited volume entitled *The State, Markets and Development: Beyond the Economist's Dichotomy,* 1994.

Linda Lim is Associate Professor of International Business at the School of Business Administration at the University of Michigan, Ann Arbor. She is one of the foremost exports on the state and economic development in Southeast Asia. She is the author of numerous articles, books and reports. Her latest volume is a co-authored book entitled *Foreign Direct Investment and Industrialization in Malaysia, Singapore, Taiwan and Thailand,* 1991.

E. Wayne Nafziger is Professor of Economics at Kansas State University. His work on entrepreneurship in Nigeria, from nearly twenty years ago, is still very widely quoted. Professor Nafziger's plethora of articles and books have focused on Africa, South Asia and East Asia. His latest volume is *The Debt Crisis in Africa,* 1993.

S. Gordon Redding is Professor and the Head of the School of Management at the University of Hong Kong. He has done extensive research on Chinese entrepreneurship. He is the author of *The Spirit of*

Chinese Capitalism, 1990, and co-editor of *Capitalism in Contrasting Cultures*, 1990.

Howard Stein is Associate Professor of Economics at Roosevelt University in Chicago. Formerly he was a Lecturer at the University of Dar Es Salaam in Tanzania between 1980 and 1982. During 1995–6 he will be a visiting professor at the Institute of Economic Research at Hitotsubashi University in Japan. His recent research has focused on structural adjustment and industrialization in Africa, institutional theory and economic reform, and critiques of models of rational choice. He is the co-editor of *Tanzania and the IMF: The Dynamics of Liberalization*, 1992.

Simon Tam is Lecturer in the School of Management at the University of Hong Kong. His work has focused on the dynamics of firm formation in Asia. His recent papers include 'Centrifugal Versus Centripetal Growth Processes: Contrasting Ideal Types for Conceptualising the Development Patterns of Chinese and Japanese Firms' in S. R. Clegg and S. G. Redding (eds), *Capitalism in Contrasting Cultures*, 1990.

Acknowledgements

One of the comments I have often heard in seminars on Africa's experience with structural adjustment is there is no viable alternative model. This volume provides one of the first attempts to challenge this assertion based on the experience of Asia. If one moves outside the realm of the neo-classical economic paradigm to interpret the lessons from Asian industrialization, it becomes possible to construct a rather different set of policies and priorities.

This project began by assembling a panel of economists and political economists with experience in Asia and Africa to examine the lessons for Africa from detailed country studies. Papers on Korea, Taiwan and Meiji Japan along with an overview of the theoretical issues were presented in November, 1991 at the African Studies Association Meeting in St. Louis, Missouri. Subsequently, additional country studies were commissioned to expand the coverage of the volume.

At the conceptual level, extensive discussions with long term collaborators Ernie Wilson and Wayne Nafziger were very helpful. I also learned a great deal from the many officials and academics who took time from their busy schedules to meet with me in East and Southeast Asia during the summer of 1991. I would especially like to thank Konosuke Odaka, Yukihiko Kiyokawa, Shigeru Ishikawa, Stephen Chee, K. S. Jomo, Nipon Poapongsakorn, Pasuk Phongpai-chit, Peter Soh, Eng Fong Pang, Anek Laothamatas, Fan Qingwu, S. Gordon Redding and Wu Xin. I am also indebted to the participants of this collection who patiently responded to my comments and questions as I moved slowly through the iterations needed to finish the volume. In addition to the two already mentioned, I would like to thank Kwan Kim, Linda Lim, Simon Tam, Deborah Brautigam and Chris Edwards. Kaye Southward was of great assistance in the preparation of the tables and the index. Finally, Tim Shaw and Clare Andrews have shown considerable support and flexibility as expected completion dates shifted with time.

HOWARD STEIN

Abbreviations

CPF	Central Provident Fund
CPI	consumer price index
DBS	Development Bank of Singapore
DCs	developed countries
DFI	direct foreign investment
DO	domestically-oriented
ECA	United Nations Economic Commission for Africa
EDP	Economic Development Board
EIDA	Engineering Industries Development Agency
EO	export-oriented
EPB	Economic Planning Bureau
EPZs	export processing zones
ERP	effective protection rates
GATT	General Agreement on Tariffs and Trade
GDP	gross domestic product
GNP	gross national product
HDB	Housing Development Board
IMF	International Monetary Fund
IMP	Industrial Master Plan
IPF	Industrial Promotion Fund
IS	import-substituting
ISI	import-substituting industrialization
ITRI	Industrial Technology Research Institute
JCRR	Chinese–American Joint Commission on Rural Reconstruction
JDM	Japanese development model
JTC	Jurong Town Corporation
KMT	Chinese Nationalists
KOTRA	Korea Trade Promotion Corporation
LDCs	less developed countries
LFR	Lewis–Fei–Ranis models
MAS	Monetary Authority of Singapore
MNC	Multinational Corporation
MP_L	marginal product of labor

NDP	net domestic product
NICs	Newly Industrialized Countries
NPC	National Productivity Centre
NPI	non-protection incentives
NTUC	National Trades Union Congress
NWC	National Wage Council
ODA	official development assistance
OECD	Organization for Economic Cooperation and Development
PAP	People's Action Party
POSB	Post Office Savings Bank
POSCO	Pohang Steel Mill
RF	Reverse Fund
SDF	Skills Development Fund
SEF	Strategic Economic Plan
SISIR	Singapore Institute for Standards and Industrial Research
SSA	Sub-Saharan Africa
TNCs	transnational companies
TQP	tariff and quota protection
UN	United Nations
UNICEF	United Nations International Children's Emergency Fund
UNIDO	United Nations Industrial Development Organisation
USAID	United States Agency for International Development

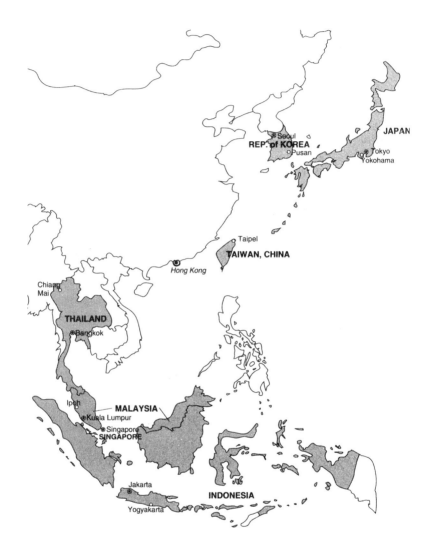

MAP 1   East and Southeast Asia

Source: World Bank, *The East Asian Miracle: Economic Growth and Public Policy* (Oxford University Press) inside cover. (Reprinted by permission of Oxford University Press.)

MAP 2   Sub-Saharan Africa

Source: World Bank, *Adjustment in Africa: Reforms, Results and the Road Ahead* (Oxford University Press) inside cover. (Reproduced by permission of Oxford University Press.)

1 Policy Alternatives to Structural Adjustment in Africa: An Introduction

Howard Stein

In many ways, the decade of the 1980s in Sub-Saharan Africa was lost in social and economic terms. Between 1980 and 1990 per capita income fell in the region by an astounding 1.1 per cent per annum (World Bank, 1992a, p. 196). This was, by far, the worst decade in the post-independence era.

The period also represented the ascendancy of the neo-classical economic model within the realm of international policy circles. Bilateral and multilateral aid agencies organized a cartel where the allocation of assistance was predicated on the acceptance of a structural adjustment program, a fairly uniform policy package. The aim of the package was to remove the impediments to growth and efficiency caused by state interference in the operation of markets. By 1987, the programs were ubiquitous in Sub-Saharan Africa with twenty seven countries initiating policy changes in exchange for the World Bank's structural adjustment loans.[1] By the early 1990s more than thirty countries in the region had adopted the Bank's program.

As the programs have spread the debate over the impact of the policies on adjusting vs. non-adjusting countries has also grown. While Africa's overall performance was quite poor the argument focused on whether countries that were 'strong' adjusters were 'recovering' more rapidly than the 'weak' adjusters in the later half of the decade. The most prominent disagreement arose between the United Nations Economic Commission for Africa (UNECA) and the World Bank, with the Bank arguing that reforming countries performed significantly better than weak-reforming and non-reforming countries (World Bank and UNDP, 1989). The ECA (1989), using the same data base, illustrated that there was little evidence of recovery and that in (their calculation) growth rates in weak-reforming and non-reforming countries actually did better overall between 1980 and 1987 than strong adjusters (UNECA, 1989, 3-8-3-10).

In a very illuminating article which revisits and updates the ECA–Bank debate, Mosley and Weeks (1993) examine growth rates from 1980 to 1991 for 44 Sub-Saharan countries. They conclude that within the limited confines of the definitions in the debate, the ECA was more accurate in arguing there was no indication of recovery in the second half of the 1980s (1985–91) and no significant difference between 'strong' and 'weak' adjusters (with other countries not in these categories actually doing better). Overall, including some Bank sources, there is mounting evidence that structural adjustment packages are not working in Sub-Saharan Africa.[2]

While much of Africa has been mired in an economic malaise, East and Southeast Asian countries have shown extraordinary growth and prosperity. During the 1970s and 1980s the policy circles were heavily influenced by neo-classical interpretations of the Asian miracle led by prominent writers like Bela Balassa (1971,1981), Anne Krueger (1978) and Ian Little (1981). More recently the Bank, at the urging (and with the financing) of the Japanese government, undertook a study to evaluate the East Asian 'miracle' (World Bank, 1993). The study, in many ways, is a restatement of the neo-classical interpretation of the policies underneath East Asia's success.[3] As argued in chapter 2 of this volume the World Bank's view of the policies behind the success of industrialization in Asia mirrors the neo-classical economic view and the model of structural adjustment closely parallels their interpretation of what was behind Asian growth and prosperity.

Led by the seminal work of Alice Amsden (1989) and Robert Wade (1990) there is a growing literature that has begun to challenge the neo-classical view of Asian development. An additional empirical question can be raised in response to the problematic experience with the adjustment model in Sub-Saharan Africa. Both of these challenges point to the need to reexamine the policies responsible for Asian growth and prosperity as a basis for developing an alternative model of economic reform for Africa. Drawing on case studies from East and Southeast Asia, the chapters in this volume begin to construct a new approach.[4] The focus of the studies is on the most successful countries in the region and on the policies responsible for rapid industrialization, a route which Africa will need to follow if it is to significantly increase the standard of living for its population. The chapters also cover the historical stages which are the most comparable to the current position of many African countries.

What are the policy lessons for Africa from industrialization in Asia? How do they compare to the neo-classical/structural adjustment view?

What are the constraints on applying them to Africa? Let us draw on the contributions to begin answering these important questions.

POLICY LESSONS FROM ASIAN INDUSTRIALIZATION: A SYNTHESIS

Theoretical Issues

Identification and Reproducibility

Chapter 2 raises two general theoretical difficulties concerning the application of policy lessons from Asia, the problems of identification and reproducibility. Identification refers to the method of pinpointing the factors responsible for industrial development in Asia. Reproducibility refers to the feasibility of replicating the model or aspects of the model once the identification problem has been resolved. Four issues concerning reproducibility are raised in chapter 2: the uniqueness of international temporal junctures, the specificity of historical economic preconditions, the irreducibility of social attributes and the peculiarity of political alignments. The case studies in the book try to deal with these problems. Identification is handled by causally linking shifts in policy positions to changes in the pattern of industrialization over various stages in each country's development. Reproducibility is discussed by laying out historical, structural and political dimensions of each case with some comparisons to the conditions in Africa.

In contrast, the neo-classicals deal with the identification problem by imposing a rationally deductive framework which presupposes the importance, dependency and outcome of the interaction between variables. The neo-classical reasoning is syllogistic. In simple terms, undistorted markets are what underlies successful industrialization. Industrialization in Asia has been successful; then it must be because they have not distorted markets or at least at some point have reversed historical distortions. Therefore the state must have been neutral allowing their countries to specialize in accordance with their comparative advantage. More recently, in response to the overwhelming evidence of wide-scale intervention by states in markets in Asia, a 'revisionist' neo-classical position has arisen on the question of identification. The argument in simple terms is that state's policy intervention did not alter what would have been predicted by a Hecksher–Ohlin–Samuelson model of static comparative advantage.[5]

The reproducibility problem for a long time was largely ignored by the neo-classicals. In a world in which there was only one successful route to achieving development, rational leaders would eventually recognize the superiority of market-led growth. The NICs (Newly Industrialized Countries) would have a positive demonstration effect. As chapter 2 indicates, this view has shifted somewhat due to the slow pace of economic reform and the resistance to structural adjustment. Neo-classicals began incorporating rational/public choice political economy arguments to explain why governments impose price distorting policies (to capture economic rents and political benefits) and in turn why there were entrenched interests impeding economic reform. As indicated below there may be perfectly sound economic reasons for resisting elements of structural adjustment packages given the contrast between the policies contained in adjustment programs and those used so effectively in Asia.

Industrial Policy

It is important to emphasize the relationship between the state, industrial organizations and markets in the development of Asia. Firms in Asia and elsewhere are institutions which provide a refuge from the vicissitudes of the market. Markets in Asia and elsewhere are social institutions which structure, organize and legitimate contractual agreements and the exchange of property rights. Their operation requires broadly defined forms of state intervention. The environment in which firms undertake investment and production can be one which is conducive to the rapid development of industry or one which is hostile. The focus of the industrial policy that has evolved in Asia has been to provide a fostering environment that has permitted industries to mature and prosper.

In contrast, the neo-classical view of markets (which underpins structural adjustment) arises from general equilibrium theory where markets arise spontaneously from the atomistic interaction of self-seeking individuals. Strictly speaking the state is completely unnecessary since markets are simply driven by utility considerations. In the more relaxed versions of neo-classical economics, there is some recognition that property rights are transferred and require some external guarantor like the state. Similarly, money is needed as a means of payment. This then provides a need for a state monetary institution like a central bank which like the guarantor of property rights would play only a neutral role (or in monetarist terms would ensure that money expansion does not cause inflation or deflation by setting its growth at the annual rate of the GDP). Beyond this role, state intervention will disrupt the ability of prices to equalize supply and demand.

The aim of structural adjustment in Africa is to reduce the distortions caused by states' interference in the operation of markets (see Quarco, 1990, for a more detailed discussion). Tax and tariff concessions need to be removed or at least lowered and equalized so that firms can choose inputs based on prices that reflect the relative scarcity of the factors of production of the country. The government needs to scale back by reducing social spending and subsidies (introducing user fees in education and health care, raising food prices etc.), deregulating markets and privatizing or closing state enterprises. Private property rights need to be carefully defined, impartially applied and guaranteed so that there is no risk of nationalization at a later date.

Exchange rate controls need to be dismantled and currencies should be permitted to float so that the exchange rates reflect supply and demand conditions and permit the unimpeded flow of investment in and out of the country. Financial reforms should focus on raising interest rates to real positive levels to attract savings and to ensure that only projects with a high rate of return will be undertaken. Credit constraints are necessary to reduce price levels and to lower balance of payments deficits (Khan et al., 1990). Reducing government expenditures helps to lower credit expansion and ensures that private sector investment needs will not be crowded out. Once private and other state impediments are removed the private sector driven economy will naturally occur and prosper.

An industrial policy is therefore an anathema to structural adjustment and neo-classical economic theory.[6] This is also reflected in the adjustment/neo-classical view of the firm. Coase and other proponents of new institutional economics describe the firm in neo-classical economics as a 'black box' (Coase, 1992). Since prices are the only information necessary to make efficient production and consumption decisions, there is no apparent reason for the existence of business organizations in mainstream theory. As we discussed, the key in adjustment is to ensure that production decisions are put into the private hands, or in other words that the public 'black box' becomes a private 'black box'. To the adjustment/neo-classical model there is no need for the state to influence the evolution and nature of the structure of industrial organization. As pointed out below and elsewhere (Stein,

1993), business organizations not individuals play the central role in the production and distribution side of the market. Understanding how the state can promote different industrial structures to encourage more rapid growth and innovation would seem to be an important part of the strategy for Africa's future development.

Industrial Strategies in Asia

It is important to emphasize that there were both constants and significant variations on the policy mechanisms used to promote industrialization in Asia. However, even in the relatively open market economy of Hong Kong, state policies were central to creating an environment which fostered rapid industrialization. Drawing on the case studies in the book the remainder of this chapter will focus on a number of policies in areas including social overhead capital (education, health care and housing), infrastructure, agriculture, labor, trade, foreign investment, credit and finance and the organization of industry. By way of conclusion we will focus on some of the questions related to the reproducibility of the Asian experience in Africa.

Social Overhead Capital

Education   One constant that runs through all of the case studies is the prerequisite for any form of industrialization is a well-educated work force. In Meiji Japan primary enrollment rates were increased from a mere 28.1 per cent in 1873 to 100 per cent by 1911. All of the countries in the a case study followed a similar pattern of early and rapid increases in enrollment rates. In addition not only did all countries rapidly raise literacy rates but the emphasis was on vocational, scientific and engineering training. Wayne Nafziger in his chapter on Japan contrasts this pattern to the educational system in Africa, where from colonial times there was an emphasis on skills that would be more useful to civil servants rather than an industrial work force. He also points out that the 48 per cent literacy rate in Sub-Saharan Africa in 1985 was very low and already reached in Japan in the first decade of the twentieth century.

In all cases, including Hong Kong, the states steadily increased their heavy support of education. In Taiwan, during the crucial phase of early industrialization, government spending increased in 1952 from 7.8 per cent of the total budget to 17.6 per cent in 1972. In contrast the austerity brought on by structural adjustment has led to a steady erosion of educational support in Africa.[7] Between 1980 and 1987 spending per student in Africa had fallen from $32 to a mere $15. This, combined with the introduction of user fees, has led to a steady erosion in primary enrollment rates which fell from 79 per cent 1980 to 67 per cent in 1990. The emphasis on government cutbacks (in education) and the introduction of user fees in adjustment packages must clearly be rapidly reversed. In addition increasing emphasis must be on educating the labor force in areas that will be useful to industry. Closely tied to this is the need for the development of capacities in science and engineering which is needed to assimilate imported technology. This has been especially important in the development of indigenous industry in Taiwan, Korea and Meiji Japan.

Housing and Health Care   Closely related to education are housing and health care which are not only ends in themselves but important to maintaining a productive labor force. The state in most of the countries examined has played an important role in subsidizing and expanding access to basic health care and housing. Singapore provided the most widespread public investment in housing and medical care. By the early 1980s it housed 80 per cent of the population in subsidized owner occupied units built by the state's Housing Development Board. Health care access was universal and also heavily subsidized. Expenditures in these areas were also important to the legitimacy of the regime, labor peace and widespread support for the state's industrial policy and steadily rose in the early period of development. For example, between 1972 and 1980 real per capita state spending on health care rose by 90 per cent in Singapore (World Bank, 1983, p. 199). In contrast, the austerity of structural adjustment programs in Sub-Saharan Africa was taking its toll on social spending. Real per capita government spending on health care in the region fell by 42 per cent between 1980 and 1987. Not surprisingly, given the rising debt load in the 1980s, the only rising component of government per capita spending was interest payments (Stewart, 1991, p. 428). Once again, any alternative model of reform based on the Asian experience would need to reverse this trend.

Infrastructure

A second constant that runs through all the case studies is the central role of infrastructure in the development of industry and the heavy direct and early involvement by the state in this area. The Meiji government in Japan invested heavily in telegraphs, postal service, water supply, coastal shipping, ports, harbors, bridges, lighthouses, railways, electricity, gas and technical research. In Korea, the government also invested in these areas with nearly 25 per cent of domestic investment between 1963 and 1979 arising from public sector allocation to infrastructural and social overhead capital. In Singapore, the state not only vastly expanded traditional infrastructure but through its Jurong Town Corporation provided low cost fully serviced factories available for the rapid establishment of new industrial ventures. In Hong Kong, the government through leasing arrangements (the Crown owns all the land) made land available for industrial estates at a fraction of their market value. The government has also been active in other areas of infrastructure with a mix of ownership, subsidization and close regulation when infrastructure has been privately controlled. In Taiwan, the KMT inherited an intricate network of roads, electrical plants and harbors but rapidly expanded them to increase the capacity in all areas of infrastructure. By 1952 the density of transport infrastructure was already many times greater in Taiwan than even middle income sub-Saharan Africa countries like Côte d'Ivoire. Clearly, one can point unequivocally to the need for a massive increase in infrastructural spending in sub-Saharan Africa.

While the World Bank, in theory, has recognized the importance of infrastructure to reducing business expenses (World Bank, 1989a, p. 115), in practice the emphasis on austerity and meeting the government credit targets of adjustment programs has led to significant declines in state investment in a number of sub-Saharan countries in the 1980s.[8] Mosley and Weeks (1993) provide strong empirical support to the importance of expanding infrastructure. As a proxy for infrastructure expansion they examine the impact of the direction of public investment in twenty-eight Sub-Saharan Africa countries between 1980 and 1990. The ten countries with increasing public investment did significantly better in the growth rate of real GDP, overall investment and exports compared to the eighteen countries with a declining rate.[9]

Agriculture   Many of the agricultural policies embedded in structural adjustment programs seem at variance to the experience documented in the case studies. From the perspective of industry, the focus of adjustment is to encourage the export of cash crops with mechanisms like devaluation, increasing the terms of trade in favor of agriculture, raising incomes which will assist industry by providing demand linkages and savings through voluntary rural credit institutions and

encouraging agro-processing as the basis of industrialization. Liberalizing input and output markets will assist this process (e.g. gains from
privatizing procurement markets, more effective allocation of fertilizer
and insecticides, etc. will encourage higher producer prices and more
efficient production). Overall, the emphasis seems to be a market-
centered strategy, with the pace and direction of industrialization
captured by the internal dynamics of agriculture.

This approach has more to do with the theoretical realm of neo-
classical axioms than the agricultural–industrial interactions of the
countries of East Asia. In general policies related to agriculture
involved heavy state intervention in the provision of inputs, procurement and pricing, land reform, significant levels of public investment
and a general subservience of agriculture to industry in the early stages
of industrialization. In Meiji Japan, a land tax accounted for more than
80 per cent of central government revenue up to 1882 with net resource
outflows through 1922. Despite this productivity rose significantly, due
largely to public investment in research, extension by veteran farmers
and agricultural school graduates who diffused the latest techniques
and seed varieties to the literate farm population. Food prices were
kept low (keeping industrial wages down) through large scale imports
from Japan's colonies.

In Korea, the policy of 'industry first' gradually evolved into a more
balanced relationship between industry and agriculture. In the 1960s
the state through forced procurement deliberately kept grain prices
low, to encourage the migration of labor to support labor-intensive
manufacturing and to keep real wages down. At the same time, there
was heavy public investment in infrastructure, research and extension
services. Toward the end of the decade, the demand for rice was
exceeding the supply leading to a rise in rice imports. The government
implemented a more balanced approach by using price supports to
prop up the income of farmers without passing on the cost to urban
workers, allowing them to contain wage increases and keep labor
intensive industries competitive. At the same time they augmented their
investment levels in agriculture, subsidized fertilizer and pesticide
inputs and assisted the organization of cooperatives.

In Taiwan, land reform played a pivotal role in promoting rural
equality. Through the removal of the landlord class, the state was in a
good position to squeeze agriculture. Once again the government
encouraged policies significantly different than those typically found in
adjustment packages. Rice prices were kept artificially low to sustain
low urban wages. Fertilizer was exchanged on a barter basis. Farmers

were also required to pay a land tax in kind and to meet a state imposed rice quota which paid prices which were 25 to 30 per cent below wholesale levels. Unlike Africa with its emphasis on extension services, Taiwan stressed state supported agricultural research. As in Korea, the industry-first approach gradually evolved toward a more balanced system using price supports to raise the income of farmers.

Despite the low prices to farmers, productivity steadily increased through the mid-1960s. Deborah Brautigam explains this as a product of policies that reduced the uncertainty of farmers while continually investing in agriculture. In contrast, adjustment emphasizes the liberalization of inputs and outputs which greatly augment uncertainty. Similarly, the emphasis on austerity and meeting government spending targets has frequently led to a decline in public investment in agriculture.

Tanzania provides a case in point.[10] In the mid-1980s, Tanzania began dismantling its state monopoly on the procurement of grain and edible oils by opening it up to private traders. While production of maize grew modestly up to 1989, by 1992 the level had fallen back to the numbers of the 1985/86 growing season (Putterman, 1993, pp. 15, 19). In many ways, the example of grain production reveals the weaknesses of the strategy of adjustment, where production becomes subject to the vicissitudes of the market. First, maize prices paid to farmers showed considerable fluctuations over the period, falling by nearly 50 per cent in real terms between 1983/84 and 1988/89 and then subsequently rising by more than one-half by 1991/92. Second, the removal of subsidies and massive devaluations undertaken to meet Fund targets, led to a tripling of fertilizer prices between 1990 and 1992. The impact of the price increases, combined with severe cutbacks in credit availability, caused reductions in already low input usage with implications to yields.

Third, due to a paucity of private traders and the vagaries of the rural road system, many farmers were being subjected to monopsony pricing. Only the wealthiest farmers had access to transportation to take grains to more competitive distant markets. Prices were often 50 per cent higher in more central locations. Some areas that were large surplus regions were in danger of becoming net importers of food (Putterman, 1993, pp. 16–18, 24, 25, 38). The low density of rural roads, lack of application of fertilizer and pesticides, absence of technologically advanced seeds, poor transportation options, paucity of irrigation infrastructure and absence of agricultural research facilities are just a few of the obstacles that are not addressed by adjustment and have in many ways become more difficult to implement in the current climate of Fund and Bank imposed austerity.[11]

Labor Policies and Wages

As opposed to the neo-classical/adjustment emphasis on the 'undistorted' operation of markets, where prices reflect their scarcity values, we find that the state constantly intervened in markets often to the advantage of industry. Labor markets are no exception. Real wages, in almost every case, were kept low and generally below productivity increases. The mechanisms used included the careful squeezing of agriculture to maintain a steady flow of new entries into the labor force, restricting union activity, setting up councils to review wage disputes, carefully regulating the price of wage goods like rice (as discussed above) and the provision of social goods (Singapore providing the most extensive example) which encouraged the acquiescence of labor. The wage policy was also part of a strategy of dynamic comparative advantage where wages were deliberately kept low until the government could induce the organization of a sufficiently large capital intensive/higher value added mass of industries.

In Africa, real wages plummeted due to a combination of devaluations, inflation and austerity. In Tanzania, for example, the minimum hourly wage had fallen to a mere $0.054 by the end of 1989 (Stein and Nafziger, 1991, p. 183). In Nigeria, in the same year, textile workers were earning only $0.16 per hour compared to $0.58 in India for comparable labor. While theoretically this should make industry more competitive, the decline has occurred without regard to living standards and the impact on productivity as formal sector salaries become insufficient to support even a subsistence level.[12]

Trade Policy and Exchange Rates

As indicated in chapter 2, the thrust of the Bank's view of trade has been that import-substitution is largely a liability. Countries that shifted more rapidly to export-orientation avoided the burdens associated with import-substitution (inefficiencies, lack of competitiveness of these industries, resistance from domestic interests to lowering trade barriers, etc.). In their view, the move to export-oriented industrialization was less of a policy shift and more a scrapping of disincentives to export.[13] In practice, structural adjustment has followed the Bank's view of policies in Asia, by emphasizing the removal of import quotas, the lowering and equalizing of tariffs and removing export taxes.[14]

In contrast, the studies in this volume indicate that import-substitution often had positive consequences and did not disappear with the emphasis on exports. As chapter 2 indicates, in places like Korea, import-substituting industries receiving protection were threatened with the removal of protection if they did not begin exporting after a period time. Successful industries were able to maintain a two-tiered system, where profits were supported by the higher prices on the domestic markets, while maintaining competitive prices on international markets.

Export orientation was not the product of neutrality but of heavy promotion which often exceeded continuing levels of import protection. In Korea, export industries not only obtained tariff exemptions, they were also the recipients of income tax reductions, state financing of imports, favorable depreciation allowances, tax rebates on imports, subsidized interest rate loans, foreign currency loans and export insurance. The government set annual targets and used a combination of moral incentives and augmented subsidization when actual levels fell below their targets. Agencies were organized to set up trade fairs, dispatch trade missions and to host foreign business visitors. Private trade conglomerates were promoted to strengthen international marketing. As opposed to the adjustment-induced rapid destabilizing devaluations of African currencies in recent years, Korea maintained a more stable nominal rate of exchange using a combination of moderate devaluations and subsidies to ensure a steady return per dollar of exports.

In the mid-1960s, Taiwan and Korea faced a similar situation to the one currently confronting Africa. After significant devaluations (partially due to pressure from US aid agencies) and the liberalization of inputs, needed to support export production, exports were still not internationally competitive. Even in labor-intensive sectors like cotton textiles, they could not compete with Japan which had higher wages but even higher productivity providing them with lower unit labor costs. The countries faced a choice: they could lower real wages and unit labor costs through further devaluations or they could subsidize exports providing time to raise productivity to lower unit labor costs (Amsden, 1994, p. 20). They chose the second option with astounding results. In Korea, for instance, exports surged from $55 million in 1962 to $27 billion two decades later.

On the import side, Linda Lim notes that the import-substitution phase was important in Singapore in the training of government officials on the usage of incentive schemes; schemes which proved important in the promotion of export-oriented industry. In Taiwan and

Korea, it is quite clear that import-substitution did not disappear with the shift toward export intensive industries. In Korea, imports were restricted up to 1967 on a positive list basis. After adopting a unified exchange rate system in 1964, the government shifted to a policy of encouraging intermediate and capital goods imports by the export sector while continuing to restrict consumer goods. After 1967 Korea moved toward a negative list system. As the government supported the development of intermediate and capital goods production in order to deepen industrialization, targeted industries were given infant industry protection. Beginning in the late 1960s, Korea began to restrict imports and were rapidly moving toward self-sufficiency in this area by the end of the 1980s. In nominal terms Korea did lower tariff levels between 1968 and 1978, but the effective rate of protection actually rose over the period showing enormous variation from industry to industry and didn't look anything like the uniformity promoted in adjustment packages (contrary to the myth of neo-classical economics). Taiwan followed a similar pattern of successful export orientation with import-substituting protectionism.[15]

Foreign Investment

Japan, Taiwan and Korea emphasized local capital accumulation and resisted large-scale direct foreign investment. In the most extreme case, Meiji Japan virtually banned foreign investment between 1868 and 1891. Adjustment, in contrast, encourages an open door policy and the institution of new legal guarantees that protect against nationalization and ensure the repatriation of profits (even with the new legislation there have been few takers).

One country seems to fit the pattern of foreign capital induced industrialization. Foreign investment dominated industry in Singapore. In 1960 less than 30 per cent of total equity in manufacturing was foreign owned. By 1980 international capital controlled 76 per cent of all output and 86 per cent of all exports in the manufacturing sector. At the start of industrialization, unlike Africa, capital was not in short supply. However, like Africa, industrial entrepreneurs, technological expertise and international marketing assets and distribution channels were in short supply. Multinationals were tapped for these compo-nents. While maintaining an open economy, the state hardly took a laissez faire approach and constantly intervened with inducements to encourage international capital to move up the industrial ladder. For this purpose they used a series of incentives including joint ventures to lower risk, tax concessions, the provision of inexpensive infrastructure, heavily subsidized training and education and by providing a stable and friendly business climate. Wages were kept low and excess demand for labor encouraged so that as capital for higher technological industries became available the country could curtail investment in labor intensive industries.

Attempts to emulate Singapore's approach have proved difficult. In Malaysia foreign capital was induced to locate into exporting zones. However, as the chapter on Malaysia indicates the zones have remained enclaves with few if any linkages to the rest of the economy. As a result, Malaysia is now looking at the strategy employed in Korea and Taiwan.

Credit and Finance

The case studies indicate that while interest rates were positive or moderately negative in real terms[16] in many of the countries over many of the years examined, the financial systems did not operate in any way like the neo-classical/adjustment view. First, interest rates on the investment side were heavily subsidized to priority sectors. In Korea, for example, interest rates were subsidized by as much as 75 per cent on loans to exporters. Second, the determination of the recipient of loans was not by market forces but through the direct allocation of credit to priority sectors. In Korea, 'policy loans' with exceptionally low interest rates and lenient repayment terms were allocated by government operated development banks. In the early days of industrialization, they accounted for half of total bank lending. In Taiwan, during the 1970s, banks extended 75 per cent of all loans to industries targeted by government planners.

Third, following its monetarist roots, the focus of adjustment is on meeting financial targets in the area of monetary growth rates and government deficits in order to maintain price stability and to ensure that private sector investment is not crowded out. In this view, countries that have low or no government deficits and expand money supplies at the rate of growth of GDP, will have higher growth rates and stable prices. What is quite apparent from even a cursory look at the data is that there was no fixed relationship between deficits, money supply growth, price levels and growth rates. While all of East and Southeast Asia on average performed better than other developing countries over the past few decades, inflation rates, government deficits and money supply growth showed considerable variation. For example, between 1970/72 and 1986/88 Malaysia's M2[17]/GDP ratio tripled while its per capita GDP grew by a half. Thailand had per capita GDP growth of two-thirds while its M2/GDP ratio doubled. However, Korea's M2/GDP ratio grew by only a quarter while its per capita GDP tripled. Yet Taiwan had similar GDP per capita growth as Korea but its M2/GDP ratio increased by two and one-half times over the period (Lindauer and Roemer, 1993, pp. 121, 136, 137)! Inflation also seemed to have little correspondence to performance and money supply growth. Malaysia with its high money supply expansion had the lowest inflation with its average CPI increasing at only 3.4 per cent per annum between 1961 and 1991. In contrast, Korea, with a much lower money supply growth and a higher GDP expansion, had an inflation rate of 12.2 per cent per annum over the same period. Sub-Saharan Africa's inflation rate, by comparison, was 20 per cent per annum between 1961 and 1991 (World Bank, 1993, p. 110). One must ask, if Africa had managed to lower the average inflation rate to the Korean level would it have made a difference in the pattern of growth and investment? It is highly doubtful. Short of the destabilizing impact of hyperinflation (which can be brought on by IMF-induced devaluations) it would appear that growth is compatible with a wide variety of inflation rates.[18]

Fourth, despite positive real interest rates, savings levels showed considerable variation with Korea generally on the lower side and Singapore on the higher side.[19] What is perhaps more important in explaining savings rates is the institutional context (broadly defined). On the savings side, one can point to a variety of factors. East and Southeast Asian countries were able to put in place secure (government-backed) financial intermediaries with low transaction costs for small savers (e.g. postal savings system). In some cases, governments were able to mobilize large pools of savings at the work place (Singapore's provident fund). In other places, such as in Japan, savings habits were part of a pattern of maintaining wealth intact for several generations. Spreads were carefully maintained by government regulation to ensure that savers received a significant part of the prevailing interest rates (World Bank, 1993, p. 217). In contrast, adjustment in Africa has often pushed deregulation with severe consequences. In Ghana, for instance, deregulation of the banking system in 1987 led to a significant rise in bank margins with a resulting drop in interest payments to depositors (Abbey, 1991, p. 524).

Despite the very successful mobilization of savings in Asia, there is growing evidence that it was not savings that led to the phenomenal investment and growth rates of the last few decades but the rise in income that led to the very high level of savings.[20] In one of the first systematic tests of savings-growth causality, the World Bank (1993) found that in five countries the causation was clearly from growth to savings (Indonesia, Japan, Korea, Thailand, Taiwan); in two it was ambiguous (Hong Kong and Malaysia); and in one it was due to other factors (Singapore where the provident fund comes into play). What is most interesting is there was no evidence to support the typical neo-classical savings to growth causality.[21]

So if high savings did not lead to growth and accumulation, then what permitted the growth and accumulation to take-off? The key is the development of accommodating financial institutions that were able to initiate and maintain a flow of credit to finance spending on investment goods. In chapter 3, Wayne Nafziger provides an excellent discussion contrasting the evolution of money and finance in Meiji Japan to sub-Saharan Africa. European colonial powers constructed the financial system in sub-Saharan Africa. In Japan, the state selectively adopted features of the American, French, British and German systems. While Japan's financial network contained virtually no foreign ownership, private banks were operated by the Europeans in Africa.

African colonial governments intervened little in the regulation of the banking system, had little or no contact with small indigenous bankers and created few if any new financial institutions. The Meiji government organized most of the banking system in the last three decades of the nineteenth century using a combination of direct ownership or indirect support of local private initiatives. Unlike the neo-classical belief that financial institutions are a product of the spontaneous evolution of the private sector, the banking institutions were 'supply leading' often created in advance of the financial requirement. With respect to state financial enterprises and industry, the Industrial Promotion Fund was set up in 1878, the Yokohama Specie Bank was organized in 1880 to provide foreign exchange to importers, the Hypothec Banks in 1896 were set up at the prefectural levels to make long-term loans to industry and in 1990 the state organized the Industrial Bank to provide medium and long-term loans to industry. The central bank of Japan was organized in 1882 only a few years after they permitted private commercial banks. The standardization of the currency, the integration of national markets and the careful financing of early industrialization all contributed to early industrialization.

Money supply expansion was rapid from 1880 to 1940 aimed at accommodating rapid growth rates while avoiding credit constraints which might lead to recessions. In contrast, adjustment and stabilization packages have imposed tight monetary targets without regard to the implications to the credit needs of sectors like manufacturing.[22]

Entrepreneurship, the State and the Structure of Industry

As noted above, a focus of structural adjustment is to encourage the movement of production decisions from public into private hands. Following neo-classical economics, there is no need to be concerned about the nature of business organizations. In contrast, the case studies indicate the important relationship between state policy and industrial organization and economic growth and innovation.

In general, business organizations are social institutions which provide a refuge from the vicissitudes of the market. In addition to reducing transaction costs, they embody habits and routines which allow companies to handle the complexity of production and exchange and develop expectations in a world of uncertainty. Different organizational forms will breed greater operational success. While authors like Oliver Williamson (1985) have stressed the role of governance structures within firms as a means of limiting opportunism and therefore transaction costs, what has been more important to success in Asian countries has been organizations that are able to encourage loyalty and trust. Mechanisms such as benefits that increase with time and lifetime employment were important in encouraging worker loyalty in Japan after World War I.

These attributes have not only been important in intra-firm relations but in inter-firm interactions. In Japan and Korea, the state encouraged the development of large conglomerates of interlocking companies which also encouraged loyalty and trust leading to transaction cost reductions.

As in Africa today there were few entrepreneurs with the experience to build large-scale industrial firms. Faced with this absence, governments in Asia set out to foster entrepreneurship. As noted above, Singapore primarily relied on foreign capital to build up entrepreneurship. In Korea, once the state identified a successful entrepreneur, cheap credit was made readily available. This would have a snow-balling effect with success breeding success since government credit was largely based on previous achievements. Given the availability of credit entrepreneurs could launch a number of simultaneous ventures. This led to a race for empire-building and the development of the Korean *Chaebols*.

To the Korean government, large-scale production was necessary given the minimum plant size to capture economies of scale in areas like automobiles, steel and shipbuilding. The government also viewed the *Chaebols* as the most effective means to compete in international markets against large foreign multinationals as well as a means of strengthening the Korean side of joint ventures with foreign partners. Finally large firms which provide refuge from the market have been important in setting up and sustaining research and development leading to innovative investment. One initial problem with the emphasis on large firms was the creation of industrial dualism with small and medium firms relegated to an inferior status. Following Japan's lead the problem has been addressed since the mid-1970s as smaller firms have been integrated into production by increasingly supplying components and semi-finished goods to the larger units.

As Gordon Redding and Simon Tam indicate, the case of Hong Kong is considerably different. While the historical structure of Chinese society limited the development of entrepreneurship, there were strong elements within the society that would encourage entrepreneurship once they were decoupled by British colonialism. The crucial legacy which played a central role in reducing transaction costs was the paternalistic power structure with a resulting dependence of subordinates and strong loyalty ties; the central role of family in determining allegiances, network structures and organizational boundaries; and the use of personalism in facilitating transactions.

Both the colonial state in Africa and the Confucianist state in China discouraged and looked down on indigenous commercial activity. The main route to upward mobility was via the public sector. In contrast, under the Hong Kong colonial government, British officials monopolized the civil service making the pursuit of bureaucratic office unavailable to the Chinese population. The pursuit of wealth became respectable and promoted by a set of policies which encouraged industrial and commercial activities.

Without even comparing the social structures of Africa relative to Hong Kong, the applicability of the Hong Kong approach seems somewhat limited. First, many of the basic components of state support for industry in Hong Kong (discussed above and in chapter 2) in areas like infrastructure and education are still absent in Africa.[23] Second, the legacy of the colonial state in Africa, with its suppression of entrepreneurship has continued in Africa. During the colonial period, legal barriers impeded the ability of Africans to engage in commerce. After independence, the choice was often between recognizing and guaranteeing the ownership rights of visible minorities like Asians or utilizing newly formed bureaucracies to usurp those rights on behalf of the general African population. Private property and accumulation were seen as evidence of exploitation which often entailed the enrichment of visible minorities at the expense of Africans. This suggests removing state barriers to entrepreneurship is insufficient. Entrepreneurship will need to be carefully fostered to build up its legitimacy. The case of Japan and Korea (as outlined in chapters 3 and 4), where the states carefully fostered industrial entrepreneurship, would therefore seem to be more applicable.[24]

The Reproducibility of the Asian Experience in Africa

The chapter has so far identified the policies used by Asian states to intervene in support of industrialization. The next question is how readily can they be reproduced in Africa given the different preconditions and histories, the current international economic environment and the political economy of African states. From the chapters on Hong Kong, Taiwan and Korea, it is apparent that in terms of infrastructure, the initial industrial base and the attitude and policies of officials, the colonial period was much more conducive to industrialization in Asia relative to Africa. In areas of Africa, after thirty years of independence, some countries have not yet overcome these inherited deficits. In addition, competition in the export of manufactures has grown steadily as LDCs in other parts of the world have aggressively expanded into new markets. Between 1965 and 1980, manufactured exports from LDCs to developed countries grew at an annual rate of 25 per cent (Sarkar and Singer, 1991, p. 334). During the 1980s, as some Southeast and East Asian countries moved up the industrial ladder, their low-wage export position was being replaced by new labor-intensive exporters like China. This further intensifies the competition that is likely at the entry level into manufacturing. These two questions provide a formidable but not insurmountable challenge. In the first case, it will require even greater levels of public spending or longer time horizons to overcome the inherited deficits. The second barrier to reproducing the Asian experience is based on too static a view; one which often permeates the dependency literature. The rapidly changing structure of manufacturing exports of LDCs illustrates how quickly the world division of labor can change.

Finally, most of the studies in this volume have contrasted the nature of the state in Asia relative to Africa. States in Africa have generally been weaker, less professional and much more subject to patronage and clientage. This greatly delimits their capacity to implement and sustain an industrial strategy.

This area also represents a formidable challenge to following the Asian route to industrialization. One reaction, as illustrated by the Lindauer and Roemer (1993) study, is that given the character of African states they should not attempt to emulate the interventionism of East Asia. Instead they should pursue the Southeast Asian approach which more closely matches their physical and social attributes and which relied on market incentives not government direction. As they more explicitly put it 'export growth came from smaller firms and from agriculture, guided by market incentives, not by government' (Lindauer and Roemer, 1993, p. 7).[25] There are some obvious problems with this approach.

First, it is not clear what the difference is between their perceived model of Southeast Asia and the structural adjustment policies used in Africa since the early 1980s with such problematic results. Second there is some question about their representation of the Southeast Asian experience. As Chris Edwards indicates, at least in Malaysia, governments did intervene heavily to promote the industrial sector. However, the reason why manufacturing has had much fewer linkages to the rest of the economy relative to East Asia is not due to a lack of support but to a lack of discipline. One approach to improving the results of support has been the usage of what the World Bank (1993) refers to as contests in East Asia. In particular, they have explicitly set out the rewards, rules and referees of the contests enhancing the competition and overall results of the support offered by the state.[26] Even the Bank admits that under some limited circumstances (particularly in the early stages of industrial development) the results of well-run contests might be superior to a market approach.

Finally, as Alice Amsden (1989) has pointed out, the enforcement of a distortion free (and rent-free) set of markets itself requires a 'strong' state.[27] Liberalization does not ipso facto remove rent-seeking in Africa. Cathy Boone (1994) in a fascinating study of trade liberalization in Senegal and Côte d'Ivoire challenges the neo-classical view. Orthodoxy argues that replacing non-tariff barriers (like licenses) with tariffs depoliticizes trade, reduces commercial rent-seeking activities and creates a level playing field which will encourage underground activities to surface in turn allowing the state to capture more revenue. The author illustrates that liberalization failed to alter commercial rent-seeking, helped to encourage the ascendancy of new politically connected capital (the Mourides in Senegal and the Lebanese in Côte d'Ivoire) and to some degree increased the tax evading underground activities leading to a further erosion of state revenue flows. The removal of rent-seeking and the creation of a level playing field leading to an effective set of markets may be more not less difficult than effective state intervention.

Many Bank officials, particularly outside the more dogmatic circle of the senior staff, recognize the central role of the state in Asia but argue that the state-led approach was tried in Africa in the 1960s and 1970s without success and therefore should not be attempted again.[28] How does one respond to this position? First, as I have argued elsewhere (Stein, 1992), you cannot explain the weakness of the industrial policy in the earlier period without discussing structural and institutional features including the international mechanisms (like Bank cost–benefit studies) that influenced the choice of industry and technology types. As Sanjaya Lall has aptly put it 'the problem with past intervention has been **non-selectivity and lack of strategy** rather than selection and strategy based on experience, analysis and economic evaluation' (Lall, 1992, p. 125). These structural and institutional weaknesses will need to be addressed.

Second, as some studies of industry in Africa have illustrated there have been industrial successes in Africa and these successes in places like Zimbabwe have often been a product of interventionist policies (Riddell, 1990, 1993). Third, and perhaps most important, if Asia is any guide, without state intervention and the development of supporting institutions, industrialization will not occur in Africa.[29]

In contrast to Lindauer and Roemer (1993) and the World Bank (1993), the central lesson of the Asia's industrialization, emphasized in this volume, is that there is no alternative to the state.[30] International agencies need to move away from the policy lending based on flawed economic theories toward financing the public goods and state capacities which are prerequisites for private initiatives in industry.[31] Performance criteria need to focus not on meeting financial targets based on some hypothetical neo-classical balances but on the professionalism and autonomy of state institutions. As economic performance improves, the legitimacy of the autonomous state will grow, creating resistance to clientalism and patronage. In the rapidly changing world division of labor, opportunities will be created for Africa's industrial exports. With the appropriate institutional setting it will be possible to respond to those opportunities.

Notes

1. The initial dates of the programs were divided fairly evenly between early adjusters (1980–84) and later adjusters (1985–87). Early countries in chronological order were Kenya, Sudan, Côte d'Ivoire, Malawi, Senegal, Mauritius, Nigeria, Togo, Ghana, Zimbabwe, Guinea-Bissau, Zambia and Sierra Leone. The later adjusters included Burkina Faso, Madagascar, Burundi, Central African Republic, Gambia, Guinea, Somalia, Zaire, Congo, Niger, Sao Tome, Tanzania and Uganda. The content and duration of the programs varied. For a good summary of the details see Mosley and Weeks (1993: Appendix A and footnote 15).

2. There is now an extensive literature (I list just a few examples) critical of structural adjustment in Africa covering a variety of topics including agriculture (Commander, 1989b; Lele, 1990), industry (Stein, 1992; Lall, 1992, Riddell, 1993), debt (Parfitt and Riley, 1989; Nafziger, 1993), basic needs (Cornia et al., 1987; Stein and Nafziger, 1991; Stewart, 1991), trade (Godfrey, 1985; Helleiner, 1990) and investment levels (Mosley et al., 1991). In contrast, the latest World Bank (1994) study, released just as the manuscript of this book was about to be forwarded to the publisher, is a strong statement aimed at reaffirming the positive effect of adjustment on Africa. The position is somewhat surprising given some of the evidence in tables in the study (Appendix B. 3). Twenty-six Sub-Saharan countries are divided into three categories based on the degree of change in macroeconomic policies. A quick glance at the data shows that countries with a 'large improvement' in policies actually did worse in median change in agricultural growth than the 'small improvement' and 'deterioration' categories and lower growth of gross domestic investment than the 'small improvement' category. The 'large improvement' group also did more poorly after netting out the oil exporters in the area of public investment compared to the other two categories (Appendix A, Table 23). GDP per capita in the large versus the small improvement category is very similar (1.8 vs. 1.5 per cent) and probably not statistically significantly different. In the text, the Bank very conveniently redefines the categories when the data are negative (e.g. in agriculture the new category is countries that have increased the real prices to exporters) and maintains the categories when they are positive. As with earlier studies its not entirely certain what is being compared here. First, there is no explanation of the reason for the choice of the dates of 1981–1986 vs. 1987–1991. Choosing other dates could lead to different results (the Bank tries a few others which hardly captures the range of permutations). Second, some countries in the categories began programs well before 1986 while others were after (see footnote one). If early adjusters abandoned adjustments due to negative economic consequences and if one assumes any lag time between policies and their effects then some of the poor results in the latter time period may be due to adjustment not due to a lack of adjustment. A similar line of argument could be used on the 'large improvement' category. Third, to determine the classification of countries, the Bank assigned the number minus three through plus three to ranges of changes in six sub-categories of macropolicies (like fiscal balances) equally weighted. The numbers used

to determine the extent of change in macroeconomic policies are arbitrary to say the least as is the choice of equal weighting. Why should a decrease of inflation of 2.5 per cent only receive a plus one and an increase of 5 per cent a minus one (a variation of 7.5 per cent) when an increase of 31 per cent leads to the assignment of a minus three (a variation of 26 per cent for the same point reduction). A few changes in the definition of the ranges can easily push five of the six countries from the 'large improvement' into the 'small improvement' category or the majority of the 'deterioration' group into the 'small improvement' category. Similar shifts would also occur using different weighting schemes. In essence, the results of the whole exercise could have been dramatically different by simply redefining the ranges or the weighting.

3. To quote the Bank study: '. . .getting the fundamentals right was essential. Without high levels of domestic savings, broadly based human capital, good macroeconomic management and limited price distortion, there would have been no basis for growth and no means by which the gains of rapid productivity change could have been realized' (World Bank, 1993, p. 23).

4. The book does not provide detailed studies of South Asia, Thailand, the Philippines or Indonesia. The focus is on the most successful cases which we believe also set the pattern that other Asian countries are attempting to emulate. Even the Malaysia chapter is written in the context of 'looking East'.

5. The two best examples of this are World Bank (1993) and Lindauer and Roemer (1993). The Bank's 'Asian Miracle' sums up this position very effectively:

> These findings do not imply that governments were not attempting to influence industrial structure. They undoubtedly were. But they suggest that, despite government intentions the manufacturing sector seems to have evolved roughly in accord with neo-classical expectations; industrial growth was largely market conforming. (World Bank, 1993, p. 315)

Similarly as Lindauer and Roemer put it:

> Industrialization in Asia followed the contours of comparative advantage determined substantially by factor endowments . . . Despite the neo-classical path the policy measures supporting industrialization were far from neo-classical in all but Hong Kong and Singapore. (1993, p. 12)

The Bank in its study provide a variety of crude tests to try to buttress their position. What is particularly interesting is that some of the results quite clearly support the opposite conclusion. For example, using Syrquin and Chenery's (1989) predicted sectoral shares of value added/GDP (based on average per capita GDP and population) for Hong Kong, Korea, Thailand and Singapore (no data for Taiwan) had significantly higher manufacturing sectors relative to the norm in the 1980s. In the

Malaysian case, there was a significant rise in the actual to predicted share between 1969 and 1981. This would seem to illustrate the effectiveness of the state's support for industry. Similarly some of the data reflects the state's heavy support. In Korea, for instance, as indicated in Kwan Kim's chapter, metal products and machinery were promoted by the government. In 1988 their percentage of value added was almost three times the norm. Of course taking global averages as a hypothetical reflection of what would have happened in a country without government intervention hardly reflects the pattern of what would have occurred given the particular endowments of each country. In a second test, they find that total factor productivity was in general higher for Japan, Korea and Taiwan than international comparisons which would give credence to the positive contribution argument. However, there was little evidence that sectors more heavily supported by the government had higher total factor productivity. Once again this is a flawed test, since it says nothing about total factor productivity in the sector in the absence of government intervention (e.g. it might have acted as a catalyst). A third test looks at the growth of the share of value added relative to the wage levels and value added per worker at the beginning and end of various periods. Hecksher–Ohlin–Samuelson (H–O–S) would predict that for low-income economies sectors that exhibit low physical and human capital to labor ratios (as measured by the low wages and low value added) would be the candidates for the most rapid expansion (negative coefficients). However, an industrial policy would target the expansion of knowledge and capital-intensive sectors as represented by higher wages and value added (positive coefficients). The results of the exercise are mixed with only statistically significant signs for Korea (negative) and Singapore (positive). First, even accepting this problematic exercise at face value, it appears that contrary to the neo-classical assertion industrial intervention did alter the course dictated by comparative advantage in half the statistically significant cases (in Singapore). Second, the results needs to be tempered by a number of considerations. First, the two digit level is rather aggregated and can hide more than it reveals. Second, there is a built-in neo-classical assumption that wage levels and value added per worker are good reflections of the relative scarcity of factors of production (for instance it assumes away the kind of state intervention in labor markets – sometimes within industries – which was prevalent in Korea and Singapore). Third, if we accept all the assumptions and say that labor-intensive industries grew more rapidly, it says nothing about the sectors selected within the broad grouping relative to what have occurred in a H–O–S world. Overall, the above quote reaffirming the neo-classical interpretation of the nature of the industrialization in Asia seems rather hollow in light of the evidence provided.

6. This is unequivocally stated in the Bank's Asian miracle study. 'Our assessment . . . is that promotion of specific industries generally did not work and therefore holds little promise for other developing economies'(World Bank, 1993, p. 24). This position also places the study squarely in the neo-classical paradigm and is contrary to the case studies in this book.

7. The Bank in the Asian miracle study recognizes how important public funding was to the expansion of primary enrolment and vocational training and in turn how central these were to the development of a suitable labor force for industry (World Bank, 1993, pp. 192–203). The recognition of this point is not new to the Bank and was emphasized in its 1989 report on Sub-Saharan Africa (World Bank, 1989a, pp. 77–84). However, the Bank seems to ignore the conflict between demand managed stabilization aimed at meeting fiscal and monetary targets in Africa and the need for supply inducing government expenditures such as increasing investment in education. So far, the emphasis has been on austerity and stabilization with consequences discussed below. Despite the Bank's comment that 'public spending on health and education did not decline in the adjustment period' (World Bank, 1994, p. 9) the data provided in tables in its new study seems to indicate otherwise. The median expenditures of education as a percentage of GDP fell in all categories between 1981–86 and 1987–90. Overall, in fourteen countries in which data was provided the median decline in the change in real educational expenditures was 4.6 per cent from 1980–83 and 1987–89 with decreases of 70.3 per cent in Nigeria and 64 per cent in the Gambia (two countries in the Bank's 'large improvement' category) (World Bank, 1994, pp. 171, 172).

8. In a rather extreme example, capital spending by the Malawi government (an early adjuster) plunged by 58 per cent between 1980 and 1989 in real terms. Malawi was one country that very heavily emphasized government austerity.(Mosley and Weeks, 1993: Appendices A and B). From a broader perspective, 17 out of 26 countries had a decrease in the percentage of GDP allocated to public investment between 1981–86 and 1987–91 (World Bank, 1994, p. 251).

9. The figures were respectively 4.0 per cent vs. 1.8 per cent; 3.2 per cent vs.−0.6 per cent; and 4.6 per cent vs. −0.2 per cent. The differences between the sample means of investment and export growth were significant at a 1 per cent level and in the case of GDP growth at the 5 per cent level (Mosley and Weeks, 1993, Table 6).

10. Tanzania, which was one of the staunchest critics of adjustment, signed a standby agreement with the International Monetary Fund in 1986. In the same year it initiated the first structural adjustment program. In actuality, a number of liberalizing measures were undertaken prior to 1986, partly in preparation for the accord. For a detailed discussion of the period see Campbell and Stein, 1992.

11. The importance of these variables are supported by empirical studies. For example, Chhibber (1989), examining data from India from 1954/55 to 1977/78, finds that the long run elasticity of supply with respect to non-price variables is three times as high as the price elasticity.

12. In Tanzania the real minimum wage fell by 33 per cent from mid-1986 to the end of 1988. In May 1988, the minimum wage would only purchase 1.3 kilograms of maize meal per day or around 40 per cent of the calories necessary for a family (using this highly unbalanced diet as a nutritional source). In household surveys the amount spent on food on average for a family of four was six to eight times the minimum wage. As a result

formal sector employment was primarily being used as a conduit for informal activities (miradi) rather than as an end in itself with negative implications to productivity. For a more detailed discussion of this see Stein and Nafziger, 1991, pp. 182–5.

13. In the new 'Asian Miracle' study, the Bank moves slightly away from its earlier view that there was a neutrality of incentives to the recognition that Asian states actively promoted exports. However, the effect was the same since they counterbalanced the protection of imports. To quote the study:

> Thus while incentives were largely equal between exports and imports this was the result of countervailing subsidies rather than trade neutrality; the promotion of exports coexisted with the protection of the domestic market. (World Bank, 1993, p. 22)

The Bank does not provide any evidence to support this assertion by systematically evaluating the level of subsidies vs. protection. The only information directly on this question is provided in Table 3.6., from a 1977 study of Korea by Larry Westphal. The table provides the ratio of the effective export exchange rate relative to the effective import exchange rate taking protectionism and subsidies into account. In every year from 1958 to 1975, the ratio exceeded one sometimes by very significant percentages. It would seem that this would indicate a bias in favor of exports which would contradict their assertion. One can only venture the hypothesis that in view of the vast evidence that indicates that the state intervened on the import and export side, the Bank wants to argue that somehow the 'distortions' were offsetting so it was as if they did not intervene at all. In effect, it can still promote the standard neo-classical based reform package of encouraging neutrality in the trade regime.

14. According to Mosley and Weeks (1993), seventeen of 23 African countries surveyed undertook adjustments of this nature.

15. The 'Asian Miracle' study argues that despite the obvious level of protectionism in countries other than Hong Kong and Singapore, there is little evidence of distortion compared to other regions. In 1985, overall tariffs plus para-tariffs in three countries (Korea, Malaysia and Taiwan) are less than almost any other developing country region. There are obvious problems here. As we argued above there has been considerable reductions in nominal levels in recent years in places like Korea. A more interesting comparison would be to examine protectionist levels used during the earlier period of industrialization particularly in Korea and Taiwan. Obviously what is important from an African perspective is how they got where they are not what the tariffs are after they have already arrived (World Bank, 1993, pp. 298–301).

16. The World Bank (1993) provides data on the real interest rates over various periods mostly between 1970 and 1991 except for Japan which is dated from 1953. Only Japan at -1.12 for 1953 to 1991 and Hong Kong for 1973 to 1991 show negative average rates. Of course, focusing on other periods such as the pre-1965 years in Korea would also reveal negative rates (p. 206).

17. M2 is a broader definition of money supply and usually includes narrow money such as currency in circulation and demand deposits as well as quasi-money which is generally comprised of savings and time deposits.

18. There was also wide variation on the level of deficits with countries like Malaysia running significant deficits into the 1980s although countries like Singapore and Taiwan after the early 1970s were very conservative. The question that needs to be answered is not what is the level of the deficit but what is being supported by the deficits and could there be a better use for the credit.

19. In 1982, for example, Singapore had a gross savings rate of 41 per cent while Korea's was only 24 per cent (World Bank, 1984, p. 227). Dornbusch and Reynoso (1993), drawing on the literature, find no evidence that positive real interest rates raise the level of savings.

20. In 1965, just prior to the big surge in industry, Singapore's and Korea's gross domestic savings rates were significantly below those in Sub-Saharan Africa. The numbers were 10, 8 and 13 per cent, respectively. By 1990 the figures were 45, 37 and 16 per cent (World Bank, 1992a, p. 235).

21. The Bank in the study uses a Granger causality test for the growth rate of real GDP per capita and the gross savings rate. For details of the results and the method used see appendix 5.1 of the 'Asian Miracle' study (World Bank, 1993, pp. 242–5).

22. In Tanzania, credit constraints imposed after the 1986 agreement with the IMF were even affecting manufacturing exports. In 1987 Texco (National Textile Company) could only meet Shs 280.7 million of a total export order of Shs 380 million due to overdraft constraints caused by the IMF credit ceilings (Campbell and Stein, 1992, p. 77). There are many examples of the impact of credit constraints on manufacturing in Africa, including attempts by small industry to finance production for exports. In a very interesting case in Ghana, reported by the Wall Street Journal, small and medium sized Ghanian textile producers were having difficulty meeting the orders of import companies like Pier One due to the tightness of credit and the lack of financial institutions to accommodate their needs. Even the normal pro-Bank Journal was lamenting how little progress had been made in Ghana, the Bank's showcase country, after a decade of adjustment (Wall Street Journal, January 26, 1994, p. A5).

23. There are some interesting cases of the private sector prospering in industry without the state's support of even basic public goods. Deborah Brautigam (1993) provides a fascinating case study of the development of mostly auto part manufacturing in the Nnewi Township in Eastern Nigeria during the 1980s. The industrial entrepreneurs substituted their own private goods such as water and power for the public goods the Nigerian state failed to provide. In the absence of financial intermediaries, they financed their operations from well-developed trading operations. Along Hong Kong Chinese lines, they reduced agency problems by incorporating family members into the management of the companies. International connections, developed over a long period in trading with mostly Taiwanese companies, reduced the effects of 'adverse selection' in the import of equipment. Clustering reduced information costs and

provided a demonstration effect which encouraged further investment in manufacturing. Long term business relations increased the trust and cooperation between different groups in the cluster. The result was manufacturing which was not just competitive domestically, but region-ally which allowed some exporting. However, given the macroeconomic instability after 1988 brought on partially by structural adjustment (e.g. devaluing naira made it difficult to plan a large investment based on imported capital goods, inflation was eroding savings, credit constraints made it difficult to obtain working capital from other sources, etc.) the surge of new industries was leveling off. Overall, given the peculiarities of the case and the threat to its sustainability, this is unlikely to be the route to industrialization. There is no substitute for the state capacity to reduce transaction costs and foster entrepreneurship.

24. Even in Taiwan where there was a greater reliance on small scale industrial production, the state played a number of key supporting roles like requiring multinational capital to use local sources as inputs into production. For a good discussion of this, see Brautigam (1994, p. 148).

25. Lindauer and Roemer (1993) in a study on Asia and Africa sponsored by the US Agency for International Development point to the Southeast Asian countries of Thailand, Malaysia and Indonesia, not East Asian nations, as examples to be emulated. Their reasoning is fairly neo-classical, relying on a combination of standard static comparative advantages and public choice arguments. First, they share similar factor endowments including unskilled labor, land and natural resources. In contrast, East Asia has poorer endowments particularly in land and natural resources. Second, the states of Southeast Asia, (unlike East Asia) have been subject to clientalism and rent-seeking which is very similar to Africa. They have not attempted interventionist strategies which would be thwarted by these features.

26. The World Bank (1993) defines the rewards, rules and referees:

> Preferential access to credit and foreign exchange have been extremely attractive rewards. Rules have centered on economic performance, primarily a well-understood imperative to export. Referees, the government officials who have designed and supervised the contests, have been generally competent and fair. (p. 94)

27. I thank Chris Edwards for pointing this out in his comments on a draft of this chapter.

28. Lindauer and Roemer emphatically concur: 'For Sub-Saharan Africa as a whole, intervention has been tried and failed' (1993, p. 13).

29. To once again quote Sanjaya Lall:

> There cannot be any 'quick fixes' for the problems of African industrialization. Some of the incentive-based approaches have given the impression that just getting prices right will launch Africa on the path to NIC-dom . . . it is the right combination of incentives capabilities and institutions . . . that will call forth a proper response . . . A great deal of responsibility . . . rests on the aid donors as well as

African governments. Donors have to ensure that funds aimed at industry are used in a policy framework which provides the right incentives (which may not, it should be reiterated, necessarily mean laissez faire or low, uniform rates of protection) and stimulates the right capabilities. The pace of industrialization should not exceed, in a general sense, the pace of capability development . . . It would also mean that action is needed on the capability front in policy formulation and implementation as well as in industry. (1992, p. 131)

30. Roger Riddell lists four areas of intervention needed to support the development of industry in Africa. They include measures aimed at improving the viability of currently operating industry; assistance in setting up new competitive enterprises which would be aimed at current domestic (to save foreign exchange, raise value added levels etc.) and external markets (particularly sub-regional); support for new enterprises which will not be competitive in the short or medium term but are useful for long-term development; and establishing a facility to monitor and assess the current viability and potential competitiveness of various industries as well as evaluating the benefit vs. cost of the other types of intervention (Riddell, 1993, pp. 240–1). In addition, one should also add the broad forms of intervention in support of industry discussed in this chapter including upgrading technical education, expanding and upgrading infrastructure, aggressive international and regional promotion of domestic manufactures etc.

31. The new Bank study of Africa argues that adjustment policies have had a positive effect on industry. Except for some rather anecdotal evidence, the main support for this position is the higher median increase in the average annual growth rate of the 'large improvement' group from 1981 to 1986 to 1987 to 1991. The argument, however, is not very cogent. First, if we ignore the classification problems discussed above and accept the categories as given, the Bank's data actually indicates that the 'small improvement' category's average annual performance in industry and manufacturing was appreciably better than the 'large improvement' group between 1987 and 1991 (mean of 5.5 per cent vs. 4.3 per cent and 8 per cent vs. 4.6 per cent in industry and manufacturing, respectively). Second, the Bank argues that the critics of adjustment policy's impact on industry must tie any declines in industrial output to Bank policies. The argument can be inverted. The Bank needs to show that if there is any improvement in industry it is due to adjustment policies. This is not done. In fact, evidence from Riddell (1993, p. 232) indicates that some of the countries in the 'large improvement' category (like Zimbabwe) improved their manufacturing by increasing the incentives to export non-traditional categories of manufactures. In contrast, Côte d'Ivoire with its reduction in tariffs undertaken in response to international agency pressure partially explains the decline in the growth of industry in the country (−2.2 per cent between 1987 and 1991) (World Bank, 1994, pp. 149–52, 247–8). In any case both the Bank and its critics would probably agree that there is little or no evidence of robust growth in industry in the last decade. The focus of the argument is on how that can be changed.

2 The World Bank, Neo-Classical Economics and the Application of Asian Industrial Policy to Africa[*]

Howard Stein

INTRODUCTION

The extraordinary industrial expansion of Asian countries in the last decade stands in stark contrast to the general economic malaise permeating Sub-Saharan Africa. Between 1980 and 1989 industry in East and South East Asia grew at an astounding 10.4 per cent per year. In contrast, Sub-Saharan Africa's industrial expansion was an anaemic 0.7 per cent per annum. This pattern of rapid industrial expansion in the last few decades has been associated with a rising standard of living in Asia leaving Sub-Saharan Africa further behind. Between 1965 and 1989, GNP per capita grew at 5.2 per cent per year in East and South East Asia while Sub-Saharan Africa could only manage 0.3 per cent per year. By 1989 manufacturing accounted for 33 per cent of GNP in East and South East Asia, while the comparable figure was only 11 per cent in Sub-Saharan Africa (World Bank, 1991, pp. 204–9).

The interpretation of the factors responsible for the growth of industry in Asia is of vital importance to students of development including those searching for ways to reverse the African malaise. Despite the proliferation of literature on the Newly Industrialized Countries (NICs) very little has been written on the potential applicability of the experience for Africa.[1] It is hoped that this paper can make a small contribution to narrowing this lacuna.

* An earlier version of this paper appeared as 'The World Bank and the Application of Asian Industrial Policy to Africa: Theoretical Considerations', *Journal of International Development*, May/June, 1994.

The paper will begin with a brief assessment of the problems of interpreting the experience of Asian industrialization. It will be followed by a presentation and critique of the World Bank view of Asian development which is heavily informed by neo-classical economic precepts. A section focusing on this international agency is important due to its current influence in Africa via structural adjustment lending. As I have argued elsewhere (Stein, 1992), adjustment as it is currently constituted in Africa, is likely to be deindustrializing. The experience of Asian NICs is seen by the bank as affirming its strategy in Africa. However, if the Bank has misinterpreted the polices responsible for industrial development in Asia, a position argued in this paper, then there will be further doubts about the usefulness of the structural adjustment model as it applies to industry in Sub-Saharan Africa. By way of conclusion the paper will point toward an alternative set of polices that can be gleaned from the experience of East and South East Asian countries.

THE CONSTRAINTS AND USEFULNESS OF COMPARATIVE INTERPRETATIONS

There are two general difficulties to consider when attempting to draw lessons from the experience of one area of the world for application elsewhere. One is the problem of identification and the other is the problem of reproducibility. The first is linked with the identification of the factors responsible for industrial development in Asia. This is an enormously complicated task which involves pinpointing not only what factors are intrinsic but also the direction of causality between those factors. The process of investigation is subjected to the continuous tension between the need for parsimony and the fear of reductionism.

The neo-classical economic literature on the NICs has tried to solve the identification problem by imposing a rationally deductive framework which predetermines the importance, dependency and outcome of the interaction between variables.[2] The presentation while certainly achieving parsimony is often misleading, misconstrued and when capturing aspects of reality overly reductionist. The reasoning is syllogistic. Most market failures are induced by government policies. Countries that have been successful are those that have allowed markets to operate 'freely' without the distortions caused by a large government sector. Any government intervention has been 'neutral' in the sense of not encouraging any particular industry. Prices internally have reflected their international opportunity costs which has permitted industries to respond to correct market signals in turn allowing the country to exploit its comparative advantage. Countries in East and Southeast Asia have had successful industrialization. Therefore, these nations have gotten prices 'right' by pursuing neutral policy regimes. It will be argued below that neutrality has been a myth even in the so called open economies of Hong Kong and Singapore.

The second problem of reproducibility relates to the feasibility of replicating the model elsewhere once the identification problem has been dealt with. The problem is both historical and structural. Four issues come to mind: the uniqueness of international temporal junctures, the specificity of historical economic preconditions, the irreducibility of social attributes and the peculiarity of political alignments. Part of the problem is the degree of endogeneity or extent to which variables can be altered through conscious policy mechanisms.

A few examples would help to amplify these ideas. In the first case it has been argued that the demand conditions for the expansion of exports were particularly propitious with both healthy world growth and easy access to developed markets, particularly the United States (Barrett and Chin, 1987, pp. 25–8; Murakami, 1989, p. 186; and Deyo, 1987, p. 227). Africa could be facing more impediments to increasing exports both due to less healthy economic conditions and growing resistance to market penetration in developed countries (such as quotas imposed on Mauritius and Côte d'Ivoire in clothing and textiles by the EC) (Cable, 1991, p. 172). In addition the movement of the World into trading blocks without the inclusion of Africa could exacerbate the situation.

The question of the preconditions relates to the economic history of countries prior to the phase of rapid industrial expansion which might be difficult to replicate. For instance, Thailand inherited a very complex network of rural roads which were developed by the United States (with the cooperation of the World Bank) for security purposes. They proved to be very important to agricultural diversification and the role it has played in supporting industry (Mackie, 1988: 299). For similar reasons, South Korea and Taiwan also received massive support from the United States. In Korea, for instance, US aid between 1953 and 1962 was the equivalent of 80 per cent of gross domestic investment. During the 1950s it accounted for five-sixths of Korea's imports. (Evans, 1987, p. 210). Security considerations are likely not to be a factor in Africa in justifying the massive inflow of support which would be required to build up infrastructure.

The irreducibility of social attributes is tied to the argument that certain variables associated with the success of NICs are linked to the character of the population which is not easily broken down into economic components that can be readily reproduced with policy surrogates. For instance there is a growing literature on oriental cultural and social values which are important to reducing transaction costs. This includes the Confucian tradition of familial obligation and trust which allows trading and investment networks to flourish (Clegg et al., 1990).[3]

There is a growing literature that is recognizing that specific political alignments partially reflecting a particular array of class, elite and coalitional interests converge to promote a set of policies. Peter Evans, for example, comparing Latin America and East Asia points to the strength of the state in foreign and domestic capital coalitions behind industrialization which was able to ensure less dependent forms of development in the latter case. This was partially a reflection of the early movement towards land reform which promoted the decoupling of the state from rural elites and the authoritarian anti-communist origins in regimes like Korea and Taiwan (Evans, 1987). The state is less autonomous and considerably weaker in many parts of Africa and if we were to adopt Evans' reasoning would be less able to direct a coalition with domestic and foreign capital.

While there are lessons that can be applied to Africa, the circumstances and conditions of their application must be carefully evaluated. To much of the early neo-classical literature, however, reproducibility was not an issue. In a world in which there is only one successful route to achieving development, rational leaders would eventually recognize the superiority of market led economic growth. The NICs would have a positive demonstration effect. The role of the neo-classical development economist was to disseminate the underlying basis of the NIC model.

There was occasional dissent in the ranks such as William Cline's admonishment (based on a simulation exercise) about the untenable market penetration (as high as 60 per cent of all manufactured imports) into industrial countries which would be required if other Third World countries were to pursue the NIC manufacturing export-led approach (Cline, 1982). The response by Gustav Ranis was quintessentially neo-classical arguing that emulating the Asian NICs was not 'exporting [manufactured goods] as much as possible but moving in the direction of market liberalization as quickly as possible'. By implication 'Some LDCs, especially those with a more generous natural resource endowment would in fact, be expected to indefinitely maintain a strong raw materials component of their exports' (Ranis, 1985, p. 544), meaning that only a few would pursue a similar manufacturing route. Thus the lesson of the Asian NICs was that they liberalized their markets so that trade would reflect their comparative advantage based on their country endowments or in other words they operated as predicted by Heckscher–Ohlin–Samuelson and thus reaped the predicted economic rewards.

With the slow pace of economic reform and the resistance to structural adjustment in other developing areas, the neo-classicals had to begin looking at the issue of reproducibility, particularly the question of political alignments. The overtly voluntaristic view of policy formation eventually gave way to a public choice political economy perspective. This school tried to explain why governments imposed price distorting policies, and the logical corollaries, the identification of entrenched interests impeding economic reform and ultimately, the coalitions that were behind successful change in the NICs.[4]

The World Bank, we will see, deals with the problems of comparative interpretation in a manner similar to the neo-classicals. First, we will turn to the World Bank's view of Asian industrialization.

INDUSTRIALIZATION IN ASIA: THE WORLD BANK VIEW

The World Bank's view of the components underlying Asia's success in industry is partially captured in its *World Development Report, 1981*, a time which corresponds to the beginning of its structural adjustment period in Africa. First, while admitting some countries pursued import substitution at early stages, the Bank argued that successful countries like Singapore and South Korea '. . . have been those that resisted or overcame the temptations to adopt inward-looking trade policies and to delay transition to greater export orientation' (World Bank, 1981c, p. 25). Thus import-substitution is seen largely as a liability in which the earlier the country shifted directions, the more '. . . they avoided the burdens to exports that extending import-substitution to intermediate goods would have entailed' (p. 25). We will see below that this overstates the case and creates a rather false dichotomy.

Second, outward orientation according to the World Bank was less of a policy shift in support of export orientation than '. . . an elimination in biases in these policies' or in other words, the '. . . scrapping of disincentives to produce for export, or disincentives to use imported inputs when they were less expensive' (World Bank, 1981c, p. 25). Similarly reform meant '. . . ending policies that favored capital-intensive over labor-intensive sectors and methods of production and placing small enterprises on an equal footing with large firms so that they could obtain credit, technical assistance and marketing support' (World Bank, 1981c, p. 25). To quote the World Bank at some length:

> Thus, policies in the successful countries have been generally supportive of industrialization and commerce but have avoided directing that support at any particular sector or method. Decisions about what activities and what processes could be efficiently and profitably built up are left to individual firms, which succeed or fail as their decisions prove to be correct or incorrect. (p. 25)

This, we will argue below, is hardly an accurate depiction of either Singapore or South Korea or for that matter any of the other countries in East and Southeast Asia. It is more a reflection of neo-classical theorems of how states *should* operate rather than how states *have* operated. As argued above, the neo-classical syllogism runs along the following lines. If undistorted markets are what underlies successful industrialization and industrialization in Asia has been successful then it must be because they have not distorted markets or at least at some point have reversed historical distortions. Therefore the state must have been neutral allowing their countries to specialize in accordance with their comparative advantage.

In the *World Development Report, 1983* we learn more about the World Bank view of the relationship between prices, distortions, government intervention and the impact on growth and efficiency. This doctrine under the relationship between pricing and efficiency has been commonly referred to as 'getting prices right'. The theoretical roots are quite explicitly outlined in box 4.1 on p. 42:

> If the economy is producing efficiently,[5] scarcity values must be equal to opportunity costs, and their common value is the efficiency price which, for imports and exports, will then be identical to the

border price. For non-traded goods, efficiency price can be measured by the opportunity cost of their production when the alternative would be to produce traded goods, or by their scarcity value in displacing traded goods.

Therefore, 'prices of goods that deviate significantly from their scarcity value (or "opportunity cost") may be regarded as "distorted " ' (p. 43). The source of distortions is typically the government, according to the World Bank. 'In most instances . . . price distortions are introduced by government directly or indirectly' (p. 57).

The result of these distortions is the loss of efficiency and growth. To prove their point they assert that 'during the 1970s, the growth rate of countries with highly distorted prices was as much as 2 per cent less than the average for developing countries' (p. 44). According to the World Bank, this is easy to understand since efficiency requires '. . . capital and labor to be priced according to their marginal productivities at international prices' (p. 43). Or in other words countries that are most successful are the ones that '. . . invest and expand in ways that reflect the relative scarcity of capital and labor-avoiding, for example, capital intensive production methods if they have abundant manpower' (p. 43).

The argument of the World Bank on the need to get prices right is buttressed with further evidence. They point not only to the higher GNP growth rates, but also higher savings rates, higher additional output per unit of investment and higher growth rates in agriculture, industry and export volumes in countries with lower price distortions. Among the countries included in the low distortion group from Asia are Thailand, Korea, Malaysia and the Philippines. Among the East Asian and Southeast Asian countries, only Indonesia is placed outside the low distortion group, (in the middle range) (pp. 60–1). Once again, success among the East and Southeast Asian countries is linked to the avoidance of price distortions.

A few comments about the nature of this exercise are in order. First, this is a very static exercise based on averages over a decade (1970s) which ignores shifts that occur in distortions in countries. For instance Chile up to 1973 was very distortionist (by World Bank standards) in its policies but went through significant liberalization after Allende was overthrown. Chile presumably because of its early period still had high enough averages to place it in the high distortion category. Conveniently Chile also had one of the poorest industrial performances of the countries surveyed.

Second the measures of distortion, to say the least, are problematic. Take their discussion of exchange rates. A high distortion is defined as a 15 per cent raise in the real exchange rates from a 1972/73 base year (Weiss, 1988, p. 36). First, there are enormous conceptual and empirical problems with measuring the real exchange rates (like the choice of deflating indices).[6] Second, even if we assume no empirical problems, an increase in the real exchange rate can either be a reduction in a distortion or an increase in a distortion, depending on whether the currency is undervalued or overvalued. A country that maintained the same real exchange rate might actually be encouraging the perpetuation of a distortion.

Third, the direction of causality, a crucial assumption in any correlative exercise, is subject to question. For instance, if the source of poor performance is structural in nature (such as low income elasticities for export products) then this might lead to the imposition of distorting policies such as import restrictions (from balance of payments problems) which would increase the real effective protection rate (one of their measures of distortion) (Weiss, 1988, pp. 60–1). One could raise these along with many other arguments which point to the inconclusiveness of this 'supporting documentation'.[7]

A final aspect of the World Bank perspective in Asia is their interpretation of the role of agriculture. 'In the semi-industrial countries in East Asia, successful development has had . . . a supportive approach to increases in agricultural productivity and growth' (World Bank, 1981c, p. 25). In the World Development Report, 1979, we learn more about their interpretation of the role of agriculture. In Asia, the World Bank cites Taiwan, Korea and Malaysia as countries '. . . which invested heavily in irrigation, land improvements, other rural infrastructure and agricultural research in early stages of development' and have reaped '. . . the benefits of high agricultural productivity' (p. 62). As a result, these countries have been able to raise rural incomes which have been an important source of demand for industrialization particularly of the labor intensive, small industry type located in rural areas. In addition, agriculture provides cheap sources of raw materials, earns vital foreign exchange through exports and provides inexpensive food for the labor force employed outside of agriculture (p. 61).

In contrast, polices such as artificially low prices to agriculture, taxation of agricultural exports, overvalued exchange rates and heavy protection of manufactured goods have turned the domestic terms of trade against agriculture, limiting purchasing power and constraining industrial development (p. 61). Korea and Taiwan, on the other hand, have used other means such as rural savings institutions to transfer resources to support industry (p. 62). Again this view of agriculture reflects the neo-classical 'getting prices right' doctrine. We will argue that as with the view of industry, it misses vital components. Moreover, many policies adopted by Asian countries, which are not consistent with their neo-classical view, have been applied with success (in terms of industry) for periods of time.

TOWARD A CRITIQUE OF THE WORLD BANK/NEO-CLASSICAL VIEW OF INDUSTRIALIZATION IN ASIA

Import Substitution vs Export Orientation: False Dichotomies?

We saw above that the World Bank/neo-classical view links successful industrialization to the early switch to export orientation in the NICs. The problem with this perspective is that it dichotomizes the choice, underplays the dynamic linkage between the two and misdirects the focus away from other components vital to successful industrialization. There is evidence to suggest that a period of import substitution was vital to creating the preconditions necessary for a switch to greater export orientation.

In Korea, for instance, Nishimizu and Robinson (1984) link the import-substitution between 1955 and 1963 to the export boom after 1963. Institutionally, Cumings (1987) points to the period as an 'easy' period which allowed the growth of the conglomerates that was so vital to the export expansion phase (Cumings 1987, p. 68). In Singapore, the ephemeral union with Malaysia (1963–1965) which led to the brief period of import substitution was important to first attracting foreign manufacturing to the city-state (Haggard and Cheng, 1987, p. 90).

In Thailand, clothing production, an important component of the country's import substitution strategy, which operated behind fairly stiff tariff barriers, was able to increase its export performance dramatically over the 1970s, becoming a leading exporter in the 1980s. In 1978, for example, clothing with a nominal tariff rate of 100 per cent and an effective rate of 243 per cent, which were among the highest rates of all products, managed to increase its share of exports from 0.5 per cent of the total in 1970 to 8.2 per cent in 1980 (Ariff and Hill, 1985, pp. 90, 201).

The World Bank/neo-classicals in studies such as World Bank (1981c) and Balassa (1984) point to the superior economic performance of export oriented regimes. But these kinds of simple distinctions hide the nature of the industrial dynamics in these countries. There is considerable evidence that import substitution has not been abandoned in the countries that have supposedly become more export oriented and that there might be a much closer integration of the two strategies than suggested by the World Bank/neo-classical view. In Korea this has been closely associated with their infant industry strategy. The standard interpretation is that, after a limited period of protection, the successful industries have been opened to competition from imports as tariffs or quotas are removed.

In Korea, an intermediate step is introduced with a much longer period of protection. In particular, infant industries are obliged to start exporting after a period of time with the threat of the removal of protection. Successful industries are then able to maintain a two-tiered system where profits are supported by the higher price on domestic markets, while maintaining competitive prices on international markets (Luedde-Neurath, 1986, pp. 177–8). This suggests an alternative to the blanket reduction in protection that the World Bank and IMF through structural adjustment is attempting to impose, with devastating consequences, in Africa.

In Taiwan, the government uses its import licensing scheme as a means of encouraging import substitution. They have been able to keep average tariffs low (although *certainly not even* as often depicted by the neo-classicals) and quantitative controls hidden (minimizing the evidence for retaliation) while obtaining significant results. In particular, they categorize imports as 'prohibited', 'controlled', and 'permissible'. In the permissible category the list is covertly divided between items that are freely imported and items needing special permission. The importer applies to a bank for a licence. The bank checks to see if the item is on the covert list. If it is, the request is forwarded to the Industrial Development Board. The Board asks the importer to provide evidence that Taiwanese suppliers are unable to meet the specifications of the importer. It forces them to approach trade association and the like. This creates communication between importers and potential domestic suppliers and can lead to cooperation between industrial supplier and would-be importers. The referral mechanism has covered both intermediate and primary good production such as petrochemicals, chemicals, steel and other basic metals, machine tools, forklift trucks and bearings, areas which the World

Bank/neo-classicals argue create the most difficulties in import-substitution strategies (Wade, 1988a, pp. 139–41). The key here is not import substitution vs. export orientation but government induced methods to increase the sophistication and depth of industrialization.

The Myth of State Neutrality: Hong Kong and Singapore

The World Bank/neo-classical view that the shift to an export orientation was one from the bias against exports to a stance of neutrality also has little to do with the policy reality in the countries of East and Southeast Asia. Governments in every country have made choices not only in support of broad strategic shifts like the move to export orientation but also to encourage very specific industries. They have backed these choices with a wide array of instruments including tax breaks, subsidies, priorities in foreign exchange, banking policies, expenditures on education and infrastructure aimed at benefiting specific sectors or even companies, tariff and non-tariff barriers and partial and complete ownership of industries.

The literature on this topic is very well developed on Korea and Taiwan and there is little need to elaborate on this here.[8] Let me instead focus on the less familiar cases of Singapore and Hong Kong, countries often cited as free market cases. The state policies in Hong Kong are less industry specific and more an example of a strong and consistent wage, infrastructure and social overhead subsidization or price control program aimed at helping the competitive position of exports.[9]

To keep labor costs down, the state has had a very interventionist food and housing policy. In the first case, a rice control scheme has been in operation since 1955 through import licensing and a government buffer scheme which is used to ensure that prices are kept low. Through state sponsored non-profit organizations, like the Fish Marketing Organization and the Vegetable Marketing Organization, prices are also kept competitive through the supervision of marketing. Low interest capital loans to groups like fisherman also help to facilitate the supply of inexpensive food.

Second, inexpensive readily available housing has been a prime concern of the state. Forty percent of the population live in government-subsidized public housing, which has been kept very low allowing high personal savings. Not only does the government fix rents for its own properties, it also intervenes heavily elsewhere. All pre-war private properties are rent controlled and since 1962, all post-war domestic private rental accommodations are under rent control (except during 1966–1970).

In all levels of education, vital for a competitive labor force, the government bears most of the costs. At the primary level, by the late 1970s only about one-sixth of all students were private paying with the rest supported by the government. After 1977, at the secondary level up to age fifteen, the government has paid for about 90 per cent of the student body with a mixture of support after that age. Post-secondary education is the complete responsibility of the government and since 1969/70 grants and interest free loans have been readily available to cover tuition and other expenses. Similarly seventy-five per cent of all hospitals are government owned or supported covering nearly 90 per cent of all hospital beds. User charges are extremely low with hospital occupants only paying HK$5 per day and only HK$3 per visit in the early 1980s at the numerous government-run clinics. (Contrast these policies with the structural adjustment induced cutbacks and user fees introduced by African governments in the 1980s.)

As in other British colonies, all land is owned by the Crown. Property rights are set by lease agreements. Land has been used as an instrument of industrial policy with land grants to industrial projects the state deems to be beneficial to the economy (lately capital intensive in nature). This policy was introduced in 1973 and organized systematically under the auspices of the Hong Kong Industrial Estates Corporation in 1977. Land rates on government estates have typically been about 6 per cent of the going market level.

In infrastructure, the government has also been active through ownership, subsidization and tight control when utilities are privately owned. Profits on the private power authority, for example, are limited to sixteen and one-half per cent. Water rates have been heavily subsidized and kept very low.

From the above description it is clear that, even in Hong Kong, the model hailed by the neo-classicals as laissez faire, there are important forms of intervention which are clearly market distorting. Policies to subsidize labor, for example, would, in neo-classical terms, unduly encourage labor intensive operations. The government, often under pressure from broad capitalist interests in Hong Kong, is interested in the competitive position of industry which means observing global market niches and creating the comparative advantage to meet them. Clearly, Hong Kong's success in recent decades in low priced labor intensive industrial exports like clothing and toys was assisted by wage subsidization.[10]

Singapore, on the other hand, pursued a set of policies that were not only broadly strategic but also industry-specific.[11] The strategy of industrialization in Singapore is unequivocally a product of conscious government intervention using a variety of tools that the World Bank would consider to be market distorting.[12] There are roughly five phases in Singapore's post-independence industrialization. The first was the attempt at import-substitution between 1959 and 1965 spurred by the prospect and union with the larger Malay market. The policy initiatives including tariffs, the huge capital investment programs of the state run Housing Development Board and the Economic Development Board, special state incentives to companies investing in government priority areas ('Pioneer Industry Ordinance') program and the establishment of a number of public enterprises in manufacturing.

The second phase, export oriented labor intensive manufacturing, occurred between 1965 and 1979. The shift was not due to the adoption of neutrality by the state, but to extensive state intervention in support of manufacturing exports. The breakdown of the union and the resulting loss of access to the Malay market clearly motivated the shift. This was formalized in the Economic Expansion Incentives Act of 1967 which lowered the tax rate on export companies to 10 per cent, removed duties on all machinery and raw materials and accelerated depreciation schedules for exporting companies.

Between 1965 and 1968 a series of anti-labor bills were passed aimed at reducing direct and indirect labor costs (further enhancing the profits from labor-intensive manufacturing for export). The Development Bank of Singapore, incorporated in July 1968, actively encouraged export oriented industrialization with low interest loans and equity participation. Later in the same year, the state organized the International Trading Company to develop overseas markets, source bulk buying of raw materials and actively participate as an equity partner in private companies. The government also formed the Neptune Orient Lines in 1969 to facilitate shipping without relying on foreign lines and the Jurong Town Corporation in 1968 to ensure a ready supply of land for industrial estates expansion. Twenty-one new public enterprises were organized in manufacturing in 1968 and 1969, many aimed at augmenting exports (shipbuilding, petroleum refining, etc.). The government also opened a number of vocational schools during this period to encourage a ready supply of skilled labor for these industries. By the early 1970s the economy had reached full employment. The government, however, maintained a policy to keep wages down through immigration and other institutional means until 1979.

With this machinery in place, the impact on export sales was impressive. Between 1968 and 1978 the export sales to output ratio in manufacturing went from 36.3 to 63.9 (Rodan, 1989, pp. 100, 109). Exports grew at an annual rate of 12 per cent during the 1970s compared to 4.2 per cent in the 1960s. By 1980, the portion of exports in food and other primary commodities had fallen from 59 per cent to 16 per cent from 1960, as manufacturing and fuel exports burgeoned (26 per cent to 55 per cent and 15 to 29 per cent respectively over the twenty years) (World Bank, 1983, pp. 165, 167).

By 1979, with the continued demand for labor from labor-intensive exports, the government decided to launch the 'Second Industrial Revolution'. The state, with a series of measures, deliberately increased wages, over three years, to encourage employers to substitute capital for labor, increase productivity and shift production to higher value added products for export. New investment incentives and manpower development programs were also introduced. This strategy was effective until the mid 1980s when a severe recession hit the economy. This led to the latest phase which is a combination of diversification into service exports (operational headquarters, information technology, financial and treasury services, leisure, entertainment, and creative services) which are considered to be more recession proof, and wage restraint with a two year pay cut to keep exports competitive (EDB, 1990a, p. 27; EDB, 1990b, p. 4). Incentives were designed to encourage the new areas.

The extent of government influence in the economy, by the early 1980s was astounding. There were 450 state-owned companies directly participating in production, accounting for roughly 25 per cent of Singapore's GNP. The government had enormous influence over investment markets through agencies like its Central Provident Fund with savings from the public sector accounting for 64 per cent of the total level of gross savings in the country. They housed 80 per cent of the population in subsidized owner occupied units built by the Housing Development Board and owned about 75 per cent of all land in the country (Lim, 1987, p. 208). Singapore has clearly gotten prices right, but they have little to do with the market signals envisioned by neo-classicals and more to do with creating incentives for the private sector to pursue a set of national economic priorities. While some would call this distorted others would call it prudent. In 1990, Singapore could boast a GNP per capita of US$11,949 from US$435 in 1960 and an infant mortality rate of 6.6 per 100,000 from 34.9 in 1960 (helped by heavily subsidized health care) (EDB, 1990b, p. 2). By contrast the US infant mortality rate is around 10 per 100,000 and 107 per 100,000 for Sub-Saharan Africa.

Agriculture and Industry: Problems with the Neo-Classical View

The World Bank/neo-classical perspective on the role of agriculture is also deeply flawed. Their analysis appears to give agriculture the leading role in a relatively unfettered market. Terms of trade constantly rise in favor of agriculture, which becomes a major source of demand for industry. Cash crop exports become an important source of foreign exchange. Agricultural processing forms the basis of industrialization and surplus voluntarily leaves as incomes expand. This view has more to do with the theoretical world of neo-classical axioms than the reality of agricultural–industrial interactions in countries like Taiwan and Korea.

Agriculture in these countries was made completely subservient to industry. Its role in the early stages of industrialization was to provide cheap sources of food for the expanding urban work force. Heavy state intervention was used in support of this objective using extra market means of procurement. To quote the economist, T. H. Lee, who later became Vice-President of Taiwan:

> The price mechanism was not considered as an incentive for adopting new technology and increasing agricultural output. Government allocation of chemical fertilizers, pesticides, irrigation water, funds and subsidy compensated for the price mechanism. Government collection of rice, sugar and other important products in addition to the unfavorable terms of trade resulted in a tremendous net capital outflow from agriculture. (quoted in Moore, 1988, p. 127)

An inexpensive readily available source of rice was vital to industrialization in order to keep real wages down. In Taiwan, farmers were legally required to grow rice on designated paddy areas and obliged to meet state quotas for procurement. A land tax in rice was also imposed. Rents on publicly-owned rice property were paid in kind as were repayments to the Provincial Food Bureau, the government credit agency. Fertilizer manufacture and importing was the monopoly of the state-owned Taiwan Fertilizer Corporation which received rice for fertilizer from rice farmers. This source accounted for more than 50 per cent of public rice procurement in the fifties. In this period state rice purchases accounted for 60 per cent of producer rice releases falling to 38 per cent by 1970. The rice market was also manipulated by the state through other means, such as trader licenses, direct allocation of rice to government personnel, and the low fixed price at which government procured rice was released to private traders (Moore, 1988, pp. 127–8).

In a similar way the state was also heavily involved in the procurement of sugar, wine and tobacco. It has also controlled a variety of food prices at the retail level including pork, and tightly regulated the import of all agricultural products. The state was responsible for almost all of the investment in infrastructure such as irrigation systems.

Overall, we can see that the policy towards agriculture was somewhat different from the one the World Bank/neo-classicals portray. Surplus was involuntarily transferred from agriculture by the state through its procurement and taxation system. The terms of trade fell during the vital labor surplus period, allowing a ready supply of workers for industrial expansion. This and the rice policy helped keep wages low (as in almost all export oriented regimes in East and Southeast Asia) permitting the expansion of labor intensive manufacturing exports. Industrial activity with its emphasis on textiles, was not particularly restricted to agricultural processing, although there was limited expansion in areas like sugar processing and mushroom and asparagus canning. Similarly agricultural goods including those processed were not the major source of foreign currency. Most of the earnings fell into the hands of the state.

By 1968, Taiwan began to be transformed from a labor surplus to a labor scarce economy with a corresponding rise in real wages. The state with a series of measures, began to improve the terms of trade in agriculture while letting up on some of its statist policies. By then industry was well on its way and staples declined as a portion of consumer expenditures. In 1974, for example, the price of rice doubled with little appreciable protest from consumers (Moore, 1988, p. 139). What is important here is that the country could afford at that point to alter its policy towards agriculture and improve its terms of trade. In the case of Africa, the World Bank through its misrepresentation of the lessons from Asia is arguably promoting an agricultural centered policy which is likely to be detrimental to industrialization on the continent. This and other related issues will be explored in the next section.

THE BANK'S VIEW OF ASIA AND ITS IMPLICATIONS TO AFRICA

The extent to which the World Bank approach to industrial adjustment in Africa draws on and parallels its view of Asian industrialization is captured by Meier and Steel's *Industrial Adjustment in Sub-Saharan Africa*, which was published by the World Bank in 1987. In line with the above view of the components of success of industry in Asia is the absence of these features in Africa. In particular Meier and Steel point to the weaknesses of industry in Africa as 'overexpansion of industrial capacity relative to agricultural production'; 'overextension of public ownership relative to the economic justification for direct public investment'; and 'overinvestment in import-substitution relative to . . . the export industries needed to generate rising foreign exchange earnings' (Meier and Steel, 1987, pp. 8–9).

The problems of identification and reproducibility as in neo-classical interpretations are non-existent.[13] As Meier and Steel (1987) succinctly put it:

> Evidence from a wide range of countries suggests that growth is better sustained under policies that minimize price distortions and are 'outward oriented' in the sense of exposing producers to international price and competition. (p. 14)

As with the above interpretation of the policy behind successful industrialization in Asia ' "outward orientation' strictly refers to neutrality of incentives'(p. 15). This means reversing the distortions in Africa and creating a 'more neutral incentive structure' which will encourage a 'shift toward industries with a comparative advantage in using the country's resources'. This 'requires reducing the level of variation of protection and increasing competitive behavior' (p. 12). As they elaborate elsewhere

> Among subsectors, distortions in the pattern of protection have encouraged overinvestment in some activities that use resources inefficiently or even lose foreign exchange and have discouraged activities based on local resources or export. Greater exposure of domestic industry to international competition requires easing quantitative restrictions on imports (replacing them with a combination of devaluation, tariffs, and taxes) and equalizing protection across subsectors. (p. 14)

Removing distortions also means avoiding the instruments that governments have used to promote specific industries such as less than positive real interest rates, investment incentives and exemptions for imported capital and raw materials (although they might permit more flexibility on exemptions for export production – which is in conflict with their strong statement on neutrality) (p. 14). It also means 'reduction in capacity under public ownership, whether through the sale to private investors or outright closure' (p. 21).

Finally on the role of agriculture in industrialization their recommendations parallel the World Bank interpretation of the success of policies in this sector in Asia

> The relatively large size of agriculture, and the evident failure of past policy biased against it, have led to a new consensus . . .: agricultural development is an essential foundation for industrial development in Africa. Improved agricultural incentives can stimulate industry by increasing raw material supplies and raising rural incomes. This stimulus, together with rising productivity, can provide the basis for sustained industrial growth . . . Agricultural production needs to keep pace with population growth as a base for industrial growth to raise income per capita. Conversely, experience shows that lagging agricultural growth eventually deprives industry of both resources and domestic demand. (p. 11)

Thus in the three areas – export orientation vs import substitution, distortions and government policy vs. neutrality and the role of agriculture – the policy recommendations for adjustment in Africa are a mirror image of the World Bank view of the factors underlying successful industrialization in Asia. We will explore the implications of this in the conclusions.

CONCLUSIONS

We have raised serious doubts about the World Bank's identification of the factors responsible for industrialization in Asia. In particular using a variety of examples we argued that the export oriented vs. import substitution dichotomy was misleading, that government policy was not neutral but active, interventionist and 'distorting' often with positive results, and that agriculture played a very different role from that suggested by the World Bank. On the latter point it was argued that interventionist state policies directed agriculture in support of labor intensive industrialization by helping to keep wages down through low food prices and migratory pressure on labor supply.

We have also shown that the strategy of industrial adjustment in Africa closely parallels the World Bank interpretation of what has been successful in Asia. This is not surprising since they both reflect a neo-classical perspective which universalizes axioms on the role of government and markets in development and applies a rationally deductive framework which presupposes the importance, dependency and outcome of the interaction between variables.

If we accept the validity of the cases that have been raised then dropping import substitution, disengaging and neutralizing government policy, including the reduction and equalization of tariff rates, and rapidly raising the terms of trade in agriculture might have serious consequences for industry in Africa.[14] Of course, this does not deal with the theoretical problem of identitification and reproducibility but indicates that the World Bank/neo-classical model of Asian industrialization and adjustment has solved neither of these.

A solution to these problems requires a consensus on what constitutes the criteria of success in industry, a careful case-by-case examination of the factors responsible in each country, a comparison of what is common in each case and the determination of what can be reproduced in Africa given its economic, political and social structure. In terms of identification the other papers in this volume begin to do this. The preliminary and partial indication from this paper is that governments have constantly intervened to set industrial priorities and to improve the competitive position of industry – a position that seems at odds with structural adjustment in Africa which believes that it should largely be left to markets. In other words governments have continuously created comparative advantage. The reason is that they realized not all specialization is created equally. No country has been able to significantly improve its living standards as an exporter of cash crops or industry based exclusively on the simple processing of these commodities. That however, is the position that logically follows from the static comparative advantage model of the World Bank in Africa.

During the past year, Asian governments have begun to reconsider the policies that have been promoted by international agencies in Africa and elsewhere. They have seen little evidence to support the contention that structural adjustment is working. Moreover, the experience of their own countries seems at odds with the policies that are being encouraged by the World Bank and the IMF. Japan, for one is currently designing bilateral programs which will layout alternatives to adjustment.[15] This is one positive sign in the otherwise grey cloud hanging over the continent.

Notes

1. There is a growing literature, on the other hand, examining Asia and Latin America. See for example Naya et al., 1989; Evans, 1987; Ranis, 1989; and Harberger, 1988. With the exception of Evans these examples are interpreted in neo-classical economic terms and are of little assistance to scholars searching for an theoretical framework for comparing Africa and Asia (more on this below). One recent paper (Ranis, 1990) not only compares Latin America and Asia but also tries to draw lessons for Africa. His argument is typically neo-classical, that Latin America went further along the road of import substitutions with more market distorting policies and therefore has found the road to exporting more difficult. His solution for Africa is to follow the Asian route, as he sees it, by first emphasizing mixed rural development (they are land-abundant) while pushing broad liberalization which will still leave room for 'natural' import substitution (pp. 23–5). The argument below will indicate 'natural' is hardly the word to describe industrialization in Asia import substitution or otherwise. The most significant exception to the focus on Latin America is Lindauer and Roemer (1993) which contains comparisons of Asia and Africa by major sectors. As indicated in chapter one, the study falls into the rubric of what I refer to as the 'revisionist' neo-classical position; it recognizes the widespread intervention of states but argues that government policy initiatives did not alter what would have been predicted by their static comparative advantage as given by their factor endowments.
2. The most influential contributions (influential in the sense of being widely cited and being in positions of considerable influence in academia or international agencies) would include Little et al., 1970; Little, 1981; Krueger, 1978; Krueger, 1981; Bhagwati, 1978; Balassa, 1971; Balassa, 1981; and Balassa et al., 1982.
3. I believe that this is one of the weaker factors pointed to in the literature given the wide array of cultures that have been associated with rapid industrial development. Even Confucianism following the tradition of Max Weber and Talcott Parsons was considered to be (as late as the 1970s) an impediment to capitalist development in Asia. For a summary of the Weber–Parson model and the literature it spawned see Tai, 1989.
4. A few examples might be helpful. In the African context on sources of price distortions see Robert Bates, 1981; 1987. On impediments to reform in Africa see Commins 1988, (particularly articles by Christianson et al. and Bates). Finally on the political economy of the NICs, see Haggard, 1988. What is common to these examples is that they add a political

dimension to the neo-classical model of development never questioning the validity of its premises.

5. The definition of efficiency is completely neo-classical using the Pareto criteria that 'an economy is considered production efficient if the supply of any good (or service) cannot be increased without reducing the supply of some other good' (World Bank, 1983, p. 42).
6. Even the World Bank admits this elsewhere. For a good discussion of these problems see Meier and Steel, 1987, pp. 270–3.
7. Weiss (1988) points to many other weakness of the exercise.
8. A few examples of the literature include Wade, 1984; Wade, 1988a; Wade, 1988b; Wade, 1990; Luedde-Neurath, 1986; Luedde-Neurath, 1988; and Reiger and Veit, 1990.
9. Some of this information comes from an interview with Prof. S. Gordon Redding, Chair of the School of Management, University of Hong Kong, which took place on August 29, 1991 in Hong Kong. An additional source is Youngman (1982).
10. How much market share is due to these policies is of course difficult to ascertain. However, given the population pressures and land scarcity one could imagine, for instance, the enormous rents which would likely arise in an unregulated market putting upward pressure on wages and hurting the competitive position of industry.
11. The discussion on Singapore is base on interviews with Prof. E. F. Pang of the University of Singapore and a Senior Planning Official of the Economic Development Board in Singapore on August 12, 1991. Conversations with Linda Lim of the Business School of the University of Michigan in Ann Arbor during 1990/91 were also helpful. Finally, the discussion draws on Lim (1987) and Rodan (1989).
12. Although it won't be undertaken here, it is fairly easy to illustrate that announced government policies in Singapore led to shifts in sub-sectoral growth rates that reflected those announced policies and therefore would be unlikely a reflection of shifting market conditions and comparative advantage as neo-classicals would like to argue. Rodan (1989) provides a fairly detailed account of political changes leading to policy shifts which in turn are reflected in adjustments in the structure of industry in Singapore. On this point, see Linda Lim's chapter in this volume.
13. Following the neo-classical literature, the World Bank has more recently focused on political economy dimensions of adjustment or the politics of reproducibility. In the introduction to a recent World Bank study of the experience of adjustment, the author notes

> Taken together, these lessons hold a moral for economists. It is that we at the World Bank – and everyone else, I believe – underestimated the political difficulty . . . We fail to give full weight in our own thinking to the fact that structural adjustment means a major redistribution of economic power and hence of political power in many of the countries undergoing this process. The politics of change is one of the reasons adjustment has taken more time than expected in some countries and one of the reasons some adjustments efforts have not been sustained. (Stern, 1991, pp. 4, 5)

The implication here is that rationality of adjustment is not in any way flawed, it is just that there might be political reasons for resisting it. This is a rational choice interpretation that is very consistent with the literature cited in the above note.

14. This is not to suggest agriculture should be neglected and completely exploited. I do agree that investment in agricultural extension and infrastructure is very important. My disagreement lies with the World Bank generalization that a rapid and significant rise in the terms of trade for agriculture is is needed in almost all African countries. If an employment generating labor intensive form of industrialization is to be developed in Africa then any increase in the terms of trade must be carefully weighed against the impact on rural-urban migratory rates relative to the supply absorption of industry and the inflationary impact on wages (or its equivalent fall in living standards). This type of industrialization also implies food oriented agriculture and state intervention in markets, along the lines discussed above, to keep prices at the retail level down. This is also contrary to broad across the board increases for all types of agricultural production and the hands off approach that the World Bank is encouraging. Finally, the World Bank recognition of the importance of state investment in agriculture runs contrary to the practice of structural adjustment where governments have cutback expenditures to meet the deficit and credit targets of the IMF standby accords.

15. During August 1991, I met with Professor Shigeru Ishikawa (a strong critic of structural adjustment) at the Institute for International Cooperation in Tokyo, prior to his meeting with aid officials to design an alternative approach to dealing with the economic problems of Egypt. I was informed that they were interested in promoting policies more consistent with the history of Japanese economic development.

3 Japan's Industrial Development, 1868–1939: Lessons for Sub-Saharan Africa

E. Wayne Nafziger

INTRODUCTION

Japan, whose 1868 level of economic development was only slightly more than other Afro-Asian countries, has had the world's fastest growth in real GNP per capita since then (Nafziger, 1990, pp. 46–7), or second fastest to Sweden if computed through the early 1950s. Africa and Asia are 'looking East' to learn development lessons from the major non-Western industrialized country, Japan. With recent US slow growth, 'modernization' theorists have emphasized capitalist Japan as an alternative model to the socialist approach.

Though the Tokugawa shogun isolated Japan from foreign influence from 1638 to the 1860s, they provided a more favorable legacy for industrialization than many present Sub-Saharan African countries. Mid-nineteenth century feudal Japan had a literacy rate about as high as England, a well-integrated transport system, a well-developed tax system, a highly commercialized agriculture whose productivity per hectare exceeded Sub-Sahara today, and guild and clan-monopoly workshops producing silk textiles, *sake*, rapeseed oil, cotton cloth, candles, and other processed products for a national market, especially the large urban populations of Edo (Tokyo), Osaka, and Kyoto (T. Nakamura, 1983, p. 51; and Lockwood, 1954, p. 4).

Japan's life expectancy in 1891–1899 was 43–44 years, lower than the level of virtually all countries (except Gambia, Guinea, Guinea-Bissau, Sierra Leone, and Afghanistan) and substantially lower than the average for Sub-Saharan Africa (51) in 1990. In 1991, Japan had the highest life expectancy (79 years) and lowest infant mortality rate (4.5 per 1000) in the world (Minami, 1985, p. 403; and Population Reference Bureau, 1991).

THE FOCUS OF THE STUDY

This chapter examines lessons from the growth of Japan from 1868, the restoration of the Meiji emperor, through 1939, the beginning of World War II, and the application of these lessons to Sub-Saharan Africa today. The Sub-Sahara is in an early stage of industrialization. Sub-Saharan Africa's share of GDP originating in industry, 20 per cent, is the same as Japan in 1887, and Africa's share of the labor force in industry, 8 per cent, less than Japan's 13 per cent in 1887 (Ohkawa and Rosovsky, 1973, p. 10; World Bank, 1989b, p. 277; World Bank, 1992a, pp. 222–3). Daily calorie intake per capita in 1868 was 1,600 in Japan (1868) compared to 2,122 in contemporary Sub-Saharan Africa (J. Nakamura, 1966; World Bank, 1992a, p. 273). Moreover, the Sub-Sahara has an average real income perhaps comparable to 1868 Japan (Goldsmith, 1983, pp. 15–16).[1]

This paper concentrates on identifying the major ways in which the pre-1940 Japanese Development Model (JDM) differs from other non-Western industrialization approaches, and how this JDM applies to Sub-Saharan Africa today. The major focus is capital formation and technology policies that contributed to Japan's rapid industrial capitalist growth: technological borrowing, product cycle, education, business assistance, financial institutions, capital markets, transfer of agricultural savings to industry, and wages. These policies even benefitted the traditional sector of the dual economy (discussed in the third to last section); most contemporary Sub-Saharan countries are also dualistic. Growth in productivity per person was increased substantially by Japan's policy of participating in the growing international specialization in the decades following the 1868 Meiji Restoration (see the next to last section). But a key to the ability of Japan to pursue these favorable policies was that, unlike most non-Western countries of the time, she was not dominated by Western imperialism (as pointed out in the next section).

SELF-DIRECTED DEVELOPENT

Despite unequal treaties with the West from 1858 to 1899, Japan had substantial autonomy in economic affairs compared to Sub-Saharan African countries, either colonized or subject to informal imperial economic controls. Although the West limited Japanese import tariffs to 5 per cent, Japan partially circumvented these protective limits through tax rebates, subsidies, government purchase contracts, and state industrial enterprises. Furthermore, the 1868–1912 Meiji government was committed to economic and military development. It promulgated laws encouraging joint-stock organization and freedom of enterprise. The Act of 1872 established a national system of education stressing scientific and technological education rather than skills for the junior civil service like schools in the late nineteenth and early twentieth century European colonies in Africa. Unlike colonial Africa, Japan virtually banned foreign investment between 1868 and 1899 (with minor exceptions like coal mining and shipbuilding in 1870–72), hiring thousands of foreigners to adapt and improve technology under ministry (or local business) direction. The Meiji government invested large amounts in infrastructure – telegraphs, postal service, water supply, coastal shipping, ports, harbors, bridges, lighthouses, river improvements, railways, electricity, gas, and technical research. In the last quarter of the nineteenth century, Japan organized a banking system (with the Bank of Japan, semiofficial development banks, and locally-run private banks), expanded bank credit for government infrastructure or private investment, regulated banks, and stabilized the currency. In contrast, even as late as the 1950s, the British, French, and other colonial governments in Africa interfered little in private foreign-dominated banks, whose power was only gradually reduced even after independence. Nor did a colonial government and foreign trading houses thwart Japanese industrial exports and import substitution, as in early twentieth-century Nigeria. The post-1868 Japanese government, in contrast, helped domestic business find export opportunities, exhibit products and borrow abroad, establish trading companies, and set marketing standards.

The experience of Japan indicates the clear advantages of domestic political and economic control, which contrasts to the experience of Sub-Saharan Africa, subject to informal imperial domination and colonial rule from the late nineteenth century through the middle to late twentieth century, and neocolonial dependence since then. Since 1979–80, Organisation for Economic Cooperation and Development (OECD) countries (the West and Japan), the major shareholders of the World Bank and the International Monetary Fund, have set in motion a new way to retain its economic suzerainty in Sub-Saharan Africa. Commercial banks, OECD governments, and the World Bank rely on the IMF agreeing to a stabilization programs (usually contingent on the borrower's reducing demand) before arranging adjustment loans and debt write-offs for African countries. Requiring this approval creates a monopoly position leaving Sub-Saharan Africa's debt-ridden stagnant economies little room to maneuver. In reality international policy enforcement is cartelized, with OECD governments, especially the United States, the European Union, and Japan, largely determining policy through their control of the Bank and Fund and their regulation of commercial banks.

BORROWING AND MODIFYING FOREIGN TECHNOLOGY

Does the JDM provide lessons for technological borrowing by contemporary Sub-Saharan Africa? To maintain political independence, the Meiji rulers adopted the slogan: 'enrich the nation to strengthen the army', a goal which the Meiji believed required adopting Western technology. But since Japan could not rely on foreign aid then, the central government and private firms had to pay the full cost for acquiring foreign technical expertise. This cost, together with introducing universal primary education and compulsory adult male military service, caused a serious financial strain. Between 1868 and 1892, the central government directed technological transfer by spending 1.5 per cent of its total expenditures for foreign employees, and an additional 0.4 per cent for expenses to send more than 4,000 students and government officials for training and education abroad. The Ministry of Industry, which invested in heavy and chemical industries, mining, and infrastructure, employed almost 1,000 foreign experts, advisors, and teachers from 1870 to 1885. The Ministry of Home Affairs hired almost 250 foreigners from 1873 through 1895 to establish agricultural experiment stations to introduce Western farming methods and products, and model factories to transfer technology to light industry. During the same period, the Ministry of Finance drew on about 125 foreign experts to help set up a modern monetary system and introduce corporate business organization. Other ministries and public enterprises hired almost 5,000, and the private sector about 12,500 foreigners during 1870–99 (Inukai, 1981, pp. 79–85).

Japan learned a lesson in the 1870s that many contemporary African countries have still not learned or only learned recently: that importing replicas of Western institutions and capital-intensive technology may exacerbate unemployment and balance-of-payments problems if the local country lacks the capital and skills needed. Foreign techniques were modified – substituting hand-powered machines in silk reeling factories and wood for iron in Jacquard weaving machines – to save capital. Japan's Ten-year Plan of 1884, the *Kogyo Iken*, advocated that projects conform to local conditions and capital available, and urged a strategy based on improvement engineering, i.e. upgrading indigenous (including artisan) production, rather than importing Western replicas (Inukai, 1981, pp. 85–95; T. Nakamura, 1983, p. 70). For Meiji Japan, foreigners were teachers, transferring technology and other knowledge, not, as in much of twentieth-century Africa, more or less permanent advisers.

In industry, both in government training schools and private firms, foreign experts were often unsuitable, importing techniques they were acquainted with, regardless of their relevance to Japan. In the raw silk industry, imported machines and equipment were too costly and mechanically sophisticated, and their capacity inconsistent with the inadequate storage facilities for the perishable cocoon. In flood control, Dutch experts introduced a system identical to that in Holland, where flood water rises from sea level, overlooking the fact that Japan had to handle flood water coming down the mountains. Repeated failures of Dutch technology to control floods convinced the Japanese government to change control measures completely. By the last two decades of the nineteenth century, the Japanese realized the necessity of questioning foreign industrial and flood control experts in light of differing local conditions (Inukai, 1981, pp. 85–88).

The Meiji government hired foreign experts directly and restricted foreign direct investment. While the immediate financial cost of limiting investment was substantial, Japan avoided the foreign restrictions placed on the transfer of technical knowledge, and continuing technological dependence on foreign sources and associated foreign technical concentration that many contemporary Sub-Saharan African countries face. Regarding direct hiring of foreign exports, the Japanese learned by the 1880s the necessity of insuring that technology introduced by foreigners be adapted and modified to fit local conditions and factor proportions.

During the Meiji period, labor was relatively more abundant in Japan than in the most advanced economies of Western Europe and the United States. Accordingly, Japan frequently substituted more appropriate labor-intensive technology for the 'best-practice' techniques available from capital-abundant Western countries.

Following are some major patterns of Japan's appropriate technology, 1868–1939:

(1) Emphasizing the production and export of more labor-intensive goods like raw silk, and silk and cotton textiles.

(2) Labor-intensive adaptation so the production process is simplified. Silk-reeling equipment appearing in 1875 consisted of a black-smith-made steam boiler, ceramic cocoon boiling and silk-reeling kettles, and a frame built by a village carpenter. Additionally, many Japanese manufacturing firms purchased second-hand machinery in good condition from Western countries. The cotton textile industry used two shifts, and substituted labor in ancillary and peripheral processes. Furthermore, much of the ancillary activities, like transport and machine repair, for large manufacturing units, were done cheaply by small firms using simple equipment and labor-intensive processes.

(3) Using manual labor instead of Western-type ancillary equipment in coal and mineral mines.

(4) Adoption of technology used in an earlier stage in the West.

(5) Adaptation of foreign technology to industries catering to tastes unique to the indigenous market, including traditional soybean sauce, and indigenous dyeing houses. As these enterprises learned through experience, many made the transition to technology needed for export markets.

(6) Substituting labor-intensive techniques to produce goods of lower quality and performance than imported goods, like bicycles (beginning in 1890), machine tools, three-wheel trucks, and small-sized cars (Datsuns in the 1930s) (Ishikawa, 1981, pp. 355–87).[2]

Meiji Japan imitated, borrowed from, and modified techniques and approaches from the advanced Western economies. A question today is: Can Sub-Saharan Africa be as successful emulating, borrowing, and adapting innovations and procedures from the West and Japan?

If anything, the contemporary Sub-Sahara has to be even more cautious than Meiji Japan in importing foreign capital and technology. Since present-day Sub-Saharan countries are even more technologically backward relative to the most technologically advanced economies than Japan was relative to the West in the late nineteenth century, it is probably more difficult to adapt technology to local conditions and indigenous production. For example, some foreign productivity-raising textile technologies available to early developing Japan were labor-using while most technologies for today's latecoming Sub-Saharan African countries are labor-saving.

Sub-Saharan African countries today are also less likely to directly control experts transferring technology than the Japanese did. A major contributor to this problem is the multinational corporation (MNC), frequently established jointly with public enterprises in Africa, but virtually absent in Meiji Japan. Foreign capital usually enters Sub-Saharan Africa only if political leaders, civil servants, or private middlemen or women are rewarded for facilitating the venture. These MNC-associated enterprises tend to use technology designed for the headquarter country, which has high wages and relatively abundant capital. Estimates based on capital resources available indicate that the appropriate capital stock per person in the United States is at least twenty times that of Sub-Saharan African countries (Stewart 1974, pp. 86–8).

Technical change requires a prolonged learning process embodied in indigenes improving capital and controlling experts transferring technology and improving capital. Under colonialism and neocolonialism, Sub-Saharan Africans have had little experience directing their own economic plans and technical adaptation and progress. Even today, African countries face externally-imposed conditions by the World Bank, IMF, and DC governments on technology use and other policies. Each successive piece of capital equipment is more productive since learning advances are embodied in new capital goods (Arrow, 1962, pp. 154–94; Nafziger, 1990, pp. 259–60).

Sub-Saharan African finance and planning officers want to rely more on government ministries and local research institutions and chambers of commerce and industry for technological policy analysis. National authorities, rather than foreign advisers from bilateral donors and international agencies, need to prepare adjustment and technological programs. Africans must direct, as the Meiji Japanese did, their planning and development for them to capture technological learning gains.

PRODUCT CYCLE

Comparative advantage may be based on a technological advantage (as in nineteenth- century Britain, the United States, and Germany and as in today's Japan, the United States, and Germany), perhaps a Schumpeterian innovation like a new product or production process that gives the country a temporary monopoly in the world market until other countries are able to imitate (Schumpeter, 1961; Schumpeter, 1939). The product cycle model indicates that while a product requires highly skilled labor in the beginning, later as markets grow and techniques become common knowledge, a good becomes standardized, so that less-sophisticated countries can mass produce the item with less skilled labor. Advanced economies, such as Britain and the United States, from 1868 to 1939, had a comparative advantage in non-standardized goods, while less-advanced economies, like Meiji Japan, had a comparative advantage in standardized goods (Vernon 1966, pp. 190–207).

Product cycle is illustrated by cotton textiles. England specialized in cotton textiles from the mid-eighteenth to late-nineteenth centuries. In the 1880s and 1890s, Japan substituted indigenous production of cotton textiles, manufactured with British machines, for imports from Britain. By 1921–39, Japan's cotton goods invaded English and other Western markets. Japan's comparative advantage in textiles was suggested by the fact that 41.0 per cent of all factory labor in Japan was engaged in textiles compared with only 20.5 per cent in Britain and 13.4 per cent in the United States in 1934. In the 1960s, Japan imported cotton textiles from South Korea, Taiwan, Hong Kong, Singapore, and China, many of which used Japanese investment and technology to compete in Japan or third countries. Shinohara (1982, pp. 32–3, 72–5, 127–8) labels this a boomerang effect, imports in reverse or intensification of competition in third markets arising from Japanese enterprise expansion in, and technology exports to, less advanced countries.

However, contemporary Sub-Saharan Africa cannot compete as readily as nineteenth- century Japan did at the bottom range of the product cycle, imitation and low-level innovation. The Sub-Sahara, unlike Meiji Japan, is competing in an integrated global economy against multinational corporations. The markets MNCs operate in today are often international oligopolies with competition among few sellers whose pricing decisions are interdependent. Large corporations invest overseas because of international imperfections in the market for goods, resources, or technology. The MNCs benefit from monopoly advantages, such as patents, technical knowledge, superior managerial and marketing skills, better access to capital markets, economies of large-scale production, and cost savings from vertical integration (Hymer, 1970, pp. 441–53). MNCs can compete in a large range of industries with today's indigenous African firm in the use of imitation or innovative technology, and unskilled or highly skilled labor.

EDUCATION

Sub-Saharan Africa's 1985 literacy rate was 48 per cent (World Bank, 1990b, p. 179), a level reached in Japan about the first decade of the twentieth century. Japan's primary enrollment rate, 28.1 per cent in 1873, reached virtually 100 per cent by 1911. Furthermore, the Japanese government made serious efforts to expand primary and vocational education, and stress Western scientific and technical education in the last three decades of the nineteenth century, when Europeans in Africa were only educating elites for service in government and foreign enterprises.

Education in the British, French, and Belgian colonies in Sub-Saharan Africa provided the intellectual skills necessary for clerks, administrative assistants, noncommissioned officers, and operatives for the colonial government, army, or European firms but not for engineers, scientists, farm and industrial managers, entrepreneurs, and government executives and technicians. With political independence in the Sub-Sahara, the primary enrollment rate (as a percentage of children aged 6–11) rose from 36 per cent in 1960 to 79 per cent in 1980 before falling to 67 per cent in 1990, and the secondary enrollment rate 3 per cent in 1960 to 16 per cent in 1980 to 18 per cent in 1989 (denominator 12–17 years old) (World Bank, 1981a, p. 181; World Bank, 1989a, pp. 274–5; World Bank, 1992a, pp. 274–5). A UNICEF study indicates that falling government spending from the external debt crisis and Bank/Fund adjustment programs of last resort in the 1980s was accompanied by declining real educational spending (Commander, 1989a, pp. 231–34). Nigeria, after a 1986 structural adjustment loan from the World Bank in 1986, cut spending, especially on education substantially; during the subsequent protest in the late 1980s, the military government closed universities, detained and dismissed university critics, and killed tens and arrested hundreds of students and academics while squashing strikes, demonstrations, and political opposition (Africa Watch, 1991, pp. 41–52).

Low literacy and primary enrollment rates have impeded labor enskillment and economic growth in Sub-Saharan Africa. Moreover, the setbacks to literacy and education during the adjustment programs of the 1980s contributed to the negative economic growth of that decade.

The emphasis on 'Japanese spirit and Western technology' meant that Meiji education stressed subserviency to superiors and the state, superiority to other Asian countries, and acquiring Western technological expertise, but not human dignity, or learning the method for developing science in Japan (Seiya, 1965, pp. 540–59). However, starting with a common language, the Meiji government developed a relatively uniform primary education that fostered national unity as well as speeding up acquiring Western ideas and technologies. While the Meiji experience reinforces studies indicating a high rate of return to investment in primary, science, and vocational education (particularly lacking in contemporary Sub-Saharan Africa), Meiji Japan provides no model for countries using the educational system to promote democracy, human rights, and female equality.

GUIDED CAPITALISM

Political revolutions in Western Europe (England, France, and Holland) in the seventeenth and eighteenth centuries reduced the power of the church and landed aristocracy, and eventually the industrial and commercial capitalist classes took over much of this power. Since most Sub-Saharan African countries, like nineteenth-century Japan, do not have the strong middle- and capitalist-class leadership for capital accumulation and technical progress, can they look to Japan's 'guided capitalism' as an alternative model to state socialism?

Following the fall of the Tokugawa *shogun*, 1860 to 1868, the Meiji government was controlled primarily by lower-ranking samurai, not merchants and industrial capitalists. From 1870 to 1885, this government owned and operated factories and mines, many expropriated from the shogunate and feudal lords (Shishido, 1983, p. 259). Throughout the late nineteenth century, the Meiji regime accounted for about half the investment outside agriculture. State investment included infrastructure, such as railroads, bridges, warehouses, lighthouses, ports, irrigation, harbors, steamships, electricity, water supply, postal services, and telegraphy. The government also invested in shipbuilding, iron and steel, other heavy industries, and arms factories to strengthen the military, as well as mines and construction, engineering, cement, soap, and chemical industries (though not textiles, the leading export sector). However, government profits proved meager and the state needed funds for armament. Thus, the state sold most industrial properties, often at bargain prices, to private businessmen, many of whom were samurai. Additionally, in 1876, the state strained its public credit to commute the pensions of 400,000 feudal lords and samurai to cash and bonds, and to pay off debts owed to relatively privileged merchants and moneylenders (like the House of Mitsui) who had financed the 1867–8 coup restoring the emperor. Moreover, the state aided private industry through low taxes on business enterprise and high incomes, a low wage policy, technical research and education, a favorable legal climate, destruction of economic barriers between fiefs, tax rebates, loans, subsidies, and lucrative purchasing contracts. (For example, the government imported spindle spinning machines, 1878–79, to sell on lenient credit terms to private enterprise in the textile industry, Japan's leading export sector.)[3] The substantial transfer of funds from the state to individuals, the high savings rates (see below), the favorable government policies, and the acquisition of already existing enterprises facilitated private industrial enterprise.

From these state-assisted entrepreneurs came the financial cliques or combines (*Zaibatsu*) that dominated industry and banking through World War II. The *Zaibatsu*'s concentration of wealth helped perpetuate high income inequalities at least seventy five years after the Meiji restoration. To be sure, the *Zaibatsu* reaped large-scale economies, managed ably, were generally frugal, invested productively, provided assistance to small industry (see below), and were partners in building national power (Lockwood, 1954, pp. 15, 61, 234–49, 285).

Both late nineteenth-century Japan and the contemporary Sub-Sahara have favored existing elites in their privatization schemes. The World Bank, IMF, and bilateral donors insisted on abrupt privatization in Sub-Saharan Africa, which created a highly concentrated business elite from newly privatized firms falling into a few hands, similar to early Japan. However, in other ways, Meiji Japan's stress on private entrepreneurs differed substantially from that of contemporary Africa's privatization. Meiji Japan provided more assistance to small industrialists. Moreover, Japan's privatization was initiated by the state whereas privatization in Africa was thrust on it by adjustment programs initiated by the IMF, World Bank, and OECD creditors. Thus emerging private enterprise in Japan was virtually all indigenous, while the World Bank insisted that the Sub-Sahara open investment to foreign private enterprise. For example, Nigeria, under two World Bank structural adjustment programs (1986–88 and 1989–91), not only sold equity in public enterprises to private investors but allowed foreign investors in most manufacturing, large trade, and petroleum sectors. Foreign investors are major contributors to high industrial concentration and (as pointed out above) to inappropriate technology.

Perhaps as many as one-fourth to one-fifth of the farmers in the late Tokugawa and early Meiji periods managed second businesses such as small bars, rapeseed oil selling, lumber vending, eating house management, bean curd making, confection making, tobacco selling, sundry shopkeeping, carpentry, and plastering. Landlords were fertilizer merchants, pawnbrokers, moneylenders, doctors, dry goods merchants, and brewers of *sake*, soy sauce, and bean paste. The landed class especially increased investment during the inflation of 1876–81, when rapidly increasing rice prices provided windfall gains when land taxes were fixed and rents received in kind. Furthermore, many merchants became landlords (Lockwood, 1954, pp. 14, 35, 286; T. Nakamura, 1983, pp. 51–61).

Empirical studies on entrepreneurship indicate that landowners and wealthy farmers in Sub-Saharan Africa today, unlike those in Meiji Japan, rarely save to invest in industry. African landlords tend to value highly consumption and real estate expenditure, lack a capital market and a savings habit (see below), and have little experience in managing and coordinating a production process with specialized work tasks and machinery and in overseeing secondary labor relations (Nafziger, 1990, pp. 290–91).

Many economists, noting the disproportional samurai representation among early Meiji industrialists and bankers, stress the spirit of the community-centered samurai entrepreneur, sacrificing for national economic progress (Hirschmeier, 1964; Ranis, 1955). But Yamamura's evidence (1968) indicates that samurai status in the early Meiji period was blurred, as many from peasant and merchant families purchased samurai status during the late Tokugawa period. The major force to establish banks and factories came from merchants and landlords motivated by profit, not longstanding samurai motivated by nationalism.

Meiji Japan's policies do provide an alternative to the Soviet approach for accumulating capital where there is no strong bourgeois class. And selling government-owned industrial properties to private firms reduces public financial losses since their bankruptcies eliminate inefficient enterprises. Yet this selling may, as in Japan, contribute to high industrial concentration, high income inequalities, and slow growth of a politically independent middle class. Moreover, today populist pressures prevent most Sub-Saharan political elites from pursuing the low-wage policies, unrestricted labor rules, low welfare spending, and large subsidies that nineteenth-century Japan used to foster indigenous capitalist development. Furthermore, few Sub-

Saharan African societies have the Japanese nexus of community reciprocal obligation that reduces the destructive power of capitalist rivalries.

Yet Meiji Japan's bourgeoisie, though weaker than that in Western Europe and the United States, were more experienced in large commercial ventures, and were not as far behind the most technologically advanced economies as Sub-Saharan Africa today. The Japanese capitalist class was capable of responding to government policies to encourage private industrial ventures. Furthermore, Meiji Japan had the vision and skills to plan programs to abet private entrepreneurs.

The irony is that while the weakness of the Sub-Sahara's elites today indicates the need for stronger government intervention and more skilled government planning to spur entrepreneurial activity, technical progress, and capital accumulation in industry, few Sub-Saharan government bureaucracies have the capabilities to facilitate these in the private sector, or to manage these in the public sector. In contrast to Meiji Japan, most Sub-Saharan African states are soft states, in which the authorities who decide policies rarely enforce them (if enacted into law) and only reluctantly place obligations on people. These states are dependent on buying political support through concessions to powerful interest groups. Regime survival in Africa's politically fragile states requires the support of urban elites (business people, professionals, executives, and high-ranking military officers, civil servants, and parastatal employees), landholders, and commercial farmers through economic policies that frequently sacrificed growth, income distribution, external balance, and the development of indigenous skills. And perhaps the easiest way for ruling elites to expand state largess to benefit allies and clients was by increased borrowing from abroad, joint ventures with multinational corporations, and cooperating with the World Bank and IMF in adjustment programs and liberalization reforms. Yet the shortage of organizational and planning skills by Sub-Saharan African elites has been worsened by their subsidiary role to that of the World Bank, IMF, MNCs, and bilateral lenders in planning the economy.

FINANCIAL INSTITUTIONS

Goldsmith (1983, pp. 4–5) thinks a knowledgeable 1870 economist would have indicated India as more likely to be economically developed by 1970 than Japan. Japan, just emerging from feudalism, had a negligible modern sector, a chaotic currency, and no modern financial institutions, while India, a British colony, possessed a unified currency, rudiments of a Western-type banking system, access to the British capital market, and British financial technology. An economist in 1870 might have observed that financial institutions in Sub-Saharan Africa, though less developed than India's, might also benefit from Europe's informal suzerainty (which later became colonial rule).

Indeed European powers constructed financial systems in India and Sub-Saharan Africa, while the Meiji government created Japan's system through conscious *selective* adaptation of features of the American, British, French, and German systems. European entrepreneurs and investors operated, owned, and organized Sub-Saharan Africa's modern financial institutions, while foreign ownership or management of Japan's institutions was practically nonexistent. Furthermore, the European colonial governments in Africa intervened little in regulating bank and financial institutions, had little contact with the small number of indigenous bankers, and created few new financial institutions. In contrast, the Meiji government organized most of the modern financial institutions during the first two to three decades after the 1868 restoration, and cooperated with and supported local private bankers and financiers (Goldsmith, 1983, pp. 55–8).

In contrast to Sub-Saharan Africa, Meiji Japan's development of currency and credit institutions through the mid-1890s was 'supply-leading', created in advance of demands for industrial loans and financial services, and private saver deposits. In 1872, the government set up national banks, and in 1876 permitted private commercial banks. Other major financial reforms were the conversion of the rights of feudal lords to negotiable government bonds, and the land tax, which provided the revenue for the government's Reserve Fund (RF), 1873–81, and the Industrial Promotion Fund (IPF) beginning 1878, for loans to industry. Other special banks established included the Yokohama Specie Bank (1880) for foreign exchange for importers, the Hypothec Banks (1896) at the prefectural level to make long-term loans to industry and agriculture, and the Industrial Bank (1900) to make medium- to long-term loans to industry (Takeda, 1965, pp. 432–3; Mahajan, 1976, p. 24). The national and private banks' high ratio of currency issues to specie, as well as the RF and IPF liberal lending policies, contributed to rapid inflation (1876–81), reducing peasant and former military real incomes, and increasing capitalist speculative profits, thus forming substantial initial capital accumulation for industrialists.

Finance Minister Matsukata Masayoshi created a central Bank of Japan in 1882 (54 years before the Reserve Bank of India, 77 years before the Central Bank of Nigeria, and at least 70 years before most other Sub-Saharan central banks) to limit paper currency, levied new consumption taxes, restrained RF lending except to export industries accumulating specie, and balanced the government budget, bringing about more stable expectations among capitalist investors (Takeda, 1965, pp. 432–6).

All in all, the new financial institutions standardized the currency, integrated the national market, and channeled savings into industry. By 1897, Japan's credit standing had improved so it could borrow in foreign capital markets. With few exceptions, the money supply grew rapidly from 1880 to 1940, enabling rapid though fluctuating growth *rates*, but virtually avoiding recessions with negative growth (Lockwood, 1954, p. 14; T. Nakamura, 1983, pp. 8–9, 60–1).

The symbiotic relationship between government and private finance strengthened Zaibatsu bank concentration, contributing to the 1920s' sharp decline in small banks (Goldsmith, 1983, pp. 58–59). While banks collected private savings for affiliated *Zaibatsu* enterprises and helped determine which firms survived, these large financial concentrations, under Japanese state guidance, still supported traditional small-scale industry and trade (T. Nakamura, 1983, pp. 97–103, 203–12). Bank concentration was not reduced until the post-World War II occupational antitrust reforms.

Sub-Saharan African states, under foreign economic supremacy during the twentieth century, suffered from at least as high a financial concentration as pre-World War II Japan, but lacked the control over local financial institutions that Japan enjoyed. The rapid growth of Japan's banking and credit institutions in advance of industrial and saver demands indicates the advantage of more than a century of self-directed financial development. In contrast, the colonial powers in Africa controlled currency from the European capitals, and banks were virtually all branches of foreign institutions until years after World War II. Even after political independence, Africa has had an externally dependent banking system, a poorly developed securities market, and little ability to fine-tune the money supply. Since 1980, Sub-Saharan states have lost further control of their foreign exchange and capital markets and their level of government expenditures under World Bank and IMF adjustment programs.

SAVINGS RATES

Japan's gross saving rates were 17 per cent of national product, 1885–1935, at no time falling below 10 per cent for a four-year period. In contrast, gross savings in Sub-Saharan Africa during the same period was no more than 5 per cent of national product.

The savings habit was a part of the average Japanese household, which maintained family wealth intact for several generations. Japan's upper and middle classes generally saved to create capital assets, not to hoard gold, speculate on real estate, consume conspicuously, or go on pleasure tours. With social services and consumer goods poorly developed, families made provisions for training and housing, and against illness, unemployment, and old age. The age-old cultivation of nonmaterial values and personal frugality was enforced by Japanese group discipline.

As the previous section indicates, Japan's capital markets were well developed; indeed they were not far behind Western Europe and North America by 1910–18. After World War I, Japan institutionalized savings in insurance and trust companies (Goldsmith, 1983, pp. 36–7; Lockwood, 1954, pp. 14, 35, 286). Sub-Saharan Africa, in contrast, has fragmented and poorly-organized financial institutions and lacked a convertible currency during the twentieth century, a period of colonialism and neocolonialism.

Japan's fast growth increased capital formation rates. Meiji Japan's rapid technological innovation, by raising the returns to capital, stimulated additional savings. Furthermore, high corporate profits, reinforced by high inequality, contributed to savings. Moreover, Japan, 1868 to 1939, had a high proportion of its population self-employed (mainly small industrialist, trader, or farmer), which spurred high savings rates. In 1930, for example, 32 per cent of Japan's gainfully occupied population was self-employed (Mahajan, 1976, pp. 69–70, 80–1; Allen, 1964, pp. 97–8).

In 1988, gross savings rates in Sub-Saharan Africa were 13 per cent (11 per cent in the low-income Sub-Sahara), a figure substantially lower than for Meiji Japan. If we assume, as UN figures suggest, net savings rates are 60 per cent of gross savings rates, then the low-income Sub-Sahara's 11 per cent savings rate consisted of 7 per cent net new capital (4 per cent replacement capital), a net rate lower than the rate Rostow indicates as the major condition for economic takeoff (UN, 1987; Rostow, 1971; and World Bank, 1990b, pp. 194–5).

TRANSFER OF AGRICULTURAL SURPLUS

Economic historians differ on the relationships between agriculture and industry in the development process, and the timing of initial sustained growth in both sectors. As in England, where an agricultural revolution preceded the industrial revolution, in Japan late Tokugawa agricultural growth (despite the substantial output share cultivators paid to the shogun) preceded the beginning of the early industrialization spurt of the 1880s.

Agricultural growth accelerated through the Meiji period before slowing down beginning in the 1910s. During Meiji, agriculture contributed to rapid industrialization. This section and the next examine how capital, labor, and food from agriculture helped industry.

A major concern for Sub-Saharan Africa is the source of early investment capital for industry. Many economists advocate relying heavily on agricultural surplus for industrial capital, since agriculture is usually an LDC's largest sector; for example, before 1928 it contributed more to Japan's NDP than any other sector (Ohkawa, Shinohara, Umemura, Ito, and Noda, 1957, p. 26). Agricultural surplus refers to an excess of savings over investment in agriculture, an amount transferred to non-agriculture (or industry). This transfer includes both private savings and taxes. Meiji centralized government replaced the feudal landed gentry (*daimyo*) who politically controlled large fiefs with smaller, capitalist village landlords who had purchased their land. These gentry remained wealthy, but lost their land and political power. The village landlords, who were often themselves farmers during the early Meiji period, frequently improved productive methods (Dore, 1965, pp. 487–93).

The Meiji bureaucrats controlling policy had no personal interest in protecting agricultural incomes at the cost of slowing industrial growth. They imposed a land tax in 1873 to squeeze investment capital from agriculture, partly through a moderate inflationary policy redistributing resources to finance state and private industrial ventures. In that year, the land tax accounted for 94 per cent of central government revenue, appropriating one-third of the total crop, only a little less than the 40–50 per cent share appropriated by the Tokugawa shogun before 1868 (Dore, 1965, pp. 487–93; Lockwood, 1954, p. 98). The land tax continued to provide more than 80 per cent of total government revenue through 1882, and contributed to continuing, though reduced, net resource outflows from agriculture to government through 1922 (Ohkawa, Shimizu, and Takamatsu, 1982, p. 10). Government investment in agriculture was only a small fraction of agricultural tax revenue used for non-agricultural investment (Mody, Mundle, and Raj, 1985, pp. 272–3). From 1888 to 1937, the significant surplus flows of private savings from agriculture to industry are concentrated during the period 1903–22, when cultivator-landlords were being replaced by 'parasitic' landlords using tenant rents to accumulate capital for industries like brewing, pawnbroking, retail shops, and village moneylending (Ohkawa, Shimizu, and Takamatsu, 1982, pp. 11–12; T. Nakamura, 1983, pp. 59). But the amount of net capital private flows from agriculture to industry is not certain, since price indices to estimate the effect of changing terms of trade on net resource flows from agriculture, and figures on private inflows to agriculture are not reliable (Ishikawa, 1982, p. 264). Part of this intersectoral resource transfer was from the colonies of Korea and Taiwan, between 1911 and 1940. During this period, Taiwan's net resource outflow from agriculture equalled its balance of trade surplus (with exports predominantly agricultural) with metropolitan Japan (Lee, 1971). Japanese investors in the colonies acquired prime agricultural land for producing food exports to Japan. These cheap rice imports from Taiwan and Korea kept Japanese food prices low, keeping industrial wages low and increasing industrial profits until World War I (see below).

Meiji Japan, like the Soviet Union subsequently in the 1930s, accumulated industrial capital by squeezing it from agriculture. With the possible exception of the Soviet Union, where the collectivization of 1929–1933 involved forcible collection of grain, confiscation of farm property, destruction of tools and livestock, class warfare between peasants and prosperous kulaks, administrative disorder, disruption of sowing and harvest, and an accompanying famine that led to the deaths of about five million people, Japan has probably relied more on a strategy of using agricultural savings for initial industrial capital formation than any other presently industrialized country.

The land tax had little or no effect on farm labor and output, both of which had low short-run elasticities of supply and low opportunity costs. The land owner, unable to shift the tax forward to farm-good middlemen or consumers, could only shift the tax incidence to a tenant, who rarely had alternative employment. The high and regressive land taxes, required in cash, the growing burden of other taxes (1890–1910), and high rents reduced farm disposable income and consumption, especially among tenants and peasants, the last of whom faced heavy debts, frequent bankruptcies, and abject poverty (Hayami, 1975, p. 48; Minami, 1985, pp. 16–17).

Dore (1959, pp. 115–25) argues that the agrarian poverty and distress from taxes and tenancy contributed to the rise of Japanese totalitarian and military expansion abroad in the following ways: (1) tenant distress and farm population pressures provided a powerful motive for securing emigration opportunities through expansion; (2) rural poverty and the interrelated low industrial wages (see below) limited domestic market size, spurring Japan to use force to acquire external markets for its industry; (3) ruling elites used overseas expansion to divert attention from agrarian distress and foster national unity; and (4) landlord paternalism and agrarian pressures for social conformity facilitated susceptibility to authoritarianism.

Other countries may find it difficult politically to extract agricultural surplus through taxes. In England, unlike Japan, the landed aristocracy maintained political influence until a relatively advanced stage of industrial development. Likewise, landlords in many contemporary Latin American countries are too powerful for the state to capture an agricultural surplus. Few low-income Sub-Saharan African countries have enough agrarian surplus and political tolerance to allow the squeezing of agriculture in excess of the substantial agriculture–industry transfers already being made.

Japan's agricultural growth relied heavily on research by local scientists (assisted by foreign experts hired by the Ministry of Agriculture), biochemical (not Western mechanical) innovations, and extension by veteran farmers and new Japanese agricultural school graduates to diffuse the best seed varieties then used on Japanese farms to a highly literate farm population. Despite the land tax, agricultural technological progress was fast, contributing to the rapid annual percentage growths of 1.8 in agricultural gross value added and 2.0 in farm productivity per worker, 1880–1920, that facilitated substantial surplus transfer to industry.[4] The agricultural surplus in many Sub-Saharan African countries is too small and growing too slowly and the material levels of living of peasants too low for industry to exploit without severe human costs.

Sub-Saharan Africa needs a thriving agriculture to produce adequate food and raw materials for other sectors. Sub-Saharan countries frequently have used policies (especially before 1980) to transfer a large share of the agricultural surplus to industry, including: (1) food price ceilings and industrial price floors to raise industrial prices relative to the prices of farm goods; (2) concentration of government investment in industry; (3) tax incentives and subsidies to pioneering firms in industry, but not in agriculture; (4) setting below-market prices for foreign currency, reducing domestic currency receipts from agricultural exports, but lowering the price of capital goods and other foreign inputs to large industrial establishments; (5) tariff and quota protection for industry, raising its prices to farmers; and (6) spending more for education, training, housing, plumbing, nutrition, medical care, and transport in urban areas than in rural areas. These policies of urban bias have contributed to farm production disincentives and high rates of rural poverty and undernourishment in low-income countries (Lipton, 1977; Nafziger, 1990, pp. 131–62).

These disincentives in many Sub-Saharan African countries have been perhaps as great as those that threatened widespread rural rebellion in Meiji Japan (Lockwood, 1954, p. 9). Rural poverty and undernourishment rates are probably no less than those in Meiji Japan. Additionally, rural populist pressures in many contemporary African countries are greater and more politically destabilizing than peasant pressures in the 1870s Meiji Japan.

In Ghana and Côte d'Ivoire, a below-market foreign exchange price coupled with industrial price guarantees resulted in the transfer of substantial agricultural savings to the nonagricultural sector in the 1970s and early 1980s – a transfer largely from poor to rich (Nafziger, 1988, pp. 140–6). Few low-income Sub-Saharan countries have the average peasant income and rural political stability sufficient to squeeze agriculture in excess of transfers already being made.

While this analysis, similar to that of the IMF, indicates that price controls and exchange-rate misalignments have contributed to Sub-Saharan Africa's stagnation and external crisis, I reject the IMF policy prescription of immediately freeing markets and contracting spending to resolve the disequilibrium. After 1981, the IMF emphasized shock treatment for demand restraint in low-income Sub-Saharan Africa, rarely provided financing for external adjustments, and cut programs from three years to one year, applying Reaganomics internationally. One year is not enough for adjustment. Demand restrictions, inflation deceleration, and currency depreciation do not switch expenditures to exports and import substitutes or expand primary production quickly enough to have the desired effect on prices and trade balance. Studies indicate, even in DCs (for example, the United States, 1985–88), the current-account improvement from devaluation usually takes about two to five years, usually beginning with a worsening trade balance in the first year. The time for adjustment is due to the lags between changes in relative international prices (from exchange-rate changes) and responses in quantities traded. Lags include time for recognition, decision (assessing the change), delivery, replacement (waiting to use up inventories and wear out machines), and production (Grubel, 1981, pp. 349–88). Even after 1988, despite increased emphasis of structural adjustment programs on productive capacity and long-term sectoral change, in practice Sub-Saharan African countries still face unrealistically short adjustment times, resulting in severe economic disruption and excessive hardship for the poor.

Bank/Fund adjustment programs in Sub-Saharan Africa increased agricultural income inequality. Agricultural export expansion, higher farm producer prices, and reduced food subsidies benefited landed classes and affluent commercial farmers disproportionately and had little impact on smallholders producing food for subsistence, whose output expansion was limited by lack of labor, land, credit, or appropriate technology. But adjustment usually reduced the surplus that monopsony marketing agencies (often controlled by political leaders and their clients) captured at the expense of agricultural classes generally (Bates, 1989, pp. 222–26; FAO, 1991, p. 97).

Samora Machel's FRELIMO government in Mozambique and Robert Mugabe's ZANU government in Zimbabwe tried to shift the terms of trade from industry (under the previous white supremacist policies) to agriculture. Zimbabwe's 1982 IMF agreement resulted in a wage freeze and real wage decline, substantial food price increases, and reduced health expenditures (1982–84). The Ministry of Health found that the percentage of underweight children less than six years old in rural areas rose from 18–22 per cent in 1982 to 48 per cent in 1984. The Zambia Basic Needs Report in the early 1980s outlined how reduced recurrent allocation after adjustment discouraged a rural woman with a sick child from walking 15 kilometers to the nearest health center, as the woman knew the center was frequently out of drugs (Parfitt and Riley, 1989, p. 33; Davies and Saunders, 1987, pp. 3–23).

Lele's study of the World Bank's approach to agricultural development castigated the shift away from integrated rural development with its emphasis on supply intervention such as infrastructure, credit, research, and extension, to private sector initiatives and adjustment programs. This shift, she argues, is flawed by its inadequate recognition of causal factors underlying growth, the effects of price-based policies on supply, the non-price actions essential to sustain policy reforms, and harmonization with long-terms goals (Lele 1990, p. 1209). Indeed World Bank economist Cleaver (World Bank, 1985) argues that farm prices have a minor role relative to state agricultural services in affecting agricultural growth.

The IMF has stressed devaluation and foreign-exchange decontrols to improve the balance of trade, increase domestic prices and terms of trade for agriculture, and reduce shortages of foreign inputs, along with market interest rates to improve capital allocation. Green (1989, p. 36) supports Sub-Saharan African states' complaints that World Bank or IMF adjustment programs fail to consider African market imperfections. However, government frequently creates market imperfections through policies of financial repression, encouraging interest-rate ceilings, foreign exchange controls, high reserve requirements, and restrictions on private capital markets to increase the flow of domestic resources to the public sector without higher taxes, inflation, or interest rates. Yet even though it helped to create these market imperfections, government cannot immediately decontrol all prices and liberalize foreign exchange and capital markets. Although devaluation raises import prices, the demand for foreign exchange may not be restrained, as relaxing foreign-exchange licenses and import restrictions spurs the use of foreign inputs and probably increases capital flight in the short run. Indeed, substantial devaluation may generate hyperinflation, as the domestic currency experiences a free fall which expectations make irreversible (Zambia in 1985–7 and Sierra Leone in 1986–7).

The effect of devaluation on the trade balance depends on demand and supply elasticities, considered by critics to be low in Sub-Saharan agriculture, especially over a one- to two-year period. The elasticity of demand for African primary products like tea, coffee, sugar, and cocoa is so low that increasing the output of agricultural exports to undertake Bank/Fund-sponsored adjustment might result in reduced revenues from increased output. On the supply side, Sub-Saharan African farmers have little short-run (one year or less) but substantial long-run elasticity (0.3–0.9) for cash crops, as farmers respond to allocate labor and land variously to commercial output, subsistence commodities, black-market activity, non-farm work, or leisure. Supply response would be at least a year or two for cotton and tobacco and between five and six years for tree crops such as coffee, tea, cashews, and sisal in Tanzania. Cost-induced inflationary pressures due to devaluation (from economic interests fighting to maintain income and consumption shares) should reduce output expansion. Inadequate infrastructure, such as poor transport for Ghanaian cocoa, limits supply increases, slowing export response to higher cedi prices for a given dollar price of cocoa. Indeed, Sub-Saharan countries remove balance-of-payments deficits quickly not from exchange-rate changes (and expenditure switching) but from reduced import demand due to a fall in real income (or a depressed economy). Still, most Sub-Saharan African countries no longer oppose devaluation, but want more control on its size, timing, structure (such as single versus multiple exchange rates), and accompanying policy measures (Green, 1989, p. 36; Godfrey, 1985, p. 32; Chhibber, 1989, p.56; Loxley, 1989, pp. 13–36; and Campbell and Stein 1992, pp. 20–2).

LOW INDUSTRIAL WAGES

From 1868 to 1915, agricultural unskilled *real* wages remained at a subsistence level. Unlike the Lewis–Fei–Ranis models (LFR), the marginal productivity of labor (MP_L) in agriculture was positive, though less than the wage (see Minami, 1973, p. 200), since the village supplied subsistence to those with a MP_L below the wage (closer to average productivity than marginal productivity). As in LFR, employers in the formal industrial sector paid a premium (say 30 per cent more than the agricultural wage) to compensate for migration costs, psychological costs of city life, and so forth. This premium remained low partly because much of industry's wage labor – female, second and third sons, or off-farm part-time – merely supplemented household income (Shinohara, 1970, pp. 342–4). But subsistence levels rose over time as the minimum maintenance level expected by society increased. The relatively stable agricultural (and thus industrial) real wages can be attributed partly to technical progress and increased productivity in agriculture (and cheap food from colonies after 1911) which enabled the industrial sector to buy food without declining terms of trade. These low real industrial wages increased industrial profits and business savings.

Over a normal range, where product and labor demand increase gradually, labor supply elasticities were high (though not infinite as in LFR), benefiting from vast reserves in the rural and informal industrial sectors (Minami, 1973; Hayami, 1975). But the 1915–1919 increase in demand for industrial products and labor resulting from World War I was too substantial to be satisfied by labor from the elastic portion of the supply curve. Wage equilibrium could only be attained at the inelastic portion of the labor supply curve, thus increasing industrial wages, and subsequently through greater food demand by new workers, increased agricultural product (especially rice) and labor prices. In the 1920s and 1930s, industrial wages, sticky downward with emerging unions, remained high, while agricultural (and informal industrial sector) wages declined from their war peak. Following the war and recovery years (1935–55), the labor surplus ended and industrial formal sector labor supply turned inelastic permanently, as innovation-led demand for industrial products and labor increased rapidly, while labor supply growth from agriculture and population growth was drying up (Hayami, 1975).

Developing Japan's labor supply grew slower than the Sub-Sahara's today. Late nineteenth-century Japan's birth rate, 22 per 1,000, kept down by farm land shortages, extended-family dissolution, and high literacy levels, was lower than Sub-Saharan Africa's 46 per 1,000 (1990), while Japanese death rates, 18 per 1,000, were higher than the Sub-Saharan rates of 17 per 1,000, lowered by access to the nutritional, medical, health, and production techniques of the past century. Japan's annual labor growth, which never exceeded 1 per cent per annum during the nineteenth century, rose to a peak of 1.3 per cent per annum in 1930, slowing to less than 1 per cent by 1955 (Minoru and Yoichi, 1965, pp. 498–9). In contrast, Sub-Saharan labor force growth was 2.2 per cent per annum in the 1960s, 2.1 per cent annually in the 1970s, and 2.5 per cent in the 1980s, and 2.6 per cent in the early 1990s (each figure slightly less than population growth). Yet Meiji Japan's density of farm population per cultivated hectare of land (higher than the Sub-Sahara today) put pressure on the nonagricultural sector. But Japan's annual industrial employment grew by 3.9 per cent of the total labor force between 1878 and 1914, compared to the Sub-Saharan figure in 1980 of about 0.4–0.7 per cent. While Sub-Saharan industry in the 1980s absorbed only 20–35 per cent of the increased labor force, Japanese industry at the turn of the twentieth century absorbed 4.5–5.0 times the labor increase. Crucial in Japan's successful absorption (or excess industrial labor demand) was slower population growth, together with rapid industrial growth (9.0 per cent per annum, 1878–1914, compared to the Sub-Sahara's negative 2.3 per cent yearly, 1980–86), highly labor-intensive, spurred by government's low-wage and appropriate technology policies (Minoru and Yoichi, 1965, pp. 497–515; World Bank, 1989, p. 236; Ohkawa, Shinohara, Umemura, Ito, and Noda, 1957, pp. 78–99, 135–49; T. Nakamura, 1983, pp. 45–9; Nafziger, 1990, pp. 215–17; World Bank, 1988b, pp. 282–3).

While Sub-Saharan Africa faces labor surpluses today from rapid population growth and slow industrial employment demand, these surpluses are more likely to be reflected in urban unemployment instead of low wages. However, wage levels must be sufficient to maintain basic living standards which in turn affect productivity levels. Of crucial importance is inexpensive readily available food supplies.

Japan had faster food output growth and more stable food prices than contemporary Sub-Saharan Africa, because of rapid technical progress in agriculture during the Meiji period, and cheap food from colonies during the early twentieth century. Sub-Saharan Africa's well-known food supply problems have greatly impeded a low wage strategy.

INDUSTRIAL DUALISM

Meiji Japan had a dual economy consisting of: (1) a traditional, peasant, agricultural sector (together with petty trade and cottage industry), producing primarily for family or village subsistence, with little reproducible capital, using old or intermediate technology, and a marginal productivity of labor lower than the wage; and (2) capital-intensive modern manufacturing and processing operations, mineral extraction, and commercial agriculture, producing for the market, using reproducible capital and new technology, experiencing high and growing labor productivity, and hiring labor commercially. This dualism was exacerbated by Japan's continuing rapid growth, especially in technology.

As implied above, the modern sector wage was more than the traditional sector wage for identical labor skills from 1868 to 1915. After World War I, these wage differentials widened, as demand increased especially for skilled labor, which large firms tried to keep through rationalization, fringe benefits, and lifetime employment policies, seniority preference, and fringe benefits. The large firms' price-controlling power in product markets and credit rationing in the capital market made higher wages possible (Yasuba, 1976, p. 253). Additionally, large firms economized on unskilled labor by hiring temporary workers, contributing to greater labor market dualism (T. Nakamura, 1983, p. 224). By 1955, in the midst of the labor shortage of the postwar economic boom, the dual market for similar labor disappeared (although there were still wage differentials for different levels of skills and experience).

In this section I go beyond industrial–agricultural dualism to discuss dualism within the industrial sector, including regional dualism. Due to geographical labor immobility, a labor market usually consisted of a village, or no more than a few districts. Moreover, poor transport provided natural protection for regions with high wage costs.

Ironically, the rapid introduction of electric motors between 1914 and 1930 spurred industrial dualism. Manufacturing establishments with 1000 or more employees were virtually completely electrified by 1914, and those with less than 100 workers by 1930. The diffusion of cheap electric motors increased labor productivity in small manufacturing, and reduced economies of scale in many industries, increasing dualism in the non-agricultural sectors (Minami, 1976, pp. 299–325).

Japan has not stressed large leaps to the most advanced state of industrial technology available, but step by step improvements in technology and capital as ministries, regions, industries, firms, and work units learn by doing. In the early Meiji period, this meant technical and management assistance and credit facilities to improve and increase the scale of small workshops, handicraft producers, and cottage industry left from before 1868, causing less social disruption, as small industry's environment was not alien. The 1884 plan emphasized improving traditional technology through applied science and favored postponing massive foreign large-scale factory transplantation until traditional enterprises could utilize new techniques (Inukai, 1979, p. 5). Factory enterprises in Japan developed faster than in Sub-Saharan Africa, but were less destructive of cottage and workshop industry than in the Sub-Sahara.

Large industry evolved, after state assistance and two wars (1894–95 and 1904–05), into *Zaibatsu* concentration by 1910, but small industry, encouraged by government to take cooperative action, was retained, even in the leading manufacturing industry, textiles. Large-scale enterprises created external economies in the supply of raw materials, working capital, and markets. Additionally, these enterprises could not manufacture every item needed, and found it cheaper to buy parts and components from independently-run small workshops. The large firms provided technical advice, scarce inputs, credit, and, where needed, access to a large international trading company *sogo shosha*, which economized on the scarce language skills of both Japanese and foreigners. Small industry (establishments with less than 50 workers) increased its real output (though not output share) from 1884 to 1930, contributing 65 to 75 per cent of Japan's employment and 45 to 50 per cent of its gross manufacturing output in 1934. But small firms were not independent, being dominated by major banks, industrial companies, and trading corporations (Lockwood, 1954, pp. 201–13, 561–2).

Many Sub-Saharan African countries use training, extension, credit, and industrial estate programs to encourage small-scale manufacturing establishments. Nigeria, since independence in 1960, has provided subsidies, tariff drawbacks, training, and extension services for the establishment of small-scale industry.

But few contemporary Sub-Saharan countries have had as well-developed a small-scale manufacturing sector as post-1868 Japan. Many Sub-Saharan African policymakers, trying to modernize industry, have emphasized capital-intensive technology representing the most advanced state of arts in rich countries, allowing small industry to decline (see Nafziger, 1990, pp. 226–32). These countries have not stressed gradual technical improvement and learning from experience among existing ministries and industries, together with dissemination of technology consistent with local factor endowment and culture. Creating small industry from scratch is not as effective as maintaining and upgrading workshop, handicraft, and cottage industry left from an earlier stage of development. Once small industry has been disrupted or destroyed, it is difficult to reconstruct.

To be sure, the technological gap between DCs and LDCs is greater today than during the Meiji period. But contemporary Sub-Saharan African countries still have many alternatives to best-practice capital-intensive techniques.

EXPORT EXPANSION AND IMPORT SUBSTITUTION

From 1868 to World War II, the Japanese had a policy (first forced and later chosen) of multilateral, nondiscriminatory foreign trade outside their empire (1904–1945). This trade policy contributed to rapid growth, even though it would be a mistake to regard Japan's drive for foreign markets as the motor force of its industrialization.

Although nineteenth-century Meiji Japan partially circumvented Western tariff limitations by providing protection through subsidies and state undertakings, it was more open to international trade than most contemporary Sub-Saharan African countries. While foreign trade was modest by Western standards during the Meiji government's first twenty-five years, its influences stimulated technological learning (Lockwood, 1954, pp. 17, 306). The large domestic economy usually absorbed most of the products of this new technology. Subsequently, as the Japanese mastered and modified innovations, they often began exporting, as with textiles, the leading export, 1874 to 1940; other light manufactures, like consumer goods and simple machines that replaced primary-product exports in second place at the turn of the twentieth century; and the leading sector after World War II, heavy and chemical manufactures (especially electronics, vehicles, and sophisticated consumer goods in the 1970s, 1980s, and early 1990s).

Unlike contemporary Sub-Saharan Africa, Japan did not discriminate against exports. Increased tariff protection in the first quarter of the twentieth century reduced the price of foreign exchange, but government export promotion through a bank to finance trade, exhibiting Japanese products overseas, sales bureaux abroad, chambers of commerce and commodity guilds for cooperative export activity, merchant-marine subsidies, and business privilege in the new empire (Lockwood, 1954, p. 531) offset the foreign exchange rate price reduction through 1937 (except for the 1920s). Japan's annual real average growth rates in exports was 8.4 per cent between 1880 and 1913 (compared to 3.2 for the world as a whole, 2.6 for Britain, and 4.2 for the United States), and 5.2 per cent between 1913 and 1937 (compared to 1.4 for the world, 0.4 for Britain, and 1.4 for the United States).

Meiji Japan's exports also benefitted from favorable international economic conditions. In 1868–97, the yen chronically depreciated vis-à-vis the US dollar. In 1882–97 the yen was on a *de facto* silver standard, as silver declined relative to gold. While Chinese indemnities after 1897 (which strengthened the yen) and the military expenses of the 1904–05 Russo–Japanese War strained the international balance of trade, World War I's export demand spurred a large trade surplus. Although the immediate postwar and early Great Depression trade balance was in deficit due to slow growth of exports, they grew well after 1931, when Japan went off the gold standard (T. Nakamura, 1983, pp. 29–36).

Today's international economic conditions are not as favorable to Sub-Saharan African export expansion. The most rapidly expanding LDC manufactured exports during the 1970s and 1980s were textiles, clothing, footwear, and simple consumer goods requiring labor-intensive technology widely available. Yet the substantial development of LDC manufactured exports was concentrated in a relatively few middle-income countries. While in 1989, the four leading newly industrialized countries, South Korea, Taiwan, Hong Kong, and Singapore, which comprised less than 2 per cent of the LDC population, accounted for 47 per cent of LDC clothing and textile exports and 54 per cent of LDC manufactured exports, Sub-Saharan Africa, with 12 per cent of the LDC population, had 1 per cent of total manufactured exports (World Bank, 1991, pp. 230–35; Population Reference Bureau, 1991). For Africa, the competition from other aspiring newly industrial exporting countries is more severe than it was for Meiji Japan.

A single country, such as Meiji Japan, exporting agricultural and light manufacturing goods, would often be a price taker with substantial scope in expanding export receipts alongside a long-run elastic supply curve. However, today a single-country analysis suffers from a fallacy of composition: What is true for one country is not necessarily true of numerous African and other poor LDCs under pressure from Bank/Fund adjustment programs to expand primary-product exports. Sub-Saharan Africa is caught in an export trap, since as these LDCs expand export supply, relative prices fall substantially. Primary-product export growth reduced terms of trade, thus reducing export purchasing power, (1977–83), and only increasing this power slightly, (1983–90). The high DC effective rate of protection also blocks technologically feasible primary-product processing and light industry, tightening the export noose blocking export expansion as an engine of growth for Africa and many other low-income countries. Widespread currency devaluations under Bank/Fund adjustment programs also spur export expansion in primary products, suggesting that the export trap, rather than anti-farm bias, may be the impulse supporting Sub-Saharan African and LDC resistance to devaluations (Nafziger, 1993, pp. xxii, 111–12).

CONCLUSIONS

Since 1979–80 the World Bank, OECD or DC governments, and DC commercial banks – whose funding for Sub-Saharan Africa depends on the IMF seal of approval – together with the IMF, have formed a policy cartel. The IMF–World Bank–OECD (Bank/Fund for short) model prefers that Sub-Saharan African countries be democracies. However, since lenders and aid-givers depend on IMF approval, the OECD and World Bank rarely provide concessional funds to compensate for the additional inflationary and external payments pressures faced by countries making the transition to democracy. In practice, the Bank/Fund provides funds to the Sub-Sahara on the basis of its economic liberalization and other economic criterion, while paying little attention to achieving political democracy (Nafziger 1993, pp. 214–18).

How applicable is the Japanese development model (1868–1939) to present-day Sub-Saharan African countries?

First, Meiji Japan received a high return from its investment priority on primary, vocational, and scientific education. Basic literacy facilitates technological adaptation and learning. Sub-Saharan Africa would benefit from a similar investment emphasis. The Bank/Fund policies toward Sub-Saharan adjustment programs contributed to low investment rates in education and literacy, especially in the highly indebted countries of low-income Africa. Many Sub-Saharan African countries, having endured years of austerity and stagnation, cannot afford to reduce consumption to effect an external transfer, and thus they shift the burden to investment (Nafziger 1993, pp. 159–60). Moreover, the Sub-Sahara needs to be selective in using pre-World War II Japanese schools as models, as they emphasized rote memory and subservience to authority and were antithetical to creativity, democracy, human rights, and female equality.

Second, high labor supply elasticities resulting from vast reserves from the agricultural and informal industrial sectors, together with low industrial wage premiums, kept Japanese unskilled industrial wage rates relatively low before World War I, increasing business profits and reducing urban unemployment. Before the Bank/Fund adjustment programs of the 1980s, minimum wage legislation, strong trade union movements, and unadaptive capital-intensive technologies in Sub-Saharan Africa contributed to wages much higher than in Meiji Japan, reducing African profits and savings. Most Sub-Saharan elites were afraid of losing political support from revising labor codes, curtailing wages, eliminating capital subsidies, adjusting foreign exchange rates, or making pay scales more flexible. Today, with austere policies essential to obtaining loans of last resort from the IMF, World Bank, or OECD, Sub-Saharan African political leaders have frequently resorted to repression to retain power.

Third, Japanese-type 'guided capitalism' is limited in Sub-Saharan Africa today, because of the inadequate government capability to spur private business, and political elite and populist opposition to large business subsidies, high industrial concentration, high income inequality between business people and others, and favorable legal and labor policies for business.

Fourth, Japanese economic history demonstrates the importance of a government role in creating and regulating financial institutions, without tolerating growing concentration of private financial institutions. However, similar to Meiji Japan, most contemporary Sub-

Saharan African countries lack the ability and will to prevent indigenous concentration.

Fifth, many Sub-Saharan African countries, like Meiji Japan, have tried to transfer large amounts of agricultural income to industry for investment capital but, like Japan, some have sacrificed rural incomes and nutritional levels, and spurred agrarian rural discontent. However, the adjustment programs of the Bank/Fund, in their rush to free markets and contract spending to restore equilibrium, failed to consider the needed complementary governmental agricultural services, the low short-run elasticities in agriculture, and the short-run effect of foreign-exchange decontrol on inflation and the balance of payments.

Sixth, Meiji Japan exemplifies the importance of improving capital and technology step by step, utilizing existing small industry, rather than making substantial leaps to the most advanced technologies available.

Seventh, given a product cycle, as goods become standardized, Sub-Saharan Africa, similar to Meiji Japan, can mass-produce items with less skilled labor. However, today's Sub-Sahara is at a disadvantage compared to nineteenth-century Japan, as Sub-Saharan firms compete against oligopolistic multinational corporations. Although today's international economic conditions are not so favorable to Sub-Saharan Africa, it could still benefit from the Japanese approach of using competitive exchange rates and export subsidization.

Finally, the Japanese experience indicates the advantages of self-directed development. However, the Bank/Fund model for Sub-Saharan Africa neglects self-direction, emphasizing a close monitor of lending and policy by the IMF and Bank. To be sure, many small Sub-Saharan countries are limited in their options of reducing dependence on DC trade and capital movements. But the JDM underlines the importance of Sub-Saharan governments controlling DC capital inflows and the employment of DC personnel introducing technology. This is especially important since the technological distance between today's DCs and Sub-Saharan Africa is large, making it less likely that foreign experts will adapt technology to local conditions and indigenous production without Sub-Saharan administrative direction.

While contemporary Sub-Saharan Africa can learn useful lessons from the Japanese development model, these lessons are limited because of Meiji Japan's historically specific conditions, and because some aspects of the Japanese approach that spur rapid economic growth also contributed to pathologies of growth, such as *Zaibatsu* concentration, income inequality, labor union repression, militarism, and imperialism. In the seven decades before World War II one can point to the indenturing of young workers by parents, the increased tenancy rates and greater tenure insecurity, the slums in major cities, the serious environmental noise and pollution problems, the cost of soldiers and civilians killed, crippled, and disabled under imperialism, the torture and imprisonment of opponents to the regime, the suffering of colonial peoples in Taiwan and Korea, the suffering of adversaries during World War II, the independence of the military command from cabinet control, the rampant militarism in the 1930s, and authoritarianism were connected to an economic strategy emphasizing low wages, a stronger military, samurai subsidies, *Zaibatsu* facilitation, capital transfer from agriculture, little spending on social welfare, and the neglect of human rights (Halliday, 1975; and Dower, 1975). These pathologies were not reduced until military defeat was followed by the democratic reforms of an occupation government, a series of events not to be recommended, nor likely to improve income equality, accelerate economic growth, and democratize the political economy in the Sub-Sahara as it did in Japan. Sub-Saharan Africa today cannot wholly adopt the Japanese model but must select components piecemeal, such as self-directed development planning, technological adaptation, scientific and practical education, state role in infrastructure and human capital investment, labor-intensive industrial export expansion, improvement capital and engineering step by step, and learning by doing.

Notes

1. Scholars have usually rejected concepts of abrupt historical thresholds like Rostow's take-off (1971) or Engels' industrial revolution. Even Kuznets' modern economic growth (1966), a rapid, sustained increase in real per capita GNP associated with capital accumulation and rapid technical change under private or state capitalism, begins so gradually that its start cannot be dated by a given year or decade. In Japan, we cannot pinpoint the beginnings of modern (or capitalist) growth more precisely than the Meiji reform era of the late nineteenth-century.
2. Nafziger, 1990, pp. 230–2, discusses possible LDC strategies for more appropriate technology.
3. In contrast, independent Siam, which in 1868 faced initial conditions somewhat comparable to Japan, did not establish government factories or

provide assistance to private industrial entrepreneurs in the latter part of the nineteenth century.
4. Calculations are from five-year moving averages from Ohkawa and Shinohara, 1979, p. 86; and Hayami, 1975, p. 228.

4 The Korean Miracle (1962–80) Revisited: Myths and Realities in Strategies and Development

Kwan S. Kim

INTRODUCTION

South Korea's 'rags-to-riches' development is often cited as a 'man-made' miracle. It is a miracle in the sense that in the span of the past three decades the country underwent the kind of structural transformation that today's industrialized countries took almost a century to achieve.[1] The transformation was accomplished with relatively equitable income distribution by international standards.[2]

South Korea into the 1960s had a backward, desolate economy based on subsistence agriculture not unlike many of today's African countries. As late as in the early 1960s,[3] the country's average real income was comparable to, or even lower than, that of Haiti, Ethiopia, Chad, Sudan, Tanzania, Yemen, and about 40 per cent below India's. With such a low-level of income, domestic savings were negligible. The population growth of nearly 3 per cent a year in an already densely populated country meant that the country had to depend on foreign aid for its survival. Unemployment and underemployment were widespread with over 40 per cent of the nation's population in poverty. Thus, the initial conditions of Korean development resemble many contemporary developing countries, including those of Sub-Saharan Africa.[4] If ever there was an economic basket case, Korea of the 1950s was it.

Korea with 42 million population and per capita income of $6700 in 1992, is the world's twelfth largest trading nation, and is on the threshold of joining the ranks of industrialized, developed nations. The government-led, outward-oriented economic strategy worked efficiently resulting not only in rapid growth but also in a gradual eradication of absolute poverty.[5]

This essay provides an overview of Korea's policies and practices and their consequences of industrial development during the 1962–80 period. This was the period of active state intervention within a market framework. The state mobilized and allocated the nation's resources to enhance national wealth and industrial strength, directing private sector activities to this end. The goal of statism was not in directing the economy toward regulatory welfarism as in the advanced capitalist countries. Nor was it meant to achieve egalitarian redistribution, as in classical Marxism. The closest historical parallels, although far from being exact, might be the developmental state of Bismarck's Germany or Meiji Japan in the late nineteenth century. The focus of this essay on development during the 1962–80 period is intentional. The Korean model of economic take-off during this period provides some useful lessons to those developing countries aspiring to industrialize, especially to those Sub-Saharan African economies whose current level of development is roughly comparable to Korea in the late 1950s.

The essay begins with an examination of the state's strategic framework which was used to direct Korea's path to industrialization. This is followed by a detailed discussion of policy in important sectors such as trade, finance, foreign investment, industrial organization, labor and agriculture. The chapter then turns to the organizational structure used by the state to implement its industrial policy. By way of conclusion the essay critically examines the myths of the Korean development model and the lessons that can be applied to African countries.

GENERAL SYNTHESIS: POLICY AIMS AND FRAMEWORKS

The Strategic Framework for Industrialization

The Korean experience in trade and development contradicts in many ways the traditional argument for free trade. The conventional argument, based on the principle of comparative advantage, emphasizes the benefits from free trade by engaging in those activities for which the country is best suited in terms of resource endowment: in particular, differences in factor endowments should determine the patterns of comparative advantage; a labor-abundant country will have a comparative advantage in labor-intensive goods relative to a capital-rich country.

When Park Chung Hee was installed in power in 1961, his policy makers, learning from neighboring Japan's experience, saw the need to build a solid industrial base as the cornerstone of Korea's future development. The long-run strategy favored diversification into manufactured exports. To pursue the policy objective for industrialization, it was felt that the state, given the initial weakness of the private sector, had to play a leading role in formulating and implementing trade and industrial policies. The basic strategy to develop industry called for targeting a few sectors of the economy that were expected to perform well in international markets. Those firms entering them would be granted special incentives, which will be discussed in more detail later.

It is worth pointing out that when Park came to power, there were no longer any strong countervailing civilian forces to check the huge military institution. The state was dominant over civil society, which enabled it to exercise a persistent and active intervention in economic affairs. In post-liberation Korea, the land reforms initiated by the U.S military regime virtually eliminated the land-owning class as a contending political force. Accused of collaboration with Japan's colonial administration, the few remaining, indigenous industrial capitalists were turned into a disorganized, weakened political force in the wake of Japan's withdrawal. The cold-war geopolitics in the postwar Korea also legitimized the use of the state's coercive apparatus to suppress civil rights, particularly labor movements, in the name of national security. The Korean state was in a position to directly appropriate a large part of the economic surplus, deploying it in bureaucratically directed activities. The state's primacy over industrial labor was critical to the success of labor-intensive exports, since it required the mobilization of cheap and disciplined labor.[6]

In Figure 4.1 the philosophy underlying Korea's earlier development strategy is illustrated using an Eatwell-style 'cumulative causation' framework (1982, pp. 48–67). The diagram shows the link between world demand and domestic output for a small, open economy. The world demand in the upper box determines the level of national output. The unit cost of industrial output is affected by the level of output, given the presence of scale economies in manufacture; namely, the greater the level of output, the lower the unit cost of production. Thus, the initial level of exports determines the country's international competitiveness, which in turn influences the rate of growth in world demand. A virtuous circle becomes complete; the more the country sells abroad, the easier it is to sell. The opposite, vicious circle is also possible. If the country loses the initial share of the world market, the domestic output level shrinks, riding upward on the cost curve. The rise in the unit cost could adversely affect the country's export competitiveness, resulting in further losses in the market share.

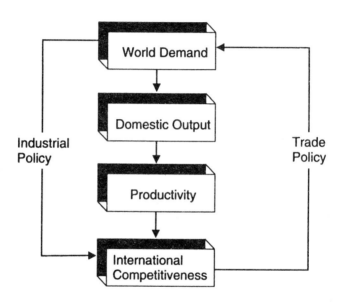

Figure 4.1   Korea's Neomercantilist Model

State interventions could prove instrumental in maintaining the virtuous circle in motion. If, for example, exports run into difficulties, the government could introduce policy measures to stimulate export demand. Such policies include exchange rate devaluation, export subsidies, or other export incentive systems. If the export sector begins to lose its competitive edge in international markets, the government may resort to fiscal or monetary policies to grant special incentives to or even to direct controls over specific sectors or firms. Imports would be confined to sectors complementary to export-sector development. Protective trade policies would be necessary to protect the country's balance of payments position.

The above model fits fairly closely to Korea's development strategy in the decades of the 1960s and the 1970s. It runs counter to the received view of market-oriented development, according to which Korea' industrialization is seen as a case of success on account of changing comparative advantage attained by 'correct' pricing and 'realistic' exchange rate policies.[7] While not denying the important roles played by market-oriented policies, the point to note is that the market system is used, when deemed appropriate and necessary, only as an instrument in achieving national developmental goals. As such, it can explain part of Korea's success.

In the earlier years of state-guided development, there was not much of a private sector to contend with. The elimination of leftist forces, which continued throughout the 1950s after the Korean War (1950–53), freed the government from the need to pursue populist policies, enabling it to focus on selected policy alternatives for implementation. Park established a system of meritocratic bureaucracy backed up by military muscle. It was simpler to get the bureaucracy moving rather than trying to bring into line the weak private sector. Although the rapid bureaucratization often distorted efficiency in resource use, the role of the state in the earlier Korean development must be judged using criteria beyond the neoclassical bounds of allocative efficiency.

The Framework of Strategy Implementation

Broad goals in a development strategy remain political window-dressing unless they are actually carried over into specific policies. Specific policies for industrial development in Korea during the period of export expansion can be grouped into two broad categories: the first was the set of macroeconomic policies aimed at influencing the general environment for industrial activities, and the second, the set of policies more directly targeted at the development of specific sectors or industries.

The Setting of the Macroeconomic Environment

One important objective of Korea's earlier industrial policy was to create an economic environment conducive to efficient resource utilization. There were two aspects of economic policy implemented for this purpose.

One aspect of this was government control of businesses and investment in infrastructural development. During the initial period of Korean industrialization, state-controlled enterprises constituted a leading sector in the national economy. They grew rapidly, increasing from 7 per cent of GDP to 9 per cent during the 1963–1972 period and accounted for as much as 40 per cent of the total domestic investment in the period between 1963 and 1979 (data from Bank of Korea). Public enterprises were created not only to provide usual public goods, but also to control most key-sector industries including all public utilities, coal, tungsten, minerals, fertilizer, steel, and transportation systems, and to indirectly exercise influence on business activities as well.

The lion's share of public funds went to infrastructural projects (highways, port facilities, electricity, irrigation, transportation, communication, etc.). New public sector firms were created specifically to serve as industrial infrastructure and to supply inputs to downstream industries. They not only made a contribution to capital formation and technological development but also created forward and backward linkages. The share of these infrastructural investments rose steadily, reaching 76 per cent of the total public-sector investment in 1977–1980 (Table 4.1). It was these infrastructure and intermediate activities that provided the foundation for strengthening vertical linkages in production.[8] A good example of the success of public enterprises is the Pohang steel mill (POSCO), which was constructed in 1973 under Japanese aid. POSCO quickly emerged as a global producer. It has been technologically modern and extremely cost-effective. Its main objective has been to provide low-cost, high-quality products to downstream industries. The cost effectiveness of this public sector enterprise was a factor contributing to the subsequent development of other downstream industries, such as shipbuilding, construction, automobiles, and machinery.

Perhaps more importantly was the second aspect of policy dealing with the price setting of such key resources as foreign exchange, investment funds (interest rate), transport, and staple grains. The Price Control Act revised in 1962 empowered the government to control the prices of most staple grains and the rates of public utilities. Given the important role of prices in the overall allocation of resources, extreme care has been exerted to reconcile the economic interests of various social classes. According to Whang, as late as 1966 some 40 per cent of total economic transactions was subject to direct or indirect forms of price control (Whang 1987, p. 83).

Table 4.1 The Industrial Composition of South Korean Public Sector Investment

	Primary Industry (%)	Mining and Manufacturing (%)	Infrastructural and Social Overhead (%)	Total (%)
First Five-Year Plan (1962–1966)	25.7	20.8	53.5	100
Second Five-Year Plan (1967–1971)	25.9	13.3	60.8	100
Third Five-Year Plan (1972–1976)	22.7	15.6	61.7	100
Fourth Five-Year Plan (1977–1980 average)	15.7	8.5	75.8	100
Total Average	22.9	14.9	62.2	100

Source: Economic Planning Board.

The first round of general price reform was attempted before the inauguration of the Second Five-Year development plan (1967–1972). The First Plan (1962–1966), largely a rehash of the ideas presented to the previous regime, was prepared in a hurry simply to show the government's seriousness about economic development and to provide a ground for more sophisticated, subsequent plans. The new measures included the exchange rate reform of 1964 and the interest rate reform of 1965. The exchange rate reform devalued the won from 130 to 255 per dollar and substantially liberalized exchange controls. The devaluation was based on a study comparing world and domestic prices, with the new rate reflecting the median purchasing power parity in international markets.

The interest rate reform of September 1965 doubled the six-month deposit rate to 24 per cent per annum (a real interest rate of around 11 per cent). Borrowing rates, except for special purposes, were comparably raised. The reform was meant to place a real rate of interest more in line with the prevailing real rate of return on capital, to enable a shift from quantitative credit rationing towards 'market' allocation. It was also aimed at encouraging domestic savings and reducing inflation.[9]

Both reforms brought key resource prices into line with relative resource scarcities. Since prices must be used to measure the value of resources in uses alternative to those being investigated, adequate resource planning becomes difficult when prices are severely distorted.

In this sense, the reforms of 1964 and 1965 were a precondition for meaningful resource planning.

Sector Policy

The basic strategies for attaining the nation's broad economic goals involved decisions over time on the shift in policy support from sector to sector. A strategy gradually evolved for upgrading the economy by shifting from dependence on relatively labor-intensive light industry to a structure based on heavy and chemical industries. This made perfectly good sense. Korea's original advantage was in cheap and diligent labor. It was therefore reasonable for Korea to engage in sectors like textiles, garments, footwear, and simple electronics. As the domestic wage rate rose and more capital was accumulated, it appeared more advantageous by the mid-1970s from the viewpoint of international competitiveness for Korea to move into more capital-intensive sectors such as steel or petrochemicals. Other developing countries, particularly in Asia, were becoming strong rivals in the export market for traditional, labor-intensive goods. At the same time, the industrialized countries were turning toward increased protection, particularly against traditional exports from the developing countries.

This progression reflects the dynamic strategy for industrialization. Korea followed the path similar to the one that neighboring Japan had pursued. To make things easier, Japan was constantly churning out long-term projections and visions for futuristic industries. By the late 1960s, the government began selecting 'strategic' industries which it was willing to back more energetically than others through a series of measures of a general supportive nature. Korea slipped into the practice later known as 'targeting industry and product' that prevailed in the 1970s.

First, the Electronics Promotion Law in 1969 recognized electronics as a 'strategic export industry'. Comprehensive plans for developing the industry attempted to direct the effort to adapt to the technological changes taking place in the industry worldwide. The government quickly established industrial estates with such suitable infrastructures as Kumi and Masan, and such specialized institutes as the Korea Institute of Electronics Technology, Korea Advanced Institute of Science and Technology, and the Electronics Industries Association of Korea for research, adaptation, and development.

In the wake of the plans for the electronics industry, the promotional policy quickly turned to heavy and chemical industries. In 1973,

President Park officially initiated the campaign for the creation of a heavy and chemical industry. The strategic branches of the industry included iron and steel, chemicals and petrochemicals, electrical and general machinery. Various projects were included in the Third and Fourth Plans with generous funding of the manufacturers who qualified. The usual support and incentives were provided for those firms that could export, and imports were restricted for those that could supply the domestic market. It seemed that no effort was spared in order to attain the targets.

Following the development of heavy and chemical industries, the choice of 'strategic' industries varied over time, ranging from sophisticated electronics to shipbuilding and to automobiles, among others. The support measures were steadily strengthened. Rather than channel funds and adopt projects as opportunities arose spontaneously, an effort was made to direct the economy along the desired path, as its development evolved.[10]

As long as private enterprise cooperated with the state in following the latter's directive, the task of developing the targeted sectors was left in the former's hands. The allocation of investment was an important part of policy but the role of planning was confined to determining where incentives for investment should be given, and to indicating and establishing an appropriate set of incentives that could guide private entrepreneurs to the right decisions. As indicated in the Plan documents during the 1970s,[11] the primary goal of planning for industrial priorities was seen as providing incentives to the private sector at a level compatible with resource needs and availabilities. The role of the public sector was, after setting incentives, to respond, where desirable, to 'private sector' requests for credit, subsidies, and foreign exchange allocation. An important task of planning at this point also consisted in developing capacity for project evaluation and decision-making at least at the ministerial level.

Once the government decided to promote certain strategic industries, all forms of incentives were made available to them (see below). These measures were administered within centrally imposed constraints by several ministries, notably Agriculture, Commerce and Industry, and Finance, and by special offices, such as the National Tax Administration.[12]

In Korea's planning overall price reform preceded the sectoral development plan. This served as a precondition for rational resource planning at the sectoral and more disaggregated level. Trade reform measures focused on shifting the economy from a strategy of import substitution towards that of export promotion. The financial reform became the classic example of a successful policy of mobilizing resources, stabilizing prices, and promoting investment.

In selecting industrial activities classified as having priority, no particular consideration needed to be given to the shadow prices of the factors of production, nor to the resulting sectoral structural distortions. The prevailing exchange rate and interest rates were used in industrial project evaluation without undue concern for excessive distortion that might result from the project. The decision to bring both the exchange and interest rates in line with market levels in the 1960s was based on the need to have prices reflect relative resource scarcities. Although price reforms provided a setting in which industrial activities could be selected, not on an *ad hoc* basis but in relation to their relative contribution to the objectives of rational economic use of capital and of foreign exchange saving. In reality they turned out to be more useful in providing information rather than in allocating resources. The Park government relied more heavily on incentives created by various forms of interventions.[13]

STRATEGY EVOLUTION IN POLICY AREAS

Trade Policy

Obviously for a small, resource-poor economy like Korea, the choice of trade strategies is bound to affect the evolution of its industrial development and structure. Historically, South Korea started with modest industrialization efforts centered exclusively on import substitution. In the decade following the end of the Korean War in 1953 the economy had largely been preoccupied with its postwar reconstruction and limited efforts for industrialization, mainly in import-substitutable basic consumer goods. By the late 1950s, the initial domestic demand for substitutable goods had been satisfied, and the heavily protected local manufacturers became too inefficient to compete in the world market. Insufficient foreign exchange, which was needed to buy foreign technologies and capital equipment, began to stymie attempts to move up on the import substitution ladder. The country only managed to survive on the basis of a meager industrial structure that could not last long without imports of essential raw materials (complicated by the US threat to cut off the indispensable flow of aid). The Park Chung Hee regime's alternative choice in 1961 thus was to consciously create an industrial base for production of exports that could be sold abroad to finance Korea's vital imports (including massive shipments of grain and fertilizer).

Export Policy

The Park government quickly instituted an offensive arsenal of material incentives to encourage exports in the nation's all-out war for survival. Various forms of direct and indirect fiscal incentive measures were provided to the manufacturers in targeted industries who qualified for assistance. The incentive measures consisted, at various times, of reductions in corporate and private income taxes; tariff exemptions for and tax rebates on materials imported for export production; financing of imports needed for producing exports; business tax exemptions; accelerated depreciation allowances; creation of various reserve funds; a fund at subsidized interest rates to promote export industries and another to encourage firms to export; foreign currency loans to finance exports on long-term credits; an export-import link system; differential treatment of traders based on export performance; export insurance; and so on.[14] The provision for accelerated depreciation allowed the manufacturing firms that earned more than 50 per cent of the revenue in foreign exchange to write off depreciation of up to 30 per cent of the ordinary rate allowed by the tax law.

Among the incentive measures, interest subsidies to exporters turned out to be of critical importance. Table 4.2 compares the interest rates charged by the banks to export-oriented, and commercial-oriented businesses. It is apparent from the table that rates were normally 40 to 60 per cent of the commercial levels occasionally dropping as low as 25 per cent. Short-term credits to exporters climbed to as high as 94 per cent of required capital by 1972. Export credits had always been excluded from credit controls – often stringent – during times of economic hardship.

Measures for moral incentives were adopted with almost equal force.[15] The Ministry of Commerce and Industry also set annual export targets for officials connected with export administration. If targets were not fulfilled, the administrative process was expedited to strengthen existing export-support schemes, to innovate new subsidy measures, and to exert irresistible pressures on businessmen to accelerate exports, even though this might have entailed losses.

The export manufacturer could obtain subsidized loans from such institutions as the Korea Development Bank, the Export–Import

Table 4.2   Comparison of South Korean Bank Interest Rates in Export vs.
Commercial Loans

	Export Lending (A)	Commercial Lending (B)	A/B
April 1962	12.78	16.43	0.78
July 1962	10.95	16.43	0.67
December 1962	9.13	15.70	0.58
May 1963	8.03	15.70	0.51
March 1964	8.00	16.00	0.50
September 1965	6.50	26.00	0.25
June 1967	6.00	26.00	0.23
May 1973	7.00	15.50	0.45
January 1974	9.00	15.50	0.61
April 1975	7.00	15.59	0.45
August 1976	8.00	18.00	0.44
June 1978	9.00	19.00	0.47
January 1980	12.00	25.00	0.48

Source: The Bank of Korea Economic Statistics Yearbook.

Bank, the Technology Development Corporation, and the National
Investment Fund. A series of legislation and regulations, such as the
Tax Incentives Law, the Government Budget and Accounting Law and
the Tariff Law, provided various forms of tax relief and tariff
reductions for imported inputs to the manufacturer.

Other institutions promoting exports were also established. One was
the Korea Trade Promotion Corporation (KOTRA), a nonprofit
government agency established in 1962. KOTRA now has over eighty
branches around the world and a home office that engages in research
and promotion. Among other activities, it displays Korean products,
participates in international trade fairs, dispatches trade missions to
potential markets, and receives enquiries and visits from foreign
businessmen seeking Korean products. It also sponsors the Korea
Exhibition Center which hosts major trade fairs, including the Seoul
International Trade Fair that attracts as many as 10,000 foreign
buyers. In the private sector, the Korean Traders Association, which
runs the World Trade Center in Seoul, provides backup to its over
2,300 member companies. Trading companies, known as *Chonghap
sangsa*, were another important institution created by the government
to specialize in export promotion. In the days of import substitution
there were many small importing firms that took advantage of the
overvalued exchange rate to profit from imports. With the emphasis on
export promotion, there was a general need for trading agencies that

could direct imports of raw materials while promoting manufactured goods exports.

Interestingly, rather than support large and small trading companies indiscriminately, the government decided to support very large ones that were generally affiliated with various industrial conglomerates as their trading arms. These large traders were not only relatively more efficient owing to their scale-economies but had access to a much broader range of foreign markets. Larger companies were enticed to enter the field by various incentives that included advantages in the areas of trade administrations, export financing, taxation, and foreign exchange control. The government in return demanded superb performance through the familiar tool of export target-setting. These export targets were broken down in considerable detail by domestic exporters, with enough disincentives to motivate them toward acceptable performance.

Moreover, the targets based on what the firms thought they could achieve were raised from year to year by the government according to their own projections of how fast exports should grow. The creation of *Chonghap sangsa* was another tool to make export-oriented strategy work well for Korea. In a short time, full-fledged trading firms emerged, quickly establishing a distribution network throughout the world. These institutions were instrumental in helping many manufacturing firms to get a foothold in foreign markets.

The official policy for creating an industrial base for export promotion, designed by Park's team of technocrats, proved immediately successful. Largely owing to the expanding international market in the 1960s, growth in exports attained an extraordinary rate that far exceeded everyone's expectations. From 1962 to 1982, the average rate of export growth was about 30 per cent a year with peaks of over 50 per cent. The nation's annual export value soared from an extremely modest US $55 million in 1962 to a massive US $27 billion in 1982. Whereas the ratio of exports to GNP was a pitiful one per cent or so in the 1950s, it rose to 30 per cent and more in the late 1970s (in current prices). Exports, considered as the country's 'engine of growth', became something of a cliché in government and business circles with its overall contribution to real GNP growth estimated at about 45 per cent for the 1962–1982 period and around 60 per cent for the 1970s.[16]

A quantitative assessment of overall price incentives given to Korean exporters was attempted in a World Bank study (Westphal and Kim, 1977, pp. 11–25). Figure 4.2 traces movements of Korea's nominal and real effective exchange rates between 1962 and 1975. The real effective exchange rate is meant to reflect the actual amount in the Korean won received by exporters per dollar of their exports. The indicator is obtained by subtracting from the nominal rate all forms of indirect taxes and by adding tariff exemptions and other subsidies given to exporters.[17]

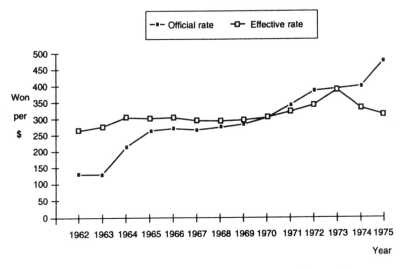

Figure 4.2   Nominal and Effective Exchange Rates for Korean Exports

As indicated in Table 4.3, the real effective exchange rate for exports was 264 in 1962 and fluctuated between 299 and 308 in the 1964 to 1970 period. It increased 30 per cent to about 400 by 1973,[18] and despite its fall in 1974 and 1975, still remained higher than its average over the latter half of the 1960s. Although these measures are only crude indicators, they suggest that the government's efforts for export push relied primarily on the incentive system (as we argued above). The government, primarily by means of periodic devaluations, continued to adjust export incentive rates to a stable level in the face of galloping inflation at home.

Toward the late 1970s, the labor shortage combined with the Park regime's quiet decision to lift the lid on wage increases caused labor costs to rise much faster in Korea than in the major exporting nations of the region. Between 1975 and 1980 the annual rate of increase of unit

Table 4.3   Effective Exchange Rates for South Korean Exports
(annual averages: won per US Dollar)

	Official Exchange Rate (nominal)	Exemptions of Indirect Tax and Tariff per Dollar of Exports	Real Effective Exchange Rates[*]
1961	127.5	—	—
1962	130.0	7.6	264.2
1963	130.0	9.1	276.1
1964	214.3	8.2	305.3
1965	265.4	11.1	304.6
1966	271.3	14.4	305.1
1967	270.7	15.7	298.8
1968	276.6	21.5	298.7
1969	288.2	22.7	299.4
1970	310.7	21.5	307.9
1971	347.7	23.1	328.6
1972	391.8	23.7	348.9
1973	398.3	21.5	396.5
1974	407.0	19.1	338.4
1975	485.0	14.0	320.9

[*] Real exchange rates that include indirect tax and tariff exemptions.
Source: The World Bank (Westphal and Kim, 1977).

labor cost was 17.5 per cent compared to 7.1 per cent in Taiwan and 0.8 per cent in Hong Kong. By 1979, textiles that alone had accounted for over 40 per cent of labor-intensive exports in the 1970s, along with eight other manufactured articles like plywood, wigs, and electrical appliances that accounted for another 25 per cent, together declined to 30 per cent while more capital-intensive heavy industrial products including iron, steel and ships began to replace light industrial products. In effect, the rise in the cost of fuel, raw materials, and capital goods imports during the decade paralleled the slump in the prices Korea could demand for its manufactured exports. The deterioration in the terms of trade obliged Korea to sell much more to gain just a little more. While the need for imports remained unchanged, possibilities of expanding exports were artificially constricted in various ways. The most menacing was the rise of protectionism in developed country markets.

Such limitations clearly cut into Korea's potential sales and made it turn toward other markets and products. This explains Korea's attempts to shift toward the Middle East, Latin America, and Africa.

An important source of Korean exports to developing countries has been the transfer of technology. For the five years from 1977 to 1981, total contracts for project-related exports amounted to $43 billion, while non-project-related technology exports[19] were estimated at about $8 billion (Westphal et al., 1984, p. 504). Among the categories of project-related technology exports, the most important one has been nonindustrial in nature, which has been transmitted via Korea's massive construction projects in the Middle East. In addition to projects to establish and operate productive systems abroad, Korea's technology transfer also included the form of capital goods exports accompanied by technical and managerial services.

The origin of Korea's ability to quickly develop a competitive advantage in technology exports can be traced back to the early 1970s when the government called for a long-term plan to build a capacity to manufacture capital goods. The plan focused on import substitution of fabricated structural elements (including shipbuilding), heavy equipment used in industrial plants, and other social overhead facilities. The earlier policy bias against the domestic capital goods sector was gradually reversed: tariff exemptions on imported capital goods were eliminated, import-licensing was made more restrictive and, among other things, the government established specialized credit facilities to provide financing on competitive terms to domestic firms producing capital goods. Economic policy beginning in the early 1970s started to encompass the development of both import-substituting as well as export activities.

Emphasis was also placed on promoting both the assimilation of imported technology and technical services exports.[20] These measures were supplemented by other provisions dealing with the promotion of local research and development, the education and training of technical personnel, and the establishment of an infrastructure of scientific and technological institutions. Promotion of technology-related industries in Korea was seen as being in line with its dynamic comparative advantage, and the government began to use capital goods and technology exports as a strategy to develop industrial competence. The acquisition of technological capability was seen as being fostered most effectively from export activity.

Once the government decided on an official policy to accelerate the development of capital goods and related services, various schemes that had already existed for other exporters were quickly reinforced to specifically benefit the producers of capital goods exports. Such measures included preferential access to credit for the financing of investment in such industries, preferential export financing[21] as well as insurance and guarantees against trade risks,[22] and the government-initiated search for and negotiation of overseas contracts by prospective exporters. In particular, producers of overseas project-related exports have received tax credits up to 50 per cent of their taxable profits and deferment of taxes on certain categories of exports-related income.

The government also used the large business conglomerate groups in Korea, known as *Chaebols*, the principal agents of capital and plant exports. Some of these conglomerates were accorded the special status of an integrated trading company that legally authorized them to combine production and overseas marketing activities. The role played by the *Chaebols* together with several Korean construction firms in expediting capital goods-related export activity has been overwhelming. According to one estimate,[23] thirteen Korean firms were listed among the 201 largest international contractors, accounting for 8.1 per cent of the value of international contracts won by these contractors.

Korea's success in technology exports was based on its technological capabilities gradually expanded through human and institutional capital accumulation. Export activity by enlarging the scope of market competitiveness stimulated indigenous technological effort. The earlier strategy of export-led industrialization thus resulted in the broadening and deepening of industrial competence, which further led to dynamically changing Korea's competitive advantage to more technology-intensive industries.[24] In this regard, government policies were instrumental in providing the driving force behind Korea's exports of capital goods and other technology-related projects, enabling Korea to rapidly adjust to dynamically changing comparative advantage.

The developing country market nevertheless could hardly replace the more lucrative markets in the United States and Europe. When President Chun Doo Hwan came to power in 1980 he had a mandate from the business community to hold the line on wage demands. Real wages in the industrial sector declined for about a year, giving exporters a breathing spell. However, Korea's planners recognized that the golden era of cheap labor would never return. Even if it did, prospects for labor-intensive export growth would remain bleak in view of mounting import restrictions, especially on textiles, in the developed countries. The nation's best hope for continued high growth, they believed, was to shift its export pattern from labor-intensive to high-technology products. This second economic takeoff was to be achieved by attracting vastly increased capital flows and technology transfers from abroad, and for this the government had to drastically liberalize its foreign investment code.

Import Policy

The Korean government's policy, although essentially export-oriented, has not been geared to the concept of a neutral free trade, an important part of structural adjustment. Up to 1967 domestic industries were protected by direct import controls: imports were permitted on the basis of the 'positive list' system, by which only the items enumerated would be allowed for import. The main items on the list were essential raw materials, energy, capital and intermediate goods. After adopting a unified exchange rate system in 1964, the government proceeded to institute incentive structures that favored use of imported capital and intermediate goods to develop efficient export industries at home. The incentive measures included the doubling of the so-called 'automatically approved' import items (mostly capital goods), tariff exemptions on capital goods (automatic for exporters and for selected import-competing industries), and liberal licensing of imported capital goods financed by subsidized credits. While liberal on essential imports, the government's policy remained highly restrictive on agricultural and manufactured products which were considered import-substitutable. The Korean government continued with measures of import restriction: an overall import quota system, foreign exchange allocation, and import legislation to discourage consumer goods imports.

After 1967 as a result of international pressures for trade liberalization, the government introduced the 'negative list' system by which the guidelines to exclude imports from automatic approval were to be stipulated. The main criteria for exclusion was the impact on the balance of payments and on the international competitiveness of domestic industries. The 'negative' system turned out to be inconsequential in actual measures of import liberalization: the proportion of imports excluded from the 'negative' list started from 61.7 per cent in 1968, falling to 49.5 per cent in 1975, and rising back to 68.5 per cent by 1980.[25] Import policy took on more restrictive features in the mid-1970s: faced with a diminished outlook for exports in the 1970s, government policy turned increasingly inward toward the domestic market. The government started ambitious programs to develop heavy, chemical, and capital goods industries to 'deepen' Korea's industrial structure, thereby reducing the domestic economy's long-term import dependence. The inevitable short-term result was increased import dependence as the areas of the priority imports had to be enlarged. The bulk of freely importable items continued to consist of crude oil, intermediate goods for re-exports, and essential components and raw materials for 'strategic industries'. On the other hand, consumer goods imports accounted for only 3 per cent of the total imports.

Along with the 'negative list' system in 1967, tariffs were added to control the patterns of imports. Table 4.4 shows Korea's tariff structures by sectors for 1968 and 1978. Since the nominal rates do not reflect the actual protection accorded to a domestic sector,

Table 4.4 Nominal and Effective Rates of Protection by Industry, South Korea (1968 and 1978) (unit = per cent)

Sectors	Nominal Rate 1968	Nominal Rate 1978	Effective Rate 1968	Effective Rate 1978
Agriculture, fishery and forestry	36.5	35.7	17.9	60.7
Mining and energy	12.2	4.0	3.5	−24.4
Food processing	61.5	37.5	−14.2	43.2
Vegetables and tobacco	140.7	139.3	−15.5	29.4
Construction materials	32.2	26.3	−8.8	−19.3
Primary - Intermediate goods	36.6	22.1	−18.8	−24.4
Secondary - Intermediate goods	58.7	31.9	17.4	2.9
Nondurable - consumer goods	92.3	48.0	−8.0	23.0
Durable consumer goods	98.3	46.3	39.8	118.9
Machinery	52.6	27.3	29.5	49.9
Transportation equipment	62.4	47.6	83.2	21.7
Total	54.3	35.3	9.0	24.1

Source: Nam, C. H. (1980).

estimated figures for effective protection rates (ERP) are also presented for the corresponding years.[26] The ERP represents the gain in value added as a result of tariffs on both inputs and outputs, as a percentage to value added under free trade.

The figures show that the average nominal rate for the entire economy fell from 54.3 per cent in 1968 to 35.3 per cent in 1978. To conclude from this that Korean imports were liberalized would, however, be misleading; in terms of the ERP there had been a substantial rise in the extent of protection accorded to domestic sectors, from 9.0 per cent to 24.1 per cent during the same period. The durable consumer goods industry, followed by primary goods sectors, were increasingly heavily protected over the period. In contrast, minerals, energy resources, primary imports, and construction materials continued to have increasingly negative protection. Thus, Korea's tariff policy was consistent with its direct import control policy. The conclusion that emerges is: Korea's import policy throughout the initial two decades of industrialization had been restrictive, and had been liberal only on imports required for its export and other 'strategic' industries.

Import substituting industries also received support like the export sectors. As discussed above, the government, in particular, recognized the strategic and economic significance of promoting a rapid development of capital goods industries. To encourage domestic production in the machinery industry, the government, already in the late 1960s, began to restrict quantitatively the import of some machinery goods immediately upon the initiation of their domestic production. Those firms using domestically produced machinery were allowed a 10 per cent tax deduction in their investment. Previously, tariff and credit policies had favored the purchase of imported capital goods. The government proceeded to abolish tariff exemptions on some types of capital goods imported, creating at the same time capital funds to support the domestic producers.

This policy resulted in active investments in the machinery sector with a wider domestic market that provided a basis for further growth. As the economy expanded with a continued need to modernize production facilities and to increase productivity, the domestic demand for capital goods registered an upward trend, particularly after the start of government support for the development of heavy and chemical industry beginning in the early 1970s. The annual average increase in the rate of domestic demand for machine tools reached as high as 24 per cent in the period between 1971 and 1981.

With a target set to fully localize the production of machine tools by 1990, the government enacted a series of provisions for promotional funds to encourage active research and development activity. Other measures included liberalization of imports of technologies mostly to be obtained through licensing agreements, and foreign assistance with production techniques. In 1977–1980, licensing agreements in the machinery sector accounted for about a third of all agreements approved in Korea.[27]

In summary, the Korean government essentially pursued a mercantilistic trade policy based on the dualistic approach of pushing for exports while advancing with import substitution. The factor deterring import liberalization has been the foreign exchange constraint. Korea's trade policy reflected a planned management which was cautious and calculating. It only remotely reflects liberalization as defined in a classical textbook sense and which is at the heart of the World Bank's model of structural adjustment.

Financing and Credit Policy

Perhaps one of the most important instruments used for implementing sector-oriented industrial development in Korea was public sector control and allocation of credits. The government itself, with a budget representing one-sixth of GNP, allocated the same percentage of its budget to the spending for development projects. The lion's share of this development spending went to transport and communication, energy, agriculture, and defense-related industries. By and large, however, the banking institutions, which were directly or indirectly controlled by the government, provided a predominant share of investment capital in industry. The domestic financing by banks, along with taxation and foreign borrowing, supported the major spurt of industrialization.[28] The prevalent form of financing was provisions of loans with subsidized interests and guarantees. Usually, these credit facilities were combined with other fiscal and tariff incentives, including public sector assistance in scientific and technical research.

A particular form of financing called 'policy loans' deserves a special mention. This type of loan had exceptionally low interest rates and lenient repayment terms. The loan was usually supplemented by other forms of incentives if the particular product was considered worthy of domestic protection or could be turned toward exports. Policy loans were administered by government-operated specialized development banks, made available primarily for purposes of export financing and supporting key industries. One estimate (Hong, 1979) shows that in 1972 the ratio of total interest subsidy associated with loans in manufacturing to the total fixed capital in that sector exceeded 25 per cent. The average annual increase in export credit reached as much as 40 per cent of the increase in money supply between 1970 and 1976.

In terms of the hierarchical structure of the financial world, the Ministry of Finance sits on top, supervising and regulating all the activities of the banking system including those of the central bank (the Bank of Korea). More indirectly involved and more concerned with implementation of financial plans is the Economic Planning Bureau (EPB), since it defines the approaches and targets that become criteria for granting 'policy loans' by the banking institutions, which are generally aimed at rendering special support to the 'prioritized' sectors. For this purpose, the government established a group of 'development banks'. They provided qualified firms with loans and also held equity in these firms. For instance, in 1984 the loans from the Korea Development Bank accounted for as much as 15 per cent of the nation's total outstanding debt. The Korea Long-Term Credit Bank has similarly been instrumental in tapping private capital to assist firms with loans and equity participation. The Korea Export–Import Bank represents another category of development banks that specialize in medium- and long-term credit for foreign trade transactions, with an emphasis on exports. These specialized banks receive funds partly from the government, from private deposits, and by issuing bonds in international financial markets.

Larger private sector banks, with a bulk of their credit given as 'policy loans,' were also drawn into the financing of industrial development and, to some extent, had to comply with orders and regulations from the Ministry of Finance. Thus, excluding the informal, curb-market loans generally available at exorbitant interest rates, the entire financial community, more or less, operated under some control and supervision of the government.

The system of 'policy loans' for providing special support to targeted industries worked well for Korea in the early days of industrialization and, in effect, accounted for half of the total bank lending. Without this public sector initiated financing it would not have been possible to develop light manufacturing industry, construction, steel, and ship-building industries, nor to build the basis for heavy and chemical industries in Korea. The system, however, contained several draw-backs. Since 'policy loans' for targeted sectors were subsidized compared to other considerably more expensive loans, many worthwhile projects failed to be undertaken simply because they were not targeted for development. The sectors targeted for promotion mostly included relatively large-scale projects. Small firms were seriously handicapped in obtaining credit. Beginning in the early 1980s, efforts began to be made to provide small firms with easier access to bank loans.

A related bias in investment decisions that resulted from the undue emphasis on 'policy loans' concerned the neglect of the microeconomic specifics in approving the worth of individual projects. The government's policy of targeting products specified only what sectors of the economy should be promoted for expansion. As a result, loans tended to be approved on the basis of superficial compliance with the administrative guidelines and not on the merits of individual projects. These weaknesses were manifest in the late 1970s when a number of government-supported projects had to be discarded. The policy aim of the 1981 bank reforms was to alleviate distortions in investment allocation by broadening the realm of managerial discretion by the commercial banks.

Finally, the policy of favoring targeted enterprises was a mixed blessing. Policy loans encouraged excessive borrowing by firms, frequently resulting in an unstable debt-equity ratio. By the late 1970s, it was not uncommon to find large firms having liabilities five to ten times as much as their net worth. Such firms were burdened with interest payments excessive in relation to their equity, which eroded their profitability and made their operation precarious in bad times.

Foreign Investment Policy

Korea is poorly endowed with natural resources. It must rely on the import of foreign resources and technologies. In the initial two decades of Korean development, the main source of financing imports had been foreign savings. Private savings in Korea were negligible, given the close-to-zero real deposit rate before 1965.[29] After the interest rate reform in 1965, which in essence guaranteed positive real interest rates, household savings soon quadrupled, reaching 3.5 per cent of GNP in 1967 and 4.5 per cent in 1976 (Bank of Korea, 1976). Nevertheless, domestic savings remained insufficient to cover the deficits of the government and the corporate sectors, which accounted for 7.6 per cent in 1976. Korea had been in continuous need of foreign capital and technologies as its economy expanded.

Until the early 1960s, capital inflow took the form of massive foreign aid for relief and rehabilitation of the economy. By the mid-1960s the concessional aid was phased out, gradually replaced by soft loans in limited amounts. In addition to the loans channeled through such donor agencies as USAID, the Japanese Overseas Cooperation Fund, the World Bank, and the Asian Development Bank, a growing share in loans took the form of supplier credit from the American or Japanese export–import Banks. The real break in financing avenues for Korea came with the conclusion of the Japan–Korea Normalization Treaty in 1965. In addition to the private-sector loan of US$300 million, the Japanese government agreed to provide Property Claim Funds (war reparations) made up of $200 million in grant aid and $300 million as a soft loan to be disbursed over the next ten years. These funds were earmarked for investments in agricultural and fishery infrastructures, for capital goods imports from Japan, and for construction of a large-scale steel mill in Pohang. The significance of this arrangement turned out to be the direct involvement of the Japanese government, which opened the door for subsequent transfer of Japanese technologies and private capital in substantial amounts. For instance, as shown in Table 4.5, Japan accounted for close to a half of the total foreign investment in the period between 1962–1980, followed by the United States with a quarter share.

During the 1970s when Korea's progress became evident and was proving its credit worthiness, it was able to obtain more commercial loans. Government policies concerning loan capital were open and

Table 4.5   Sources of Foreign Direct Investment in South Korea (1962–82)
(unit = million dollars)

	1962–1966	1967–1971	1972–1976	1977–1980	1981	1982	Total	Share (%)
Japan	0.7	40.8	376.9	180.3	34.6	41.6	675.9	47.1
USA	21.9	12.4	67.9	122.9	85.2	107.6	418.0	29.0
Netherlands	0.0	6.3	58.7	37.6	1.3	1.5	105.3	7.4
Hong Kong	0.0	0.3	3.5	8.8	8.1	24.5	45.1	3.2
W. Germany	0.3	2.4	2.8	12.2	3.1	3.1	24.1	1.7
Others	0.1	10.5	55.4	80.5	13.1	9.4	168.1	11.6
Total	23.0	72.7	565.2	442.4	145.3	187.8	1436.5	100

Source: Ministry of Finance.

unrestrictive. There were no shortages in the demand for loans with reasonable terms. The inflow was massive in the late 1970s, with the outstanding external debt rising to $37 billion in 1982 from a mere $4 billion in 1972. The debt burden remained manageable as export earnings continued to grow rapidly: the debt-service ratio was 18 percent in 1972 and fell to 15 percent a decade later.

Direct foreign investment was a more recent phenomenon in Korea,[30] and was not important compared with such countries as India or Brazil. The first serious efforts to attract foreign investors were made beginning with the launching of the First Development Plan in 1962. Although foreign ownership was restricted to less than 50 percent,[31] reasonable conditions that included tax relief, duty-free imports of capital goods, easy remittance of profits, and other incentives were offered. It took some time for an appreciable amount of direct investment to flow in. As Table 4.5 indicates, by the end of 1981 total direct foreign investment amounted to US $1.4 billion. The basic policy on foreign investment followed the line of an outward-looking strategy for development. The Korean government, however, had a clear purpose for foreign direct investment: foreign operations would be allowed so long as it conformed to the national interests perceived by the government (Kim, 1988). As such, despite the appearance of a fairly liberal environment for investment, foreign firms were subject to the high degree of restrictions and interference by government. In general, except for special cases of investment in the strategic sectors of the economy, foreign firms could not compete on equal terms with local firms on the domestic market. As a result, the prevalent form of foreign direct investment has been a joint venture with the domestic partner.

Foreign capital was thus welcomed as long as it could contribute to the development of 'priority' sectors, the transfer of technologies, and the enlargement of marketing contacts. While investment opportunities were open in most sectors, there was a clear preference for investment in manufacturing industry. As a result, manufacturing received a predominant share of foreign investment; then textiles in the early period, and electronics and petrochemicals in the later period.[32] Direct investment played a particularly important role in the vital area of Korean development. Foreign investors have been instrumental in introducing new production and management techniques, and in facilitating the transfer of overseas information and knowledge.

Beginning in the 1980s, in a bid to facilitate the realignment of industrial structure, the government further intensified measures to attract foreign investment by dismantling many restrictions on capital inflow.[33] Korea's investment policy started to aim at inducing the import of technical knowhow through joint-venture projects, as Korea entered into a new specialization in more sophisticated capital goods and high-technology industrial products. Emphasis on exports was not forgotten either. Foreign investment in export-oriented industries has always been welcomed in Korea.

To conclude, what then is the overall assessment of foreign capital inflow in Korea? As a result of the earlier borrowing, Korea in the early 1980s turned into a major debtor nation and had to remit interests, profits and royalties in substantial amounts to foreign investors. Although over the years the amounts involved in foreign debts and investment rose rapidly, so did the ability to handle them as the economy grew more rapidly. Unlike the situation in Latin American countries, however, Korea has actually been freeing itself of external dependence. While savings from foreign sources were three times as large as the domestic counterpart in the early 1960s, two decades later the relationship was reversed with domestic savings contributing the most to capital formation. In Korea, foreign borrowing has been put to use mainly for development of industry and vital infrastructure. Direct foreign investment, although relatively unimportant in amounts in relation to the loan, has been instrumental in promoting the development of indigenous industry in a different way. The expansion of direct investment has meant opportunities for technological adaptation rather than opportunities for employment. Again, this is in sharp contrast to the view of the World Bank which emphasizes the removal of all barriers to direct foreign investment.

Business Policy and Industrial Organization

An important aspect of Korean industrial policy concerns the government's relationship to business. In Korea, the large industrial conglomerates known as *Chaebols*, usually represented by the most dynamic and aggressive entrepreneurs, play the crucial role in the industrialization process. They have often in the past been used as an instrument of government policy, and in return the government inadvertently strengthened the hand of these conglomerates.

Currently there are some fifty major conglomerates with each unit composed of half a dozen to fifty member firms that are horizontally and vertically integrated in the industrial structure.[34] The breadth and speed of the rise of the *Chaebol* in Korea seems unprecedented in the history of enterprise. As Table 4.6 shows, in the period between 1973–1978 the annual rate of growth in value added contributed by the 10 largest conglomerates was as high as 30 per cent. In terms of the share of their contribution to GDP, they accounted for 14 per cent in 1973, rising to 23.4 per cent by 1978. The top 46 firms, taken together, accounted for 31.8 per cent of GDP in 1973, which rose to 43 per cent over the same period. These measures clearly show the extent of progress in industrial integration as well as the process of concentration of wealth in Korean industry.

The phoenix-like rise of the *Chaebol* was mainly caused by government policies. In the earlier days of industrialization, the business environment was conducive to opportunities for forward or backward integration in industry. A broad spectrum of sectors opened up for entrepreneurs to participate in, as export demand suddenly rose in diversified areas. Access to financing was made easy, as the government provided easy credit in efforts to promote exports. Once the government was convinced the entrepreneur could succeed, this would usually have a snow-balling effect, success breeding success, since the government credit was largely based on past achievements. This type of credit policy made it possible for successful entrepreneurs to launch several ventures at the same time, which eventually led to a race for empire-building in business.

Trends toward concentration in manufacturing industry can be discerned from Table 4.7, which reports the annual average growth rates in manufacturing output and employment during the 1967–79 period. The data show that larger firms had grown much faster than smaller ones, indicating trends toward concentration in Korea industry. In terms of output, the largest group of firms employing

Table 4.6 Contribution to Value Added by Conglomerates in South Korea

Number of Conglomerates	Annual Growth Rate (1973–1978)	As Percentage of GDP 1973	As Percentage of GDP 1978
5	35.7	8.8	18.4
10	30.0	13.9	23.4
20	27.5	21.8	33.2
46	21.4	31.8	43.0
GDP Total	17.2	100.0	100.0

Source: Korean Development Institute.

more than 500 persons grew at an annual rate of 27.6 per cent during the period compared to 11.1 per cent for the smallest units employing fewer than nine persons. In Korea any establishments employing less than 500 persons are considered as small and medium units. The table thus implies the cumulative decline experienced by small and medium firms in Korea. Despite the alarming trends of concentration, the government continued to support larger units. Larger firms with scale-economies and cost-efficiency could be counted on to more successfully complete crucial projects for national development. Funds flowed more readily into larger companies, since they were generally in a better position to outbid smaller firms in government-financed project contracts.

Policies for promoting industrial integration appeared necessary for the development of heavy industry, as Korea was preparing to move into advanced sectors. Economic logic also favored large-scale production. A minimum scale in plant size was required in such heavy sectors as automobiles, steel, and shipbuilding. The *Chaebol* had to compete in international markets with foreign multinationals which tended to be large in comparison with their Korean counterparts. Firm size was also an important factor to consider in joint ventures with foreign partners, since there was a danger that, if too large, the latter might dominate and control their domestic counterparts.[35]

The government's preferred method of supporting a project was to make credit available on favorable terms to specific borrowers. During

Table 4.7   South Korean Growth Rates in Manufacturing Output and Employment by Size of the Firm (1967–1979)

Firm size in persons	Output (%)	Employment (%)
5 – 9	11.1	−1.5
10 – 19	13.9	2.1
20 – 49	20.1	7.7
50 – 99	22.7	9.9
100 – 199	25.8	11.8
200 – 499	22.1	12.4
over 500	27.6	15.0
Total Average	24.0	10.4

Source: Economic Planning Board, *Report on Mining and Manufacturing Census and Survey.*

the period of rapid growth, the banks, whether public or commercial, had remained under the government's tight control, and credit was distributed mainly in line with the planned priorities. The credit standing and connections of businesses played a key role in obtaining credit, and naturally large firms had the edge over small, unknown ones.

While the policy to support big business may have been a factor contributing to rapid industrial growth and the success in the world market, it also served to cause a serious structural imbalance in the Korean economy. It led to the creation of industrial dualism, in which large and powerful conglomerates had the virtual control of the market and the remaining masses of small and medium firms were initially relegated to an insignificant status. Beginning in the mid-1970s, efforts have been made to integrate small and large units in the process of production. Small and medium firms have been given increasingly specific roles in supplying components and semifinished goods to large units.

There is another problem with large companies in Korea today that is attributable to the government's support of big business in the past. As a result of easy access to bank-lending, large enterprises in Korea have been accustomed to depend heavily on external funds. According to one survey (*Hankook Ilbo*, September 27, 1981) in 1980 external funds – those borrowed from domestic banks and foreigners – for the top 50 enterprises in Korea accounted for as much as 85 per cent of the total. This ratio was much higher than that of Japan or the USA, which showed 38.1 per cent in 1977 and 29.1 per cent in 1974, respectively. Furthermore, the degree of dependency on external financing by large companies generally increased over the recent years. High debt–equity ratios have adversely affected profitability in large companies and raised the risk of bankruptcy in bad times.[36]

Labor Policy

Korea's early strategy of emphasizing labor-intensive manufacturing exports resulted in rapid increases in labor demand in the industrial sector and rural labor quickly began to be absorbed into the urban industrial sector. Excess labor demand caused upward pressure on industrial wages. This threatened Korea's competitive advantage in labor-intensive exports. As a result, the government's labor policies had to cope with the changed labor market conditions. This section examines government policies that have affected the labor market, employment conditions and wages, and their implications for industrial development in Korea.

Productivity and Wages

In Korea, growth in output and employment in the industrial sector has been much faster than that in the non-industrial sector. Rapid growth in industry has exerted upward pressures on industrial wages. Nonetheless, except during the past two years, real wages, in a sluggish response to labor markets, tended to lag behind productivity increases.

The industrial real wage rate remained virtually unchanged during the earlier period of industrialization (1961–1966). Between 1967 and 1978 the real wage rate increased by more than 370 per cent (Table 4.8 and Figure 4.3).

It rose, however, in a pattern of lagged response to spurts in productivity growth throughout the period. It is significant to note that labor productivity grew almost 50 per cent faster than the real wage rate. After 1977 real wages gained some ground over productivity increases. These gains in wages reflect the impact of the government policy to respond more readily to labor markets. For one thing, as labor markets became tighter, the hitherto dominant Korean labor unions were becoming increasingly militant.

Table 4.8   Real Wages and Labor Productivity in Manufacturing, South Korea (1967–1977)

	Rate of Change (%)		Index (1966 = 100)	
	Real Wage Rate	Labor Productivity	Real Wage Rate	Labor Productivity
1967	10.4	17.7	110.4	117.7
1968	13.9	19.8	125.7	141.1
1969	21.7	26.5	153.1	178.4
1970	11.5	12.6	170.6	200.8
1971	2.4	09.8	174.7	220.5
1972	1.9	09.0	178.0	240.4
1973	14.4	10.4	203.7	265.4
1974	08.9	11.2	221.8	295.1
1975	01.5	11.6	225.1	329.3
1976	17.7	11.9	265.0	368.5
1977	20.6	3.9	319.6	382.9

Source: For wage series, Bureau of Labor, and for productivity series, Center of Productivity.

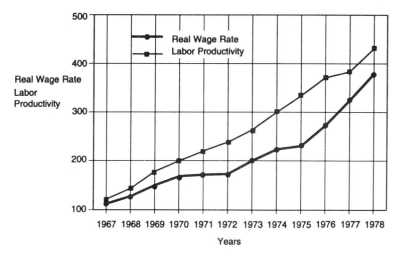

Figure 4.3   Real Wages and Labor Productivity in Manufacturing, South Korea (1967–1978)

The slower growth in real wages relative to that in productivity has been reflected in labor's declining share in output.[37] As shown in Table 4.9, wage earnings as a percentage of either gross output or value added in manufacturing steadily declined in the period from 1958 to 1976. For instance, labor's share in manufacturing value added declined from a high of 36.6 per cent in 1958 to a low of 23.0 per cent by 1975. The recent data show only slight increases in labor's claim on output.

Another aspect of Korea's low-wage-based growth strategy relates to the long work hours of a Korean worker. Up to the early 1980s, the Korean worker on average worked 50–53 hours per week, which exceeded the averages in other industrializing countries in Asia (Table 4.10). Hard work and efficiency have become the hallmarks of the Korean labor force. These workers were, nonetheless, underpaid in relation to their productivity. The cheap labor argument is thus plausible in accounting for Korea's competitive edge in labor-intensive exports, especially during the early industrialization period.

The declining wage share can be explained by the repressive wage policy of past regimes in the context of the weak, ineffective roles played by Korean trade unions. Also, the stagnant real wages in the 1960s can be attributed to the excess supplies of rural labor to industry at that time. The argument of redundant rural labor cannot, however,

Table 4.9   Wage Earnings in Relation to Gross Output and
Value Added in Manufacturing, South Korea (1958–1976)

	Wages as percent of Gross Output	Wages as percent of Value Added
1958	—	36.6
1960	11.3	30.9
1963	9.7	26.2
1966	9.1	24.4
1967	9.7	25.8
1968	10.0	25.5
1969	10.2	25.1
1970	10.3	25.1
1971	09.7	23.4
1972	09.4	23.5
1973	08.7	24.8
1974	07.9	24.2
1975	08.0	23.0
1976	08.6	24.8

Source: Korean Industrial Bank, Census on Mining and Manufacturing, and
Economic Planning Board, Annual Reports.

Table 4.10   Per Worker Man-Hours in Selected East Asian Countries

	1963	1964	1965	1966	1967	1968	1969	1970
South Korea	50.3	56.0	57.0	57.4	58.8	57.6	56.3	52.5
Philippines	43.6	43.4	45.6	46.7	46.7	—	—	—
Singapore	47.7	47.3	47.2	47.4	47.4	48.3	49.2	—
Thailand	45.7	45.7	45.7	51.3	51.3	—	47.8	—

Source: International Labor Office.

explain the declining trends in the relative position of industrial labor
in subsequent periods. The rural sector in Korea began to experience
shortages of its work force after about 1967 when the urban labor
market started to tighten, exerting upward pressures on industrial
wages. Nonetheless, the 'hard state' under the Park regime continued
to guarantee profits and to reduce entrepreneurial risk by keeping real
wages below productivity.

Labor and the State

Trade unions in Korea have never been a strong political force throughout the period under consideration. Historically, Korean unions had not been concerned so much with the issues relating to working conditions or wages as with such abstract ideas as the cooperation of labor in working towards an egalitarian industrial democracy. Also, there had been no strong tradition of labor movements in Korea. Workers in general had too low a level of class consciousness to join trade unions. As late as 1986, officially registered union members accounted for only about 20 per cent of the total industrial work force. The general pattern of labor organization in Korea is that unions tend to be organized at the enterprise level. Collective bargaining is carried out by local unions within an enterprise. There has been a general lack of coordination of union activities at the national level. This internal company unionism precluded the possibility of the unions creating a united front on common economic and social interests, thereby diminishing the unions' impact on national policy decisions. Moreover, critics have argued that the existing unions that claim national representation have more or less played the role of political puppets subservient to management and the government. For this reason, a feeling of apathy and insensitivity towards union activities has prevailed among rank-and-file union members.

The past authoritarian regimes in Korea actually promoted internal company unionism as a useful means of controlling labor movements. Park's regime in the early 1960s was apprehensive that trade unions might develop the ability for mass mobilization in political affairs. It actively prevented unions from formulating and promoting policies on issues related to national development.

Within the private sector enterprises, both management and labor are supposed to reach mutual agreement on matters related to working conditions and wages. But the enterprises where these matters require an agreement between both sides have in reality constituted a small fraction of the total and in other firms the management has simply informed the union of its decisions on wage- and work-related issues. Even in cases where joint consultation between both parties was allowed, union representatives were passively included in decisions. For practical purposes, joint consultation has often worked as a rather one-way communication from management to labor. In the cases of a dispute deemed of relevance to national security, the government has frequently intervened as an arbitrator. It has usually taken sides with business interests, since to do so has often been considered to be in the national interest. The state's lack of interest in labor is evident if one examines the modern history of Korean labor legislation. As compared with industrializing countries in Latin America, the scope and coverage of legislation related to welfare conditions of the worker have not been extensive in Korea. Even the minimum wage legislation in Korea is of relatively recent origin.

Reflecting such tendencies in both labor-government and labor-management relations, labor conflicts steadily increased from the early 1960s. Between 1966 and 1971 the total number of industrial disputes that involved negotiations with labor unions was 675, out of which in 66 cases actual work stoppages took place.[38] In about 70 per cent of these cases, the main cause of dispute concerned wages. The rather low proportion of work-stoppages seems to be explained by the government's heavy handed methods of settlement. In an attempt to expedite the settlement of disputes, the government has provided various institutional mechanisms, such as Wage Boards, Industrial Tribunals, and the Labor Adjustment Committees. These mechanisms have not, however, offered a fitting means for direct involvement of workers. The available evidence indicates that in the majority of these settlements workers' substantive interests have not been satisfactorily defended.

During the early 1970s, as the average real wage rate began to rise in response to tight labor market conditions, Korea was newly threatened with the rapid deterioration of its competitive edge in labor-intensive exports. The government quickly enacted a series of measures to restrain increases in wage rates by curtailing the power of the trade unions. An example of this was the 1971 Special Emergency Law enacted under the umbrella of a series of national security provisions: in a situation of emergency threatening national security, the settlement of labor disputes would automatically fall under the jurisdiction of the government-controlled Labor Tribunals; open walk-outs would then be illegal; other forms of restrictions would be imposed on collective bargaining; and special rules were stipulated in dealing with the foreign-owned or publicly-owned enterprises, which would prohibit walk-outs by workers employed in these enterprises.

In an attempt to appease labor, the government introduced a series of paternalistic labor laws, including the upgrading of wage structures more in line with the market conditions. As Korea shifted its comparative advantage into more capital-intensive industries it no longer had much to gain from a policy of wage restraint. The average real wage rate in fact rose quite rapidly, in contrast to the early period of export drive. Despite these new measures, the frequency of labor conflicts continued to rise. For example, between 1975 and 1979 more than 5,000 cases of labor disputes were reported. In about 10 per cent of these cases, work stoppages took place. As before, the predominant cause of the disputes was demands for higher wages.[39]

Agricultural Policy

South Korea is one of the most densely populated countries in the world.[40] With the arable land covering a third of the total country, per farm household arable land comes to about one hectare, which is less than half of what one finds in Japan. The soil is largely acidic, requiring heavy inputs of both limestone and fertilizers. Farming has been fairly labor-intensive in Korea. The viability of the farm economy hinges crucially on sustained improvements in land productivity.

When the Park government decided to focus on industrialization, it was largely because of the planners' perception of limited potentials in Korean agriculture. With the process of rapid industrialization beginning in the early 1960s, the relative importance of agriculture, which had been the mainstay of the economy, continued to diminish: agriculture accounted for about two-thirds of the total population, producing some 40 per cent of its GDP in the early 1960s. In 1981, it employed only a quarter of the total population, producing 18 per cent of its GNP. This section examines the nature and extent of state intervention in agriculture, and in particular, the role of agricultural policy in Korea's industrialization.

From the policy perspective, the initial period throughout the 1960s under the Park regime was characterized by exploitation of the agricultural sector for industrial development. This was followed in the early 1970s by the policy reversal to support agriculture. Korea's industrialization started with the promotion of export activities in such labor intensive industries as textiles, plywood, processed food and other light manufactured goods. The strategy was to squeeze agriculture to support labor-intensive manufacture export activities. This 'industry first' strategy reflected the overriding national concern for industrialization; it called for increased food production while keeping rural real income at a low level to guarantee sustained inflows of cheap labor to urban factories. Farmers had to deliver obligatory quotas of rice to government at prices below the market. Low grain pricing was also necessary for financial stabilization in the economy. Allied to the low wage policy, the government also initiated programs for rural infrastructure development (roads and irrigation dams),[41] agricultural research and extension services to increase rice output for urban consumers.

Although food production expanded in the 1960s, food demand increased more rapidly due to growth in the population and income, coupled with the growing use of grains for commercial and industrial purposes. This led to increased food deficiency in the country, as the self-sufficiency ratio in food continued to fall throughout the 1960s from a 99 per cent high in 1960 to a 76 per cent low by 1971. As a result, government policies to extract surpluses of cheap food had to be combined with policies to import foodgrains in order to maintain low industrial wages and production costs. The adverse terms of trade imposed against the farm sector, however, caused the real farm income to lag behind increases in agricultural productivity. While the rural income as deflated by actual prices paid to farmers remained stagnant, the disparities in urban–rural income widened.

Coming to the late 1960s, the relative decline in rural living standards became an economic as well a political concern of the Park government, as it was seeking its legitimacy through economic success. While the 'industry first' strategy continued to widen the urban–rural gap, the decline in the agricultural population[42] and food production posed the threat of inflation and exacerbation of the balance of payments. It was in these circumstances that Park decided to reverse the 'industry first' strategy. For the Third Five-year Plan period (1972–76), the plan's broad objective sought a balanced development between industry and agriculture. Concerned with increasing food imports and the resulting balance-of-payments difficulties, the plan also called for self-sufficiency in food, agricultural infrastructural development, farm mechanization, and improvements in the overall distribution of income through rural development.

To achieve the new goals, the government attempted a three-pronged approach. First, it initiated programs of price support in rice and barley. Beginning in 1968, the government purchased these grains at income-support prices while maintaining a subsidized grain price system for urban consumers (a policy completely opposed by the World Bank in their structural adjustment programs in Africa). The difference between purchase and delivery prices were financed by government budget deficits. According to Ban et al. (1980), during the period of 1970 and 1975, while the real price of non-government supported agricultural products rose 12.5 per cent, that of rice paid to farmers rose by 28.5 per cent. On the other hand, the price of rice as the main wage good to urban workers continued to remain low. The farm price support, in effect, contributed to the marked rise in domestic production of food grain and in farm incomes. For example, the price support programs initiated in the early 1970s led eventually to the narrowing of the urban–rural gap: the average annual real income of farm households rose from 68 per cent of that of urban wage-earning households in the period of 1965–67 to 80 per cent of the latter in the period 1971–79 (Kim, Kajiwara and Watanabe, 1984, p. 132).

Secondly, drawing on surpluses from the industrial sector, the government started to increase investments in rural infrastructure, agricultural research, provisions of extension services and subsidies on fertilizer use (generally eliminated in adjustment programs). The TFYP called for investment in agriculture which were four times that of the SFYP, and eight times that of the FFYP. Public investment in land and water development projects accounted for 27.5 per cent of the rural projects. Particularly noteworthy is the cost-effective method of investment aimed at raising land productivity. Introduction of high-yielding rice varieties through government-supported agricultural research and extension services, along with subsidized provisions of fertilizer and pesticides, contributed to rapid gains in per acre yield in food production.3

Thirdly, what really made the government intervention effective was the launching in late 1969 of a self-help community development movement called the *Saemaul* ('New Community') Movement. The idea resembles that of the Kibbutz in Israel. The purposes of the Movement was to uplift rural living standards by encouraging villagers to voluntarily participate in income-generating projects. The government provided incentives to share resources with the villages that participated in cooperative work efforts. The Movement was intended to minimize direct interventions of state agencies in the domestic agricultural economy and to ultimately substitute for costly public investment in rural infrastructure. In the 1970s it was an important factor contributing to rural development in Korea.

The efforts to raise land productivity through cost-effective interventions largely paid off. Between 1968 and 1979, agricultural output, although slower than that in industry, grew at an average annual rate of 10.35 per cent , doubling the rate of the previous period (1962–67)'s (Kim, Kajiwara and Watanabe, 1984, p. 116). While neither arable land nor labor showed significant growth,[44] output expansion was accompanied by increases in land productivity. This growth in productivity, in turn, stemmed from land-saving, technical progress on improved plant varieties, and increased use of fertilizers. As a result, Korea, albeit short-lived, was able to attain self-sufficiency in food toward the mid-1970s.

Toward the end of the 1970s, the government began to accumulate sizeable deficits resulting from farm support programs. The financial cost of subsidies on farm inputs and on the differences between the producer and consumer prices became staggering. Moreover, as the world recession began to hit the Korean economy in the late 1970s, its industrial growth was decelerated with the resulting retrenchment of the agricultural sector. The small-farm economy, once functional to industrial growth, became a hindrance in the open market economy.

In summary, in the case of Korea the economic link between agriculture and industry was by no means one-sided. Agriculture contributed to industrial development by serving as the source of cheap wage goods and labor supplies in the initial stage of industrialization. With the success of industry, the latter, in turn, provided inputs and infrastructure for rural development. The growing urban economy also generated consumer demands for high-valued cash crops, thereby contributing to increased rural incomes. The government continued to play the intervening role in effecting the transition between the phases. This is very different from the strategy of African adjustment with its emphasis on rapidly rising terms of trade in favor of agriculture, removal of subsidies and austerity leading to a reduction in public investment in agriculture.

POLICY IMPLEMENTATION: APPROACHES AND INSTITUTIONS

Organizational Structure

Plans and strategies exist elsewhere. However, what is probably unique in the case of Korea, and certainly different from most other countries, is the ability to get the plans and strategies put into practice. The idea of effectively organizing and managing an economy started with Park Chung Hee when he came to power in 1961.

Among his earliest policy measures was the creation of the Economic Planning Board (EPB), as a mechanism for examining the state of the economy and drawing up appropriate plans for improving it. The EPB has a substantial budget of its own with talented and technically trained bureaucrats as well as access to support from other ministries and academic institutions. The director of the Planning Board also assumed the position of the Deputy Prime Minister of the cabinet, which enabled him to pull rank on his colleagues. This assured the EPB's effective coordination with each ministry which had its own special planning unit for designing and implementing the plans at the ministerial and lower levels. Moreover, since both the economic planning and budgetary functions were performed under the aegis of the Deputy Prime Minister, this helped merge the process of planning and implementation effectively. The biggest strength of the Planning Board has, however, been the interest and support of the President. The Board usually dealt with what he considered to be the most important policy matters.

The bulk of the planning work since the early 1960s has been carried out by young Koreans trained in economics and planning. Before the existence of the Planning Board, foreign experts had been invited to draw up more sophisticated plans along the lines of Western economic doctrines, which could hardly be faulted on technical grounds. Apart from the problems of government commitment to economic development, what made these plans inadequate was their lack of understanding of the indigenous society and culture, in particular of how Koreans thought and behaved.

Although the entire process of planning gives an appearance of a highly centralized organizational structure, it has been the ministries and public-sector enterprises that were entrusted with the responsibility of getting specific projects done effectively and efficiently. Among the ministries, more heavily involved in the design and execution of national planning have been such ministries as Finance, Commerce and Industry, Construction, Agriculture and Fisheries, and Energy and Resources.

As mentioned already, public enterprises were often entrusted with the task of meeting the governmental need to apply policy action to a particular problem area. Although supervised and controlled in financial matters by one of the special development banks, they generally enjoyed a certain degree of autonomy to do their job as professionally as possible. Their tasks, in all cases, were intimately related to the planning of economic development, provision of basic transport and communications, essential services, utilities and banking, and sometimes even engagement in productive operations like mining or manufacturing.

The Framework for Policy Formulation

At the outset, it must be emphasized that all Korean governments since independence in 1945 had to be ideologically committed to maintaining a capitalist economy in which the private sector played a central role. Politically and economically, the regime had no options but to remain comparatively liberal. Thus, as delineated in the First Five-Year Plan document, the economic system officially adopted by the military regime was dubbed as 'guided capitalism', in which the government is allowed to guide the directions of the macroeconomy and the basic industries in a free enterprise system (Republic of Korea, 1962).[45]

Thus in principle, planning in Korea played the role of providing a framework for policy directions, leaving most practical decisions in the hands of private economic actors. Plans were supposed to indicate the directions in which the economy would be headed and what its goals should be, offering incentives to those who complied with them. In this context, the annual Overall Resource Budgets and management plans drafted by the EPB indicated precisely what the government intended to do during the planned period and what contribution it expected from the private sector and general public. There were also documents like the Korean Development Institute's fifteen-year projections for 1977–1991 and the EPB's projections up to the year 2000, which provided a longer-term framework consistent with various five-year plans. Of course, aside from the role of planning in providing a general framework for policy directions, more specific laws, regulations, and directions had to be formulated to promote exports or other priority sectors, channelling the efforts of various ministries and those of the individual enterprises dependent on them in the direction consistent with the planned goals.

Any national plans, if they are to be implemented, should be based on as much of a broad-based social consensus as possible. That is, however sophisticated and well-designed the plan may be, if it lacks a broader view that integrates and reconciles diverse social interests, it is likely to fail. In the case of the Korean planning, the first task faced by the planners was obtaining the views and feedback from diverse interest groups. This implied receiving feedback from and interacting with local leaders and various advisory committees that usually consisted of officials, industrialists, businessmen, and academics. What proved most effective in influencing the process of decision-making turned out to be myriad lobbies established by various interest groups, such as agricultural cooperatives or trade associations. And, while usually reticent on political issues, the press, interest groups, and politicians freely expressed their views on economic issues.

Once the goals of the policy were agreed upon or at least understood by the private sector leaders, the planning process focused on the internal consistency between the overall policy framework and the goals set at sectoral or firm levels. Here again, the planning was based on both the 'top-down' and 'bottom-up' approaches. In the early plans (the First and Second Five-Year Plans), the drafted plans with the details on the sector-level targets[46] were subject to the reviews of industry committees typically composed of engineers, economists, technical experts, ministerial officials, and industrialists before the targets and estimates of the coefficients of variables in the plan model could be accepted for implementation. The preparation of planning for the sectoral profile gave industrialists a needed opportunity to review investment prospects for various industries.

Implementation

Given the basic policy orientation of 'guided capitalism' in Korea, the plans provided a framework for the directions of policy and the overall procedures of implementation. Incentives were offered to those who complied with these but there were, in principle, no mechanisms for enforcing a complete cooperation from the private sector. In reality, however, the extent of government intervention in Korea has often gone beyond the stated framework of 'guided capitalism.' The Park government frequently used power and authority to directly influence the economic behavior of the private sector.

The implementation of the plans was of course more effective when executed within the public sector, which included myriad state-run enterprises. Heavy pressures were exerted on bureaucrats to execute their jobs well and, in many cases, to complete at least the agreed-on targets. In dealing with the private sector, the most coercive administrative institution has been the tax authorities, which periodically inspect the returns of all companies.

Thus one way or the other, the post-military government prevailed over the private sector to comply with government policies. Of course, getting the private sector to fall into line could not be accomplished without a great deal of social tension. For instance, when import-substitution was the government strategy, firms were urged either to produce import substitutes or to make purchases from local manufacturers even if their prices were higher and the quality not quite as good as imports. With the switch to export promotion, industrialists were encouraged to sell more abroad even if this was a completely new activity for them and did not look profitable. Strategic industries were advised of the advantages of diversifying and upgrading, and quickly reprimanded if they did not.

Apart from the strong hand the government wielded over the private sector, what really held together the close public-private sector cooperation was a shared interest in a strong and prosperous economy from which all would benefit. The recognition of priority for economic development was not solely the result of determination at the top. In the earlier phases of modernization, it was conceded by all segments of society that there were indeed advantages in working together for the good of all. It was considered desirable to set suitable priorities, if necessary, by planning and policy. It was helpful for everyone to know in which direction the economy was heading even if some did not care to follow. No businessman would have made his own decisions without at least some understanding of development plans and strategies.

If the coherence of the planning as well as the effectiveness of policy implementation are to be judged on the basis of how closely the targeted goals have been achieved, the Korean case can be claimed as a success. Comparisons between planned targets and actual performances are shown in Table 4.11.

In all the plan periods except that of the Fourth Plan,[47] which mainly coincided with the recent world recession, the economy's performance in GNP, exports, and industrial output actually exceeded the target goals by substantial margins.

FINAL REFLECTIONS: MYTHS AND REALITIES

The Myths of Korean Development

This chapter has made a point of the instrumental role played by Korea's development strategy and approach to policy implementation in attaining such phenomenal success. In summary, the Korean government's role in development can be discussed in terms of the firm and stable commitment of the political leadership to economic development and the effective exercise of power in influencing economic behavior, while maintaining flexibility in the structural adjustment process to cope with changing global markets. The 'growth-first-via-industrialization' strategy adopted during the initial stage of development made

Table 4.11 Comparisons of Planned Targets and Performance (1962–1981) (unit = real annual growth rate –%)

	First Plan (1962-66)		Second Plan (1967-71)		Third Plan (1972-76)		Fourth Plan (1977-81)	
	Planned	Actual	Planned	Actual	Planned	Actual	Planned	Actual
GNP	7.1	7.8	7.0	9.7	8.6	10.1	9.2	5.5
Agro-Forestry and Fishery	5.7	5.8	5.0	1.5	4.5	6.1	4.0	0.1
Mining	15.0	14.3	10.7	19.9	13.0	13.0	14.2	9.7
Alone Manufacturing	15.0	15.0	—	21.8	13.3	18.7	14.3	9.9
Social Overhead and Others	5.4	8.4	8.8	12.8	8.5	8.5	7.8	5.2
Population	2.8	2.7	2.2	2.2	1.55	1.7	1.8	1.8
Per Capita GNP	4.2	5.0	4.7	7.3	7.0	8.2	7.5	3.9
Fixed Investment	14.8	25.7	10.2	17.9	7.8	11.1	7.7	9.9
Export of Commodities	28.0	38.5	17.1	33.8	22.7	32.7	16.0	12.0
Import of Commodities	8.7	18.7	6.5	25.8	13.7	12.8	12.0	10.8
Employment	4.7	3.2	3.3	3.8	2.9	4.5	3.2	2.3

Source: Economic Planning Board.

good sense in a resource-poor economy with widespread poverty.[48] The dominant courses of government action under 'hard state' rule consisted of eclectic recipes of 'carrots' based on an extensive private incentive system and 'sticks' based on regulation and planning by direction.

A larger issue that remains to be answered is: Why has Korea succeeded while other developing countries pursuing similar policy measures have been less successful? In drawing lessons for other countries, it is important to keep in mind the interacting nature of various socioeconomic factors that directly and indirectly contributed to the positive outcomes of government polices. Nonetheless, some factors seem to stand out as representing a situation unique to Korea, with its replicability in other country contexts questionable. At the same time, some myths about Korea's development must be dispelled in order to place its lessons in a proper perspective. The following evaluation will begin with dispelling some popular myths about the Korean experience.

In common with the rest of the so-called 'Gang of Four' (Taiwan, Hong Kong, and Singapore), Korea shares the Sino-cultural, Confucian heritage. It has frequently been argued that the 'right' values of Confucian ethics were instrumental in promoting Korea's development. The Confucian value system essentially governs nonreligious, ethical codes of social behavior. As such, certain of its virtues can be considered supportive of economic development. Among them would be: the intrinsic value placed on education as a vehicle for self-gratification; extolment of diligence and self-discipline; respect for social order, hierarchy, and authorities; and absence of religious or ideological dogmatism inhibiting the pragmatic pursuit of ends.

However, one must also note other aspects of the Confucian heritage that can be considered inimical to economic development. For instance, in the Confucian hierarchy businessmen and merchants typically occupy lower social classes in contrast to the high prestige accorded to government officials, scholars, and even farmers. The argument of cultural influence does not go hand in hand with the abrupt surge of the entrepreneurial class since the start of Korea's modernization efforts. The entrepreneurial class in Korea emerged as soon as the right incentives and sociopolitical environment for business were secured.

Another culture-related myth is that the East Asians have a hard-work ethic. It is true that the Koreans have in the past worked long hours. So would, however, Latin Americans or Africans under propitious conditions. The Koreans did so only because opportunities for a better livelihood were made available. It is worth pointing out that the same Koreans had often been the target of ridicule by the Western media for being an extremely indolent and uninspired work force in the 1950s, when the economy was stagnant. The puzzling question is: Why with the start of the development process, have the negative factors in the cultural heritage suddenly withered away, with only the positive influences retained?

As regards the role of foreign aid in Korea's development, it must, first of all, be admitted that South Korea had received an inordinate amount of American aid, particularly during the 1950s – however, mostly in the form of food and basic consumer goods. The concessional aid rapidly diminished after the mid-1960s, being gradually replaced by loan capital. In the case of Korea, both positive and negative effects of foreign aid have been present. While part of the aid Korea received may have been spent on infrastructure building for subsequent industrial development, in other instances it had adverse impacts on the economy. For instance, American food aid in the 1950s deterred the possibility of self-sustained development in agriculture. While aid can be a great help, it can easily lead to a state of self-complacency, inaction, and dependency.

As regards the factors contributing to Korea's success, its experience, in particular from the perspective of comparing with non-East Asian countries, can be considered *sui generis* in the following aspects. First of all, the society of Korea is culturally and ethnically homogeneous, and relatively less structured. No strong social discriminations are discernible because of differences in religion and no deeply-rooted class structure exists. The social mobility of labor is relatively unrestricted, and the sociocultural environment can be viewed as largely conducive to economic development.

Secondly, a relatively well-educated labor force has been a key feature in Korea's transitional growth story. Given its cultural tradition in which education is socially valued, Korea's transition to a high-growth economy started with an already relatively well-developed educational system far in advance of that existing today in other developing countries. The nation has one of the highest literacy rates in the developing world,[49] although public expenditure on education has not been particularly high by international standards. Society's emphasis on human capital investment has yielded a high-quality skilled work force, to which can be attributed the sustained growth in labor productivity observed throughout the period of Korea's transition.

Another feature of the Korean experience that must be noted is prolonged political stability, paradoxically brought about by the authoritarian regimes. Beginning with the military coup in 1961, Korea had strong and stable governments motivated and able to implement far-reaching economic policies. With the help of competent technocrats,[50] the governments were able to formulate and effectively execute policy plans articulated for concrete action. When deemed necessary, they intervened in labor markets, countering organized labor and thwarting its effort to emerge as a political force, although wages were as a rule allowed to rise in response to labor market conditions. It was during the early 1960s that real wages were severely suppressed in order for Korea to gain a competitive edge in exports of its labor-intensive goods.

The final point to note is that Korea's earlier export success was achieved under rather unusual international circumstances. The two decades following the Bretton Woods system until the first global oil crisis in the early 1970s represented the 'golden age' of international trade and investment. During this period, not only were supplies of international capital at reasonable borrowing terms relatively abundantly available, but also many industrialized countries could attain and sustain near full-employment growth, which further stimulated expansion of the world market. The world trade volume in manufacturing goods grew by more than ten per cent per year. The fruits of the expansion were also shared by the newly industrializing countries in East Asia, including Korea.

Particularly worth noting is an historical event in the world that influenced the pace of Korea's industrialization. South Korea participated militarily in the Vietnam conflict during the late 1960s and the early 1970s, and provided war-related offshore supplies to the American troops. Korean participation in the war efforts immediately resulted in substantial foreign exchange earnings, which subsequently facilitated the rapid development of Korea's basic industries. In particular, steel, machinery, and other heavy manufacturing industries benefitted from offshore procurement.[51] The changed global environment today in which the developing countries find themselves plagued by mounting external debts, insufficient foreign savings, and industrialized countries' protectionist trends would, however, make the attempts to replicate the Korean-style, export-oriented strategy much more difficult.

Lessons from the Korean Model: with Special Reference to African Countries

These factors, more or less unique to the Korean situation, are not sufficient in themselves to explain Korea's success. In the final analysis, it was essentially a set of industrialization strategies carefully designed and effectively implemented that set in motion the whole process of development. A combination of historical and cultural circumstances conducive to development already existed, and this only helped government policies to work.

There are a number of traits in Korea's development strategy that can serve as lessons – both positive and negative – to other industrializing countries, especially within Sub-Saharan Africa:

1. The Korean model exemplifies the continual process of interaction between government and market. As pointed out by I.J. Whang, 'the interaction took place not necessarily in the context of competition over resources but rather in the context of complementarity for economic development' (Whang, 1987, p. 86). A good example of this was the role of Korean public enterprises: they were established mainly in infrastructure activities that required massive capital-intensive technologies or where the private sector would be unwilling to bear the risk. In some cases, they dealt with the cases of market failures involving entrepreneurial inadequacies or imperfect capital markets. Korean public enterprises were rarely involved for long in activities commercially competitive with the private sector. In essence, while relying on the market mechanism whenever suitable, the Korean government persistently intervened to expedite the attainment of the national goal, which was rapid industrialization. Thus for instance, the short- and long-term success in Korean exports was the result as much of realistic exchange rates, low wage policy and government subsidies as credit allocation policies to support the 'winners.'

   In Africa, the mix of government and market has in general been ill-defined: the abuse of non-market instruments and discretionary state powers has often turned into bureaucratic corruption and mismanagement. Also, the public sector tends to own the lion's share of the formal economy, frequently engaging in commercial activities that could be done more efficiently by market forces. Many of these public-sector firms have failed to run their operations efficiently, thereby contributing to governmental budget deficits (Kim, 1981 and 1988b).

2. The Korean government's role continued to provide direction to the economy by participating directly or indirectly in basic economic activities and by coordinating or guiding private sector activities. The government's strong commitment to economic development and its competent bureaucracy encouraged the formation of a rational incentives structure which helped nudge market agents into collaboration. Although the Park government played the role of a dominant partner by determining the policy goals, the private sector with a possible interest in the outcome was, as a rule, consulted with for advice and feedback.

    In Africa, social contact between the state and private sector is not often found: it is not unusual to find the situation in which government and business – in particular, foreign multinationals – attempt to outmaneuver each other to its own advantage. The government-business interactions have not generally been productive; the government prefers to engineer the economy at every level from a dictating position and the business community has little confidence in the civilian bureaucracy.

3. The Korean experience shows the importance of a dynamic policy. Structural transformation of the economy will not come automatically by market forces. It calls for the conscious, long-term strategy for industrial restructuring in order to create comparative advantage in high value-added industries with potentials in markets and scale-economies. Korea's sectoral planning, designed in a manner consistent with encompassing macroeconomic policies and flexible enough to reflect changing circumstances, was concerned with the dynamic sequencing of sectoral development that could be adapted to shift the patterns of comparative advantage.

    Although the policy of targeting strategic sectors encouraged a capital-intensive production process and resulted in factor-market and other forms of structural distortions in the economy, it led to the creation of new patterns of comparative advantage in industry. The point to emphasize is that it was not the factor endowment conditions that influenced the evolution of Korea's industrial development. Rather it was a set of articulate, conscious policy measures that contributed to a dynamic sequencing in industrial development for comparative advantage.

4. There are a few lessons to learn from Korea's experience with outward-looking orientation. First of all, the stage of export

promotion was preceded by the period of import substitution in the 1950s which provided the industrial infrastructural base for the subsequent export expansion. It was during this period that many exportable industries of the 1960s, especially the shoes and textile industries, matured. The success in industrial exports did not come overnight through some quick-fix, magic formula. Moreover, even during the period of export expansion, the development of internal market-oriented industry that could complement an export industry was not overlooked. The Korean model is an eclectic one that while emphasizing outward orientation, considered the protection of selective import-substituting no less important. The coherent set of policies aimed at integrating producing sectors by means of the strengthened production of intermediate and capital goods, led to the establishment of a viable industrial structure that proved adaptable to shifting international markets. Vertically integrating the production structure has also lessened the economy's dependence on imports. In this context, Korea's outward orientation must not be interpreted as liberalization of trade in the sense of neoclassical economics. Perhaps the lesson worthy to note is that the outward-oriented model provides an effective instrument with which to gauge performance of the domestic sectors, thereby forcing them towards increased efficiency and technological progress. This is a much more nuanced view than the simple dichotomy of export vs. import-substitution found in structural adjustment programs.

5. The Korean case shows the importance of concrete but flexible planning and management of policy action. The distinctive virtues of Korean management were the pragmatism and flexibility of its policies as well as the effectiveness of implementation. Detachment of the policy makers from straight-jacket economic ideologies and their willingness to experiment on what would work best at a given time and place seem to have been the key to Korea's success. There were really no traditional textbook models that could be used to adequately describe the Korean experience. Its distinctive trait lies in the ability of policy makers to quickly and flexibly manipulate both positive and negative external factors to promote their own goals, formulate plans to realize their goals, and effectively implement these plans under an efficiently functioning bureaucratic system. Typically, once a development project was approved, government support would be continuous and consistent from the beginning until its eventual withdrawal. There were constant evaluations of industrial performance and industrial dynamics,

which would eventually be built into the process of government mobilization of support and assistance.

In post-colonial Africa, policy makers have often shown themselves assiduous in the pursuit of nationalistic, strait-jacket economic policies, thereby tending to be rigid and inflexible in managing the economy.

6. The Korean model is not industrialization alone at the expense of other areas. For instance, despite the priority for industry, the agricultural sector has not been totally ignored. In fact, there were periods, during the earlier part of the 1970s, when agriculture was the prominent part of the development strategy. The goal of government policies has been avoidance of an excessive urban–rural disparity in income. The fairly equitable pattern of income distribution that emerged from the earlier success in land reform obviated much of the policy makers' concern with distributional issues in implementing rapid-growth strategies. Specifically, from Korea's experience in agricultural development, *three* aspects of its policy are worth noting.

(a) The Korean experience shows that the market forces alone cannot facilitate sustained agricultural development. On the contrary, state action violating market principles can play a positive role in agricultural development. The policy of particular relevancy to African nations would be Korea's agricultural pricing policy. Korean policies of subsidized grain and fertilizer prices provided necessary incentives for increased farm production and incomes, making it also possible to prevent excessive fluxes of migration to cities. Contrary to the conventional, dual-economy model, in which the transfer of the so-called, 'redundant' rural labor to the urban sector is seen as the way to raise rural incomes for the remaining, the Korean experience tells us the importance of rural, grass-roots development. Rural income does not rise simply because of fewer mouths to share the food. The Korean experience shows that urban migration reduced only the productive labor force in rural areas; as more productive, younger males tend to migrate, labor productivity declines which needs to be countered through government programs.

(b) The Korean experience shows that the availability of arable land relative to the population is not an absolute deterrent to self-sufficiency in food. To those capital-poor African nations, the Korean case demonstrates the possibilities of cost-effective government aid to increase agricultural productivity. Land productivity can be enhanced without requiring substantial overhead costs. The Korean experience shows that productivity in agriculture can be increased without necessarily incurring large overhead costs. Government assistance took the form of land consolidation, creation of production cooperatives, introduction of applied research results through extension services and rural education, self-help community development movements, and farm price support.

(c) The Korean experience shows that agricultural development would be much easier to attain in a rapidly industrializing economy. Contrary to the conventional belief that industrialization in a developing country would be at the expense of agriculture, Korea's initial policies to squeeze agriculture ended up with fostering faster industrial growth. This in turn contributed to faster agricultural development, for the capacity to raise per acre yield is closely related to the level of manufacturing activity. Without an expanding industrial economy, it would be extremely difficult to expedite the transfer of resources to the agricultural sector and to finance programs for farm-price support. Also, diversification of farm production to high value-added cash crops (fruits, livestock, etc.) from the exclusive reliance on land-intensive grain cultivation would have been difficult without increased urban incomes and expanding urban markets. On the negative side, the Korean experience, even with an extremely successful industry financing agricultural development, also illustrates the problems inherent in unbalanced growth: budget deficits, rural impoverishment, urban congestion, and distributional inequity.

Korea's 'industry first' model is not, however, applicable to contemporary Africa. Many African countries, as a result of urban-biased policy and excessive zeal for industrialization in the past, have neglected to encourage agriculture on a par with industry. African economies currently face the prospects of their industrial exports and of foreign investment that are very different from Korea in the 1960s. The inevitable option facing contemporary Africa is to diversify and promote agriculture in order to be able first to feed itself, and then to generate surpluses in quantities sufficient to accommodate industrial growth; this policy is different from structural adjustment with its emphasis on increasing the export of cash crops and cutbacks in agricultural support and subsidies.

7.   Perhaps the most tangible lesson from Korean experience is the importance of human capital investment. Koreans, in common with other East Asian NICs, have shown an awesome commitment to investment in human capital by way of both the quantity and quality of education. The unusual educational zeal is partly cultural, but also reflects the result of policy measures to increase the efficiency of public education. Related to the issue of human capital is efficient management at the firm level and the high quality labor force. Both have been the basic strengths in Korea's industrialization process as its manufacturing sector is characterized by efficient factor use and high rates of capacity use. For instance, although such capital-intensive industries as steel, petrochemicals, shipbuilding, and machinery have only recently been developed, the average capital-output ratio for the manufacturing sector is very low by international standards.[52] Moreover, labor productivity grew at an average rate of about 7 per cent per year during the 1966–76 period. These gains were accompanied by small increases in the stock of capital per worker, reflecting large improvements in productivity.

Contemporary Africa with widespread illiteracy provides a sharp contrast to the East Asian situation. Clearly, the future development of African economies in the high-tech, post-industrial age will depend critically on how they succeed in developing their vast human resources. Once again the emphasis in structural adjustment on austerity and user fees in education have placed any educational strategies in jeopardy.

Notes

1.   From 1954 to 1986, the mining and manufacturing sector increased its share of GDP from 12.0 per cent to 30.2 per cent with the share of agriculture in GDP decreasing from 44.6 per cent to 13.5 per cent. There was also a rapid change in the structure of foreign trade. In 1962, primary products accounted for almost three quarters of total exports with industrial products accounting for a quarter. By 1982 manufactures reached 94 per cent of the total exports. Heavy machinery and chemical

products began to comprise an increasingly larger share in composition of exports, reaching close to a half of the total exports.

2. See Adelman (1974), Mizoguchi, et al. (1976), and Choo (1987).
3. Per capita income for 1962 was recorded at $87 in 1979 prices.
4. For the unique features of the Korean development, including the quality of the labor force, see the concluding section.
5. Since 1962 the real income of the poorest groups has risen at about the same rate as GNP with actual declines registered in their relative share in the total population: the proportion of the population considered poor fell from 40.9 per cent in 1965 to 9.8 per cent in 1981 and to 5.1 per cent by 1987. The land reform in 1949 provided a foundation for equitable growth. For instance, between 1947 to 1964 tenant farmers fell from 42 per cent of the total farm households to a mere 5 per cent, while tiller-owners increased from 16.5 to 72 per cent. Although the incidence of absolute poverty has diminished, the distribution of income in the relative sense seems to have worsened in recent years.
6. See discussion below on labor policy. Also Kim (1992).
7. See for instance, Balassa (1985), Bhagwati (1985), and Krueger (1980). For opposing views, see Amsden (1989), Jones and Sakong (1980), and Sen (1983).
8. The active government investment support, however, gave rise to budgetary deficits and exerted inflationary pressures on the economy in the early 1970s.
9. Real domestic savings doubled in 1965 and again doubled by 1967. The velocity of money was reduced, halving the rate of inflation over what it would have been without the cut in velocity induced by the change in the interest rate; the incremental capital output ratio declined by 30 per cent; and the investment rate rose as fast as the increase in savings permitted.
10. In passing, it must be noted that the practice of sector targeting, beginning in the Fifth Five Year Plan during the 1980s, has been gradually phased out as the economy becomes increasingly sophisticated and complicated to manage. Except for the high-tech sector which continues to receive government support, measures that can benefit all indiscriminately are now being implemented.
11. The earlier Second Five Year Plan (1962–1966) was fairly comprehensive in scope and rigorous in contents as it relied on sophisticated input-output tables. This framework was an attempt to provide an intersectoral investment plan consistent with accelerated growth of the economy. Because of inadequate resources devoted to the planning, the framework quickly became inadequate for projections after two years of use. Subsequently, top policy makers in Korea did not find that comprehensive, centralized planning would be of much material assistance in executing policy decisions. Instead, they adopted a more decentralized 'indicative' planning method.
12. For the details of incentive measures, see Hong, W. (1979) and World Bank (1981b).
13. The Korean experience thus differs from the neo-classical argument that price reforms are necessary for both informational and allocative purposes. I thank Howard Stein for reminding me of this difference.

14. Real export incentives were maintained at a relatively constant level after 1964, while sporadic efforts were made to reduce import restrictions. A World Bank study (1977b), demonstrated that, despite market variations from industry to industry, the average tariff rates were quite low (averaging about 9 per cent in 1965) even by international standards.

15. The public was constantly reminded of the importance of exports through cermonies, monthly export promotion meetings, and the presentation of awards to those who achieved most. Exporting was considered a patriotic duty.

16. This export success, however, should not make one forget that imports also kept growing at a quite considerable pace. From 1962 to 1980, imports attained an average growth of 20 per cent. This was much slower than export growth. It was not easy for Korea to hold imports down since the bulk of them were fuel, raw materials, and intermediate goods that went into the production of its exports.

17. A more meaningful indicator should incorporate other incentive and disincentive instruments, such as all forms of subsidies including interest subsidies, access to imported inputs or price reductions on overhead inputs.

18. This was largely caused by the appreciation of the Japanese yen that contributed to a two and a half fold increase in the real value of exports during this period.

19. The term 'technology exports' is used here in a broad sense to include the transfer of all forms of technical and engineering know-how including intergovernmental technical assistance and training.

20. Two legislative acts passed in the mid-1970s, the Technological Development Promotion Act and the Engineering Services Promotion Act, contained such provisions.

21. According to a study (Westphal et al. 1984, p. 510), in 1980 the basic interest rate charged to exporters of capital goods and related services by the Korean Export–Import Bank was 8 per cent and that charged to the buyers was 8.5 per cent, while the preferential rate on ordinary exporters was 12 per cent and the nonpreferential rate was 24.5 per cent.

22. The Korean Export–Import Bank, established in 1976, operates insurance and guarantee schemes, along with provision of export credit.

23. The Hyundai group (ranked eighth), followed by two other Korean firms, were the largest contractors among the developing countries (Engineering Export Promotion Council of India, 1981).

24. Direct foreign investment and international subcontracting have not been important in most Korean exports. Nor was the technology transfer emanating from foreign investment a significant factor.

25. Korea's import policy in the 1980s became more liberal, particularly after 1985 when the country began to generate trade surpluses vis-à-vis the United States. The import liberalization ratio rose to 80 per cent in 1983, and to 95 per cent in 1988 when the number of the restricted items under a negative list system, in which import-prohibited items are to be listed, was drastically reduced to a few hundred. The tariff rate coninued to be reduced with the average rate for all imported products falling from 24 per cent in 1983 to 18 per cent by 1988. These measures notwithstanding,

some imports, mainly the products in agricultural, chemical, machinery, and pharmaceutical industries, remained subject to restrictions either by inclusion in the negative list or through a series of protective laws and regulations. The basic thrust of Korea's trade policy continued to be a cautious and calculated management: nonessential imports would be allowed so long as the country could afford it and as long as they would not severely injure domestic industries.

26. For the formula used, see Nam (1980).
27. The total number of agreements during the period was 1974.
28. Major financial reforms in 1964–5 drastically enhanced the intermediary role of banks in private capital markets.
29. Domestic saving as a percentage of GNP rose from a mere 3 per cent in 1962 to 16 per cent a decade later.
30. The government, confident of an improved investment climate in Korea, set itself an ambitious target of attracting US $2.5 billion in foreign investment during the Fifth Plan period (1982–1986).
31. Except in the free export zones where full ownership by foreigners was permitted.
32. Of the 855 industries listed in Korea's Standard Industrial Classification, 521 items including large-scale projects in capital-intensive industries such as machinery, metals, electronics equipment, and chemicals, energy related or export-oriented projects, projects for manufacturing foodstuffs and medical products, or projects contributing to the development of domestic resources or the commodity distribution system, have all been open to foreign investment.
33. In this regard, the recent Foreign Capital Inducement Act (1982) added three important benefits to investors. The first benefit was allowance for foreign equity sharing up to 100 per cent. This provision applied to those projects introducing high-level technology into Korea, or those undertaken in free export zones or otherwise contributing to increased exports. The second provision exempted foreign invested enterprises from income and corporate and capital gains taxes as well as from import duties under reasonable conditions. The provisions covering a technology contract were more generous. Foreigners could be exempted from wage and salary income taxes. Finally, the legislation guaranteed the outward remittance of dividend and the repatriation of capital.
34. The largest four conglomerates are Hyundai, Dae Woo, Samsung, and Gumsung, which together recently accounted for close to 10 per cent of total exports. Furthermore, 10 Korean conglomerates were recently listed among the top 500 corporations in the world excluding the United States in Fortune magazine.
35. Another important benefit from supporting big business was the political funds the President could count on from them. While industrial capitalists' survival and prosperity depended on the goodwill of the state authority, it was not unusual for the benefitted to return the favor by financial contribution for political causes.
36. Alarmed by the trends in industrial concentration, the government, beginning in the early 1980s, instituted policy reforms to pursue countermeasures against trust formation and to support small and medium firms.

They currently account for more than 95 per cent of the total number of enterprises in Korea, employing roughly a half of its industrial work force and producing about a third of the total industrial output.

37. Note that the rate of change in labor's share of GDP reflects the difference between the rates of change in real wages and productivity.

38. For data on industrial disputes, see the Bureau of Labor (1978).

39. The labor movement in Korea took on a new dimension in recent years as the country entered a period of political liberalization. The state strategy of labor containment worked well in the earlier days of labor surplus under a political regime possessing a highly developed repressive capacity. In the environment of political liberalization, the grip of the state apparatus over civil society is being loosened, and in the case of Korea a labor shortage, particularly for unskilled workers, has been growing for some time. Thus, the sudden eruption of labor disputes witnessed recently was a natural consequence of these developments.

40. As of 1982, it has a population of 38.7 million in an area of 98,000 square kilometers.

41. In the FFDP the agricultural sector received close to 10 per cent of the total investment.

42. For example, the agrarian population declined an average annual rate of 2.98 per cent between 1967 and 1979 (Kim, Kajiwara and Watanabe, 1984). One reason for the widening gap was that more productive labor consisting mostly of young, male workers tended to migrate to higher-wage urban areas, leaving behind older, female and child workers. The argument of rural labor-redundancy in the neoclassical development model is a myth when applied to the Korean experience.

43. Despite the initial success with new varieties, they proved very susceptible to disease and cold weather. The government's overpromotion without careful research and planning was the main cause of the poor harvest in 1980.(Steinberg et al., 1982)

44. For example, throughout the 1970s the total arable land increased 12.7 per cent.

45. Subsequent plan documents have not referred to the explicit role of government to avoid any misunderstanding with foreign businesses.

46. For instance, in formulating the Second Five-Year Plan, a comprehensive resource planning framework based on a sophisticated dynamic input-output model was employed to calculate the required amount of investment at the sectoral level.

47. By the late 1970s, however, it became clear that the implementation machinery was working too effectively. Private companies blindly followed the government's lead without paying much attention to the underlying economic ills characteristic of inflation and distortions in the economy; too many production units were crowded into too few strategic sectors, resulting in too much capacity too fast. Some of these sectors did not really possess a comparative advantage, revealing distortions in the allocation of resources. Excessive aspects of the command structure were gradually being discarded in favor of more initiatives from the private sector, and businessmen were urged to pay more heed to market signals and profits.

48. There is no implication that the Korean model would not apply to resource-rich developing economies.
49. In 1949 for the first time in the history of the nation, the universal compulsory education system for six years of primary schooling was adopted. This paved the way for an educational revolution based on individual initiatives during the 1950s, boosting the 30 per cent literacy rate in 1953 to 80 per cent ten years later. By 1970, the country's literacy rate was one of the highest in the world: the median period of formal education of Korean youths (25–34 age group) was 6.76 years, which was slightly lower than that of Japan (7.84) but higher than that of France (5.01) and far above that of India (0.70) (UNESCO, 1973). Since public funds were limited to the elementary level of education, higher-level education had to be financed mostly from private sources. Nonetheless, enrollment in high schools rapidly increased in spite of a high rate of unemployed high school graduates and the limited absorption of the graduates by colleges. The strong aspirations for education among the Koreans have been a factor contributing to a relatively well-educated labor force.
50. Under the centuries-old Confucian ideology in East Asian societies, civil services have been accorded highest social hierarchy as a position, attracting the best minds to enter.
51. According to an estimate (Kim, 1970, p. 28), Vietnam-war related revenue accrued to S. Korea for year 1967 alone reached as much as $185 million, accounting for about 4.0 per cent of Korea's GDP in that year.
52. For instance, the gross incremental capital-output ratio was estimated at around 2.4 (Westphal and Kim, 1977, pp. 5–11).

5 The State as Agent: Industrial Development in Taiwan, 1952–1972[*]

Deborah Brautigam[1]

INTRODUCTION

Sub-Saharan Africa's industrialization experience has been marked by considerable unevenness and uncertainty over the past generation. Buffeted by changing international market conditions, and by the instability of domestic policies, African manufacturers have generally been unable either to substitute successfully for manufactured imports, or to break into increasingly competitive export markets. The austerity conditions of the past decade have led to massive retrenchments for industry in most African countries: faced with shortages of foreign exchange, tight money supply, and depressed local demand, few industrial sectors have avoided significant reductions in capacity utilization and employment.

The contrast with the Asian NICs (newly industrialized countries) is stark. Over the 1980s, facing the same difficult international environment, the developing countries of East and Southeast Asia experienced consistent growth of industry and of exports. Living standards continued to rise, as did real wages and productivity. The contrast has challenged African leaders, development agencies, and analysts. The Asian experience is all the more compelling, because it provides a model that contradicts some aspects and reinforces other aspects of

* This chapter draws on Deborah Brautigam's 'What Can Africa Learn from Taiwan? Political Economy, Industrial Policy and Adjustment', *Journal of Modern African Studies*, 32 (1), 1994.

orthodox structural adjustment policies as promoted in conditionality-based lending across Sub-Saharan Africa.

Are there lessons Africa can learn from the East Asian NICs? Evaluating the relevance for Africa of an Asian country's experience is fraught with difficulties inherent in making comparisons across regions, during different time periods, with different preconditions. Yet Taiwan's successful combination of industrial development and 'growth with equity' reflects goals that are important for African policy-makers. Growth rates over the past four decades brought Taiwan's GNP per capita from $143 in 1953, to $7284 in 1990, while most African countries followed a path more similar to Congo ($170 in 1962; $1010 in 1990), or even Zaire, which registered $170 in 1962 but only $220 in 1990 (EPC, 1975; EIU, 1993; Wade, 1990, p. 35; World Bank, 1992a). Even during the debt crisis of the 1980s when growth rates turned negative across much of Africa, Taiwan continued to expand production of goods and services at an average annual rate of 8.2 per cent (*The Economist*, 1992, p. 66). This sustained growth has been widely shared by all income groups in the country. Indeed, in Taiwan the share of income held by the top twenty per cent is only 4.5 times as much as the bottom twenty per cent of households (Li, 1988, p. 161). This compares favorably with a selection of African countries for which such statistics exist: in Ghana, the top twenty per cent hold six times as much as the bottom twenty per cent; in Côte d'Ivoire, the top twenty per cent hold almost eleven times the share of income of the bottom twenty per cent; in Botswana, the share of the top is almost twenty-four times the share of the bottom.[2] In Taiwan today, literacy is nearly 100 per cent, infant mortality rates are at European levels, and unemployment rates so low as to be negligible.

The purpose of this chapter is to explore the experience of Taiwanese industrialization, compare Taiwan's policy choices in an earlier period with some of the choices made by African countries more recently, and finally, to attempt to extract some of Taiwan's lessons with relevance to African industrialization strategies in the era of structural adjustment. First, however, we have to make the case that Taiwan can be a useful model for Africa.

Observers have argued that Taiwan is a special case, that its common language and common Confucian culture, history of Japanese colonialism, large transfers of US foreign aid in the 1950s and early 1960s, the stimulus of the perceived threat of communist China across the Taiwan Straits, and the fortunate timing of its export push during the prolonged economic expansion of the 1960s and 1970s make Taiwan an inappropriate or unrealistic model for African countries. These aspects of Taiwan's history *are* very different from Africa's current crisis. Yet in other respects Taiwan's history looks very familiar. Taiwan suffered in the 1940s and 1950s from many of the problems African countries have faced more recently: a difficult transition out of colonial rule, civil war and refugee resettlement, inflation of 3500 per cent, a severely overvalued exchange rate, a large public enterprise sector with inefficient production, extensive rent-seeking and corruption, and an economy dominated by agricultural commodity production. This chapter argues that some aspects of Taiwan's strategy for overcoming these constraints are transferable.

The chapter focuses on the period between 1952 and 1972, when Taiwan's level of development and consequent policy decisions are most likely to be relevant to African countries. By 1952, recovery from the war period was well underway. After 1972, the economy had become very competitive and the country had a comfortable cushion of accumulated wealth. It is important to note that Taiwan's economic decisions of the past twenty years, which reflect an increasingly liberal approach to economic policy, are *not* the decisions that supported the rapid development of broad-based industrialization.

In order to put Taiwan's policies between 1952 and 1972 in perspective, I first review the preconditions for industrial growth in Taiwan: the colonial period, and the US foreign aid program. Then I focus on the set of macroeconomic and industrial policies that provided the underpinnings for Taiwan's extraordinary growth. The chapter concludes that Taiwan's experience – in broad outline – has significant relevance for African countries, reinforcing structural adjustment recommendations that African governments cut budget deficits, raise real interest rates, and avoid overvalued currencies. However, Taiwan's experience calls into question current recommendations for the sequencing of stabilization and adjustment in Africa; trade liberalization, and wholesale privatization, including public utilities, marketing boards and agricultural input supply programs, and market-determined interest and exchange rates. Taiwan's economic policy stressed stability over liberalization. Stability was reinforced by state control of key economic parameters, including electricity production, interest rates, and exchange rates, and by extensive use of quotas and other nontariff barriers to stabilize and protect production for the domestic market. This emphasis on the state as a developmental agent may mean, however, that some aspects of Taiwan's experience will be difficult if not impossible for African countries to emulate. The reasons for this have to do with critical differences in state capacity and ideology, as reflected in domestic political structures and state institutions in Sub-Saharan Africa and Taiwan. We will return to this issue later in the chapter.

PRECONDITIONS FOR INDUSTRIAL DEVELOPMENT

The Colonial Period 1895–1945

Mainland China was forced to cede the island of Taiwan to Japanese control in 1895. Japan rapidly introduced a number of critical institutions, intended to assist Japanese investors and industrialists. Within the first ten years, standardized weights and measures were in place, and the Japanese had carried out both a comprehensive cadastral survey and an initial land reform. The colonial state's deep penetration of Taiwanese society, by way of establishing tightly controlled farmers associations and neighborhood committees, enabled effective control over society and a well functioning rule of law that protected private (particularly Japanese) property. Few African countries have experienced similarly extensive institutional development, either during or after colonialism.

To support the island's early role as a supplier of rice and sugar – produced primarily by smallholders – Japan built up agricultural institutions, irrigation structures, and farmers associations, and built roads and railways where almost none had existed before. Agricultural research introduced technological change to improve yields of rice and other crops; rice yields per hectare increased by 50 per cent between 1923 and 1937 (Thorbecke, 1979, p. 136). Under Japan, total irrigated area more than doubled; the colonial government financed almost half of the construction cost (Ho, 1978, pp. 36–7).

Initially, industrial development was protected for Japanese nationals, with rules and regulations restricting entry for Taiwan's native population. Japanese investment in power generation between 1926 and 1941 increased local capacity for electricity generation by 700 per cent (Fei, Ranis and Kuo, 1979, p. 25). Beginning with agricultural processing for export – sugar refineries, rice mills, and pineapple canneries – industry under the Japanese shifted toward primary import substitution, growing by 6 per cent per annum in the 1930s and including textiles, bicycles, cement, paper, fertilizer, metal products and petroleum refining (Ho, 1978; Ranis, 1979). As World War II began, the Japanese introduced heavy industry to the island, initiating capacity in industrial chemicals, machine tools, and aluminium.

Japan's investments and infrastructure development in Taiwan were broad and deep enough to sustain Taiwan's first several decades of post-colonial development. When the Chinese Nationalists (KMT) retreated across the Taiwan Strait and took stock of the island's productive capacity, they found some ten thousand registered factories, more than half of which were processing non-agricultural products. Approximately 27 per cent of the population was literate (in Japanese) due to programs of free and compulsory primary education; primary enrollment rates were 71 per cent by the end of the colonial period.[3] Investments in sewage systems, sanitation services, and vaccination programs had cut the death rate in half. Despite the destruction caused by World War II, the immediate task facing Taiwan's post-colonial government was, like Europe's, more one of reconstruction than development, and with repairs to infrastructure and factories, growth resumed.

Sub-Saharan Africa's colonial experience was quite different. Investments in transport infrastructure and electricity were generally much lower for African countries, both in absolute numbers, and relative to population. Lower investments in education led to lower literacy levels: in the Portuguese colonies, for example, only one out of a hundred people was literate in 1945. On the average, fewer than ten per cent of African children were enrolled in primary school by 1945 (Davidson, 1983, p. 81).

The Role of U.S. Aid 1950–1965

What role did foreign aid play in Taiwan's economic transformation? On balance, U.S. economic aid was critical for controlling inflation in the early post-war years. It effectively filled the classic gaps of foreign exchange and domestic savings, allowing a higher level of imports and of domestic capital formation than would otherwise have been possible. Aid was substantial, it made a positive difference, and it did not create dependency, terminating in 1968 after a relatively brief period of only eighteen years.[4] In contrast, most African countries have been receiving foreign aid since independence in the 1960s, a period of some thirty years, with little in the way of concrete improvements in living standards or productivity.

United States economic aid amounted to approximately six per cent of Taiwan's GNP through 1961, totalling US$ 1.3 billion in non-military assistance between 1950 and 1968, and averaging $67 million per year (EPC, 1975).[5] In 1987, Sub-Saharan African countries received the equivalent of approximately eight per cent of the continent's GNP in official development assistance (ODA) (World Bank, 1989a). As a percentage of GDP, ODA in 1990 ranged from 0.7 per cent in Nigeria, to 13.3 per cent in Kenya.

Filling the two gaps of domestic savings and foreign exchange, US aid had a critical role in Taiwan. US aid financed more than 40 per cent of Taiwan's imports between 1950 and 1957, and it enabled the Taiwan government to undertake postwar reconstruction and expansion of the human and physical infrastructure (Kuo, Ranis and Fei, 1981, p. 25). Aid financed an average of 40 per cent of Taiwan's capital formation per year, 37 per cent of infrastructure development and 26 per cent of its human capital development over the fifteen years between 1950 and 1965 (Simon, 1988, p. 148).

As important as the quantity of this aid was its quality and timing. During a major period of crisis, when Taiwan was absorbing more than 1.5 million mainland refugees, battling hyperinflation, and rebuilding infrastructure heavily damaged in the war, the United States provided heavy support. The support continued at high levels as Taiwan undertook its reform program in the late 1950s and early 1960s. Timing was also important in building up the agricultural base and the foundation of equitable income distribution: in the first three years of the aid program, half the aid ($267 million) went toward agricultural development, underwriting a major land reform effort (Thorbecke, 1979, p. 172). The US aid program in Taiwan invested heavily in productive infrastructure. Assistance for electric power generation projects took up 36.5 per cent of project-type aid (EPC, 1975). Nearly 59 per cent of net domestic capital formation in agriculture – largely water use and control – was contributed by US aid (Jacoby, 1966, p. 180). In their efforts to promote production, US officials helped establish the China Productivity Center, offering management and production assistance, and credits targeted to upgrade technology and equipment. Many of the imports financed under US aid were of capital equipment and over 73 per cent of commodity aid came in the form of raw materials ready for industrial processing (EPC, 1975). For example, U.S. surplus agricultural commodities, delivered under the P/L 480 program, were additional to the regular commodity aid, which comprised not only foodstuffs (wheat and flour (19 per cent), and milk products (0.8 per cent)), but also raw materials for industrial processing: raw cotton (19.4 per cent), soybeans (9.3 per cent); and ores and metals (8.1 per cent) (EPC, 1975).

Like African countries in the past decade, however, Taiwan was unable to avoid conditionality and the pressure for structural policy reform. After five years of funding Taiwan's policies of import substitution with overvalued exchange rates, the US aid agency began strongly pushing for devaluation and other policy reforms. US advisers used loans and grants as incentives for policy change: 'on a number of occasions, AID offered to increase the level of aid if proper government actions were taken and threatened to reduce it if the government failed to act' (Ho, 1978, p. 118). Taiwan's first significant structural adjustment in 1960 was accompanied by conditionality-based loans. The new policies, the Nineteen-Point Program of Economic and Financial Reforms (discussed below), were promoted by the large number of American advisors present in Taiwan, and in favor of the program, and a new US$20 to $30 million loan was made conditional on the program's 'prompt implementation' (Ranis, 1979, p. 245, fn 45).[6]

US aid to Taiwan was offered on very generous terms, with a grant ratio of 84 per cent. In 1980, across Sub-Saharan Africa, the grant ratio of net ODA was 71 per cent, and in 1987, only 66 per cent (World Bank, 1989a, p. 251). In 1974, almost ten years after aid ceased, Taiwan's ratio of debt service (almost entirely aid loans) to exports of goods and services was only 2.7 percent, compared with ratios of up to 55 per cent in some African countries.

Aid has both quantitative and qualitative dimensions; Taiwan not only received more aid on average than other developing countries, it probably received better quality aid. In the early days of the aid program, development economists argued that aid should fill two gaps, the foreign exchange gap, and the savings gap. In contrast, aid to Africa, influenced by a new generation of theories, was more experimental in nature. During the first post-colonial decades, the World Bank and other agencies gave substantial loans for African integrated rural development projects, many of which failed the test of sustainability (Ruttan, 1984). Instead of traditional infrastructure projects, the New Directions of USAID emphasized technical assistance and direct aid, primarily as social welfare transfers to 'the poorest of the poor'. A critic of AID's shift noted at the time that 'projects intended to build the institutions or infrastructure of developing countries are now undertaken surreptitiously, if at all' (Cotter, 1979?, p. 107). In Kenya, World Bank lending for transport infrastructure sank from 66 per cent of loans in 1970 to 27 per cent by 1980, with a large portion of funds shifting into 'not always usefully applied' experimental rural programs (Hazlewood, 1991, p. 137).

Likewise, shifting large proportions of the World Bank's lending to structural adjustment over the past decade has meant fewer funds available for the kind of productive infrastructure investments favored by development agencies in an earlier period in Taiwan. Structural adjustment emphasizes lowering trade barriers as an important stimulus to greater efficiency and economies of scale. However, as former World Bank economist Larry Summers noted, 'Improved transportation, beyond its benefits in reducing travel time, must have the same types of effects [as lowering trade barriers], yet such considerations have not been fully or even partially accommodated in our analyses of the attractiveness of this type of lending' (Summers, 1991, p. 4).

The next sections examine the major aspects of Taiwan's economic and social investment policies as they evolved from the post-colonial period through 1972. We begin with agriculture – industry's foundation.

Agriculture as the Foundation

Taiwan benefited from the irrigation construction, research, cadastral survey and agroindustries developed by the Japanese in order to boost production and export food surpluses to Japan. Rural infrastructure contributed to the rapid, sustained growth in agriculture under the KMT, but the improvements in income and asset distribution are a function of land reforms implemented several years after the KMT took control of the island and which required all landowners to sell all their land above a specified acreage.[7] The government's appropriation of Japanese lands and investments after the end of the war supported the land reform by providing extensive public land (25 per cent of the arable land in Taiwan) to sell to smallholders on easy terms, and by allowing landowners to be compensated by industrial bonds based on confiscated Japanese factories. By redistributing assets to the poorest of Taiwan's population, the land reform underwrote the remarkable income equality still felt today in Taiwan, an important lesson for African countries, many of whom are already feeling the pinch of increased population pressure and unequal access to land.

The land reform also enabled the government to better squeeze resources from agriculture without the need to compensate a 'parasitic' but politically powerful landlord class. Net capital outflows from agriculture averaged almost four per cent under the Japanese, and rose to ten per cent under the KMT (1951–1960) (Amsden, 1979, p. 353). Although agricultural productivity increases eased the burden of these transfers, growth was not the result of letting the market set prices. African structural adjustment packages typically promote market prices for agricultural produce, abolishing marketing boards and government control of agricultural trade, raising agricultural prices to farmers, reducing government subsidies and privatizing agricultural inputs such as fertilizer. None of these characterize Taiwan's agricultural development during this period.

As one of its first economic policy decisions after arriving in Taiwan, the KMT government set the terms of trade between the main staple – rice – and fertilizer, with fertilizer sold on a barter basis. Rice production received an implicit tax, with fertilizer overpriced in rice terms. Additional surpluses were transferred through land taxes farmers were required to pay in kind, and through the requirement that farmers sell a fixed quantity of rice to the government at a price set 25 to 30 per cent below wholesale (Ho, 1978, p. 180). Through these mechanisms, the government channelled agricultural surpluses to other activities throughout the period under discussion. The low prices for rice, the primary wage good, meant that wages could be lower, assisting industry. The US surplus commodity aid program, valued at 28 per cent of the total aid ($436.7 million between 1951 and 1968) supplemented the low rice prices by supplying substitutes of wheat and flour but appears to have done little to suppress local production (EPC, 1975).

In the first fifteen years of its existence, the rice tax provided more government revenues than did income taxes; some 25 per cent of annual rice production was delivered to the government (Amsden, 1979, p. 358, 1976; Ho, 1978, p. 182). Although farmers lost from the price squeeze, they enjoyed the clear benefit of stability: assured and timely access to fertilizer supplies, with reduced price risk, since the price was fixed in terms of rice.[8] Also, as beneficiaries of the land reform they were able to keep more of their crop without the landlord as an additional layer between the producer and the market.

Primarily out of fears of inflation, Taiwan's government emphasized stability in the agricultural sector: though rice prices were low, they were stable, and markets were stable, enhancing predictablity. Rice output increased steadily at about 3 per cent per year from 1952 to 1964, until farmers began switching to higher value asparagus and mushrooms.[9] The government guaranteed prices for high value export crops to encourage farmers to diversify production.[10] With the greater political strength of farmers by the 1970s, and once industry was on a self-sustaining growth path, the in-kind land tax was reduced in 1972, the rice-fertilizer barter program was eliminated (in 1973), and the government purchase price for rice was tripled in 1975, converting the rice tax into a price-support program, and effectively liberalizing the rice market.

The government – with the support of foreign aid – invested considerable resources into institutional capacity and agricultural research. In 1948, the Chinese–American Joint Commission on Rural Reconstruction (JCRR) was established, with US funding, as a semi-independent '*de facto* superministry of agriculture' (Thorbecke, 1979, pp. 172, 184), the major institution responsible for the land reform and for agricultural planning and development. Supported by JCRR, the government invested in knowledge. In 1960, Taiwan had 79 agricultural research workers per 100,000 farmers, compared with Japan (60 workers) and India (1.2 workers) (Ho, 1978, p. 178). In Africa, government policy and foreign assistance both have been biased against research in favor of extension. A recent review of USAID's program of agricultural assistance in six African countries found that only 2.3 per cent of assistance was channelled to research, and criticized the 'lack of continuity', calling the programs 'short-term and fragmented efforts that could not be expected to make a significant contribution to the necessarily long-term task of building a national capacity for research' (Johnson et al., 1992 p. 120).

In Taiwan, land reform, investment in research, protecting farmers from risk and assured fertilizer supply all supported agriculture, enabling it to support industrial growth in the 1950s and 1960s by supplying cheap rice and inputs for agroprocessing and by serving as a market for industrial goods – small power tillers, pumps, etc. – produced in local workshops and small factories. The JCRR, an insulated, semi-public agency, financed by US aid but staffed predominantly by local expertise, shaped policies and programs in agriculture. Decentralization of factories was made possible by the excellent rural road network, enabling farm families to supplement farm incomes by working in factories. By building up agricultural exports during the 1950s, the nation was able to finance necessary imports for agricultural production (fertilizers, for example) as well as inputs for industry; the agricultural export surplus, over and above the cost of imported agricultural inputs, was US$12 million in 1952 and rose to US$120 million in 1965 (Thorbecke, 1979, p. 139). Finally, although the net transfer from the agricultural sector into the rest of the economy amounted to some 15 to 22 per cent of total agricultural production between 1952 and 1969, the sector itself received consider-able investment and recurrent resources from government, enabling it to increase productivity and serve as the basis for economic transfor-mation (Thorbecke, 1979, p. 203).

Infrastructure

In developing the island as a supply depot, the Japanese built an extensive network of rural roads to carry agricultural products to the island's ports. The KMT government inherited 16,000 km. of roads (mostly unpaved), 6000 km. of railroad tracks, 32 electric power plants and two harbors able together to process 4 million tons of seafreight annually (Long, 1990, p. 25). The government (with military and non-military funding from the US) paved an average of 450 km. of road per year after 1952, raising the percentage of paved roads from 7 per cent in 1952 to 50 per cent in 1972. The government also invested in additional power facilities – particularly the extensive rural electrifica-tion that helped enable so much of Taiwan's industry to be decen-tralized in the rural areas; by the mid-1970s, rural electrification was virtually universal. In the 1960s, the government built and provided infrastructure for more than seventeen rural industrial estates (Ranis, 1979, p. 226). The density of transport infrastructure – roads and railways – was still more extensive in Taiwan in 1952 than in many African countries today. Taiwan had 434 meters of highway per square km., compared with 165 meters in Côte d'Ivoire, 134 in Nigeria, and 94 in Kenya (EPC, 1976; Kurian, 1992).

Electricity in Taiwan was provided by a government-owned utility and appeared to be priced at 'realistic' levels ('no profit, no subsidy') much as the World Bank advocates for African countries.[11] Raising public utility rates was one part of the reform package implemented in 1960. However, subsidized interest rates to utilities still enabled the price of electric power 'to be kept lower than otherwise would be the case' (Lundberg, 1979, p. 293). Perhaps as a result of these subsidized loans and capital construction subsidies resulting from the heavy aid investments in power generation, in 1961, the power rate in Taiwan was considered by local planners to still be 'relatively low', at about US$0.01/kwh (Li, 1961, p. 5).[12] By contrast, almost thirty years later, 1989 power rates in Nigeria were less than US$.008/kwh, and heavily subsidized. Poor performance of the system meant that 50 per cent of Nigerian factories in a recent survey experienced between 5–10 power outages per week. Every firm over twenty employees, although connected to the NEPA grid, had invested in its own power supply, costing on average $US.51/kwh to generate (Lee and Anas, 1989).

Infrastructure deficiencies such as uncertain electricity supply are a significant implicit 'tax' on industry in Africa. Costs of operation and investment are said to be some 50–100 per cent higher in Africa than in South Asia, for example (World Bank, 1989a, p. 3). Although policies in many countries have kept the rates charged to business consumers low, the resulting budget inadequacies have meant an inability to maintain existing infrastructure, resulting frequently in businesses having to invest in private, supplementary electricity generation, roads, and water supply. In comparative perspective, Taiwan's 'low' rates were relatively high, and the system performed quite well, lending some support to the push for realistic utility pricing in Africa (although clearly significant investment is also badly needed to expand and refurbish infastructure).

Education, Labor, and Social Welfare

Taiwan's industrial growth was fueled in part by government investment in universal literacy, vocational and science-based learning, and by policies that kept employment high, urban–rural wage differentials low, and real wages rising at or below average productivity. As we have seen, Japan's colonial policies led to a substantial base of literacy in the Taiwan population. Under the KMT, primary school (six years) was both free and compulsory, and in 1968, nine years of schooling were made free and eventually, compulsory. Funding, social values, and legal compulsion brought literacy rates to almost 87 per cent by 1972 (CEPD, 1989). On the average, middle-income African countries reached Taiwan's 1952 primary enrollment rate of 84 per cent by 1970, but low income African countries are still at or below 68 per cent enrollment (World Bank, 1988a, p. 131; World Bank, 1989a, p. 274). Taiwan's emphasis on education finds reflection in budgetary priorities of African governments, who have clearly valued education. Between 1960/61 and 1975/76, the percentage of GNP in Taiwan spent on public and private education rose from 2.5 per cent to 4.2 per cent. For Sub-Saharan Africa as a whole, the percentage of GNP spent on public education alone rose from 3.5 per cent in 1970 to 4.5 in 1980, dropping to 3.9 in 1983 (World Bank, 1988a, p. 138). As a percentage of total government expenditure, spending in Taiwan rose from 7.8 per cent in 1952 to 17.6 per cent in 1972 (EPC, 1975). In Africa, the average has remained close to 17 per cent since 1970. However, in the grim economic climate of the 1980s, most African countries have had to reduce per capita spending on education. Mauritius cut per capita spending by 17 per cent between 1980 and 1988; Sierra Leone by 62 per cent, and Tanzania by 73 per cent (United Nations, 1992). Overall, spending on education per student declined from $32 in 1980 to $15 in 1987 (UNESCO, 1990). Furthermore, austerity programs have brought in efforts to collect user fees in attempts to provide revenues for services when government cutbacks caused short falls in allocations.[13]

Taiwan's government invested heavily in planned, vocational education. Vocational training in Taiwan as a percentage of all senior high school enrollments rose from 37 per cent in 1950 to 66 per cent in 1980 (Woo, 1988). An exam at the end of the ninth year of education determined which educational track continuing students would be able to follow: vocational or university. Like most African parents and students today, Taiwan's families in the 1950s and 1960s did not envision their educated children becoming blue collar laborers, but rather in white collar office and government jobs. Yet the government did not provide the education demanded by society, but rather the education it saw would be needed to support skilled labor demand by growing industries. After 1966, Taiwan's planners mapped out estimates of manpower demand by sector and channelled students into educational streams needed by the economy. Woo notes that state capacity made a difference in translating plans into action: 'an important feature of these plans was that they were actually implemented . . . according to a strict timetable with deadlines. Specific agencies were made responsible and other agencies were required to oversee them' (Woo, 1988, p. 9).

Taiwan's manpower development plans also mandated a shift in university and college discipline from law, agriculture and the humanities into the sciences and engineering. Enrollments in the natural and medical sciences and engineering in 1972 totalled 40 per cent (CEPD, 1989). In a recent study of thirteen African countries for which similar data could be obtained, 1985 enrollments for natural and medical sciences and engineering amounted to 32.6 per cent of the total (Zymelman, 1990, p. 27). The difference between Taiwan and Africa appears to be less in the structure of enrollment than in the percentage compared with the population at large, and this is in part a consequence of low levels of income. By 1985, Taiwan had 65 enrollments in natural sciences, 767 in engineering, and 198 in medical sciences per 100,000 population (Woo, 1988, p. 33). The thirteen African countries averaged 13, 9 and 7 respectively per 100,000 population. For comparison, the OECD countries averaged 214, 369 and 260 respectively per 100,000 population (Zymelman, 1990, p. 27).

Education statistics give some indication of how government and society value technical education and skilled labor, but there are other important aspects of the quality of labor, and the nature of the labor market. Whether from experience gained under Japanese industrialization, better training, or from cultural patterns, labor productivity has been high in Taiwan. By 1972, the productivity of labor of Taiwanese workers was almost equal to that of workers in Japan and the U.S. (Gold, 1986, p. 79). Unlike many African countries, Taiwan maintained a fairly competitive labor market: strikes were prohibited, unions weak, and there was effectively no minimum wage.[14]

In theory, a competitive labor market absorbs 'surplus labor' (often rural labor released by higher productivity in agriculture) at a fairly constant wage rate in real terms, up until the turning point where unemployment virtually ceases to exist and real wages begin to rise. In Taiwan, real wages were slightly under the growth rate for labor productivity, which kept unit labor costs low during this period (EPC, 1975; Little, 1979, p. 477). By 1972, wages in Taiwan were still only US$.20 per hour (Scott, 1979, p. 360).[15]

African wage trends are very different from this experience, and represent both colonial decisions, the bargaining power of major unions, and, more recently, the effect of devaluation on labor, as a 'nontraded input'. Before the current economic crisis, wages in African countries tended to be considerable higher than the average in low-income Asian countries such as India.[16] Government employees were estimated to earn 2.8 times their (low-income) Asian counterparts, and unskilled wage levels were 1.4 times those in Asia (Nash, n.d., p. 40). At present, real wages have fallen below Asian levels. In Nigeria, the hourly wage for textile workers in 1989 was approximately $0.16/hour, compared with $0.58 in India, and $0.30 in Indonesia.

Taiwan's experience of very low levels of unemployment was undoubtedly assisted by the corollary of market-established wage levels. The structural adjustment policies that advocate elimination of dualistic wage structures (a highly paid urban labor force versus low, informal sector wages for everyone else), while undoubtedly painful for those families bearing the cost of lowered wages, are predicted to lead over time to greater employment and more labor-intensive industrialization, and eventually to the elimination of the labor surplus and consequently, sustainable increases in real wages. However, labor absorption requires additional investment and economic growth – outcomes that are probably assisted more by focusing more directly on growth, than by the demand reduction policies now characteristic of structural adjustment. There are also concerns in efficiency wage terms of ensuring that real wages are sufficient to support productivity levels (the opposite of the usual neo-classical argument).

The government in Taiwan provided only limited social security, health and welfare to offset the low wages, investing three times as much in education as in health over the two decades of this study. Public health rose from 1.5 per cent of government expenditures in 1951–55 to only 1.7 per cent in 1971–73 (EPC, 1975). No unemployment compensation existed, although there was a labor insurance scheme, which by 1976 covered some 50 per cent of all employees (Galenson, 1979, p. 444). Although other of the NICs – Singapore, for instance – invested in public housing, Taiwan provided very little public housing, although the national government has subsidized twenty-year home mortgages at 3 per cent for government employees.[17] This appears to indicate that the government in Taiwan disaggregated human resource development into investment in education as a public good, and investment in other forms of social welfare as private goods.

POLICIES FOR INDUSTRIAL DEVELOPMENT IN TAIWAN, 1952–1972

After taking control of Taiwan from the Japanese, the KMT continued to promote industrialization via a protected domestic market, direct subsidies to public sector industries, and overvalued and strictly controlled foreign exchange. Taiwan followed the classic pattern of moving first into primary import substitution (agricultural diversification and nondurable consumer goods: food processing, textiles, leather, etc.). Economic activity gradually shifted from the agricultural sector (36 per cent of GDP in 1952, 14 per cent in 1972) to the industrial sector (where manufacturing rose from 11 per cent of GDP in 1952 to 32 per cent in 1972) (CEPD, 1989). Structural changes within manufacturing were often rapid. Textiles, for example, moved from 7.3 per cent of manufacturing production in the late 1950s to 27 per cent in the late 1960s, dropping to 12 per cent in the late 1970s when machine tools, petrochemicals and other more technology intensive industries were coming on stream (Fei, Ranis and Kuo, 1979, pp. 10–11). The industrial sector grew at 12 per cent from 1953 to 1962, accelerating to 20 per cent from 1963 to 1972 (CEPD, 1989). In the pattern now common for East Asian NICs, much of this growth can be directly linked to exports; the share of industrial products in exports rose from 8 per cent in 1952 to 83 per cent in 1972 (EPC, 1975).

In the first ten years after the post-war recovery (1952–1962), Taiwan dealt with many of the same macroeconomic imbalances that faced African countries in the 1980s. Not surprisingly, then, the Nineteen Point reforms implemented around 1960 resembled in some ways structural adjustment policies currently in place in many African countries. In particular, they led to a unified exchange rate that did not discriminate against exports. They also promoted preferential treatment for the private sector in finance, foreign exchange and taxes; and led to some relaxation of state economic controls. Public utility rates were raised, and some subsidies removed. Exports as a per cent of GDP increased 67 per cent in the first four years after the reforms. While the direct impact of the reforms on industrial output cannot be calculated, average annual growth rates in the seven years before the 1960 reforms were already a healthy 11.5 per cent; this increased to 14.2 per cent for the seven years after the 1960 reforms (EPC, 1976).

Exchange Rate Policy

Fixed exchange rates were one of the foundations of the Bretton Woods system. When the developed countries went off fixed rates and began to float their currencies in 1973, Taiwan maintained a fixed rate. There are several difference between Taiwan's experience and that in most developing countries over the past several decades. In particular, Taiwan's experience stressed stability while at the same time guarding against overvaluation.

Exchange rate policy followed a gradual path that led to liberalization only after almost two decades of fixed nominal (and stable real) rates. First, Taiwan introduced a multiple exchange rate system in 1951 where the public sector and importers of raw materials and intermediate goods enjoyed a sharply lower cost of foreign exchange. Concerned from a very early date about overvaluation, the government devalued the yuan several times before moving to a unitary exchange rate gradually between 1958 and 1961. Once the exchange rate was unified, Taiwan kept it fixed (with some slight adjustments) at NT$40 to the US dollar for the rest of the period under discussion, allowing it to float only in 1978, when it was linked to a trade-weighted basket of Taiwan's major trading partners' currencies. This stability – an important boon to domestic industry – was possible only because Taiwan's expenditure and monetary policy and trade surpluses kept the real effective value of the yuan within a range of NT$44 to NT$30 to the US dollar (Levy, 1986, p. 2). When the real value deviated from the nominal value, it was generally in the direction of undervaluation, which discourages imports, while promoting exports.

Second, the government controlled all foreign exchange and allocated it almost entirely for development purposes. Spending foreign exchange on travel for pleasure was not allowed, for example (Wu, 1978). Exporters were required to surrender all receipts to the Central Bank, although after the early 1960s, under a marketable foreign exchange linkage system, many exporters could regain 100 per cent of export earnings (Ranis, 1979, p. 220). Importers applied to the Central Bank for foreign exchange allocations. This system was also implemented by many African countries, which, however, generally suffered from overvalued currencies which tend to promote capital flight, and the creation of a parallel exchange market, effectively reducing the amount of foreign exchange controlled by the government and raising the scarcity rents. By 1983, overvalued exchange rates in Africa led to average parallel market rates of some 250 per cent above official rates (Nash, n.d., p. 11). Although overvalued exchange rates are clearly unsustainable in Africa, allowing the exchange rate to float may not be the most sustainable strategy; already by 1990, four of nine African countries to have established floating rates dropped them in favor of greater controls (Rodrik, 1990, p. 940).

Credit and Interest Rate Policy

Taiwan's experience of credit and interest rate policies during this period was, again, one of extensive government direction and control. Interest rates were kept high, and positive, in real terms. At the same time, Taiwan's financial system, while providing capital to fuel the industrial expansion in the post-war decades, functioned with significant constraints, including heavy reliance on short-term credit for factory construction, and the use of postdated checks, backed by criminal penalties for insufficient funds, as the island's 'principal credit instrument' (Wade, 1990, p. 163). In addition, the government set targets for the state-owned banks to meet in directing finance to particular industries and subsectors. Banks extended some 75 per cent of bank loans to industries targeted by government planners, in the 1970s (Wade, 1990, p. 167). Had the market allocated credit, it is likely that traders would have cornered a larger share of bank loans. As it was, traders generally paid a higher rate of interest than manufacturers, and the curb market for unsecured loans in Taiwan offered substantially higher rates, with a nominal rate of around 30 per cent in the mid-1960s (Wade, 1990, p. 58). Further, the government limited competition among the banks, restricting private and foreign-owned banks to a small role.

The government in Taiwan kept real interest rates high during the entire period under discussion, once the hyperinflation of late 1949 and early 1950 was contained. Secured bank loans were offered at a real rate of interest close to 13 per cent in the 1950s. Real interest rates on bank savings deposits averaged 3.2 per cent for most years between 1952 and 1972. Taiwan's rates were clearly high, even compared with the higher rates prevalent in Africa under structural adjustment programs. The 'new NIC', Mauritius, has followed a similar policy recently, with real interest rates on secured loans of 10.8 per cent, and on savings deposits of 5.3 per cent (IMF, 1992), but in many African countries, the rates have been sharply lower, often negative in real terms. Taiwan's former finance minister K. F. T. Li named high real interest rates as one of the cornerstones of Taiwan's development management, and the basis of its high savings rates (Li, 1988). While the World Bank has recommended positive real rates of interest, it has cautioned against the high real interest rates experienced in many of the NICs there (Bhattacharya and Linn, 1988, p. xi). Although the high interest rates in Taiwan seem to have been healthy there, we cannot be sure that they would have the same beneficial effect in Africa. As Robert Wade points out (1990, p. 172), it is not entirely clear how high interest rates in Taiwan failed to 'undermine export competitiveness, cause dangerously high debt/equity ratios, crowd out new borrowers, and fuel inflation' as they have done elsewhere. Nevertheless, the successful early years of Taiwan's labor-intensive industrialization must be partly attributed to policies that made capital relatively expensive.

Government control over interest rates was relaxed only in the early 1980s. The Central Bank – exceptionally autonomous, and answerable only to the president – refrained from resorting to printing money to finance deficits, and kept inflation very low after 1952, aside from the price surges imported with the oil price hikes of the 1970s.[18] The government's ability to keep the budget in surplus after 1964 no doubt assisted the lion's share of finance capital to flow into industry, rather than into government deficit financing.

In Sub-Saharan Africa, Central Banks have rarely been autonomous, and have had great trouble controlling inflation. Governments in Africa have frequently resorted to the printing press to finance government expenditures, and have expanded credit to meet the demands of their private sectors. Annual inflation between 1980 and 1987 was at double digit rates in almost half of the countries in Africa (World Bank, 1989a, p. 268), a result in part of the liberalization of exchange rates and, subsequently, higher domestic prices for imported goods, and in part a consequence of unrestrained domestic money supply expansion. When stabilization and structural adjustment programs in Africa emphasize positive interest rates that reflect the real cost of capital, and restrictions in government expansion of the money supply, industry in Africa benefits from a healthier macroeconomic environment. However, liberalization when extended to deregulation and decontrol of banks, and allowing the market to set interest rates, does not reflect the pattern followed by Taiwan during the first twenty years of postwar industrialization and export growth. Taiwan's combination of government control and positive real interest rates emphasized the stability and predictability important for industrial investment. Keeping real interest rates strongly and consistently positive on savings deposits encouraged domestic savings to finance industrial investment. Financial liberalization, as part of structural adjustment programs, generally implies allowing the market to set the cost of capital. An alternative, suggested by Taiwan's experience, is for the government to maintain fixed rates, but to keep them positive in real terms, i.e. above the rate of inflation.

Domestic Taxation Policy

Consistent with neoclassical recommendations, taxation in Taiwan has been biased in favor of consumption taxes, with low rates of business and personal income tax. In 1962, for example, 8 per cent of tax revenues came from income taxes, 22 per cent from customs duties, and 6 per cent from business taxes, while almost 50 per cent of tax revenues were collected on consumption: domestic goods and services (EPC, 1975). Taxation policy in Taiwan has reflected both government capacity and economic policy. Reflecting the high level of capacity in

Taiwan, the tax system was computerized after the Tax Reform Commission of 1969, which probably lowered evasion (Little, 1979, p. 481). In keeping with the emphasis on savings in Taiwan, for individuals, interest income from savings accounts has largely been tax-free. The regressive consumption taxes shifted income toward production activities; however, other aspects of tax policy compensated for regressive consumption taxes. Most low income households, for example, paid little or no personal income tax, and a progressive business income tax started at only 5 per cent for small businesses (Lundberg, 1979, p. 305).

Furthermore, business taxes were themselves skewed in favor of manufacturing. The 1960 Statute for Encouragement of Investment that followed the Nineteen Point reforms provided a five year tax holiday for manufacturers, a cap of 18 per cent on business income taxes for manufacturers (as compared with 32.5 per cent for traders), and tax deductions for reinvested profits and some export proceeds (Kuo, Ranis and Fei, 1981, p. 75).

Trade Policy

The controversial area of trade policy is perhaps where the experience of Taiwan is most contradictory to the policies advocated in structural adjustment dialogues with African countries. Taiwan's trade policy was both highly protectionist, and outward-oriented.[19] Taiwan's export success was not a matter of 'free trade' but of a dual incentive regime, where exports were promoted but local production was heavily protected, although often for strictly limited periods. According to one of Taiwan's top planners, the country erected a 'high tariff wall' alleviated somewhat by tariff rebates and export processing zones (Li, 1988, p. 136). However, trade policy in Taiwan was carried out by institutions with considerable implementation capacity, unlike the present situation in most African countries where many already weak public sector institutions have been further weakened by austerity cutbacks.

Protection for Domestic Producers through Tariff and Import Controls

Import restrictions such as quotas, and nonquantitative restrictions such as investment regulations are considered by neoclassical economics to be the poorest way to support industry. Preferred methods are explicit fiscal subsidies, followed by tax exemptions, and (a poor third), tariff protection. Few countries actually reflect this type of pattern, and Taiwan is no exception. Throughout the period (1952–1972) under review here, exports surged and yet the trade regime was a model of controls, high and variable tariff protection, quantitative restrictions and administrative allocation. Although nontariff barriers were supposedly set for limited periods of time, with the expectation that after that period, tariff protection would take their place, Robert Wade demonstrates that even in 1984, nontariff barriers covered more than half of imports (by value), and tariffs were still 'minutely differentiated by product, ranging from zero to well over 100 percent' (Wade, 1990, pp. 117, 122). In addition, during the period under review import licenses were controlled for two-fifths of imported commodities, with permission given only if the prospective importer could certify that domestic supplies were not available.[20]

Currently, nontariff barriers in Sub-Saharan Africa are far higher than anywhere else in the world, and their lowering or elimination is a key element of liberalization.[21] Although discouraged by neoclassical economists, Taiwan's experience indicates that nontariff barriers may have some advantages over tariffs. For example, they can reduce important information uncertainties, thus lowering transaction costs. By ensuring that only a certain number of units are imported, quotas and other quantitative restrictions allow for greater predictability and market stability, an advantage for domestic producers. In addition, in Taiwan, as perhaps in other countries, tariffs changes were generally possible only through legislation, whereas quotas were more flexible and could be changed by executive order.

Until 1979, nominal tariff rates in Taiwan averaged 44 per cent (Wu, 1985, p. 99). However, when all trade related taxes and subsidies and nonquantitative restrictions are taken into account, effective protection for manufacturing in 1966 averaged 44 per cent, while effective protection for the portion of output sold domestically averaged 126 per cent for consumption goods, 48 per cent for intermediate goods, and 32 per cent for capital goods (Scott, 1979, p. 334). Manufactured goods in Mauritius, for example, had average effective rates of protection of 89 per cent in 1983 (Gulhati and Nallari, 1990, p. 11) and Zambia in 1975, had effective protection on a quarter of consumer items over 500 per cent (World Bank, 1989a, p. 116). In addition, the structure of protection in Taiwan is not flat, as economists recommend, but cascading, with lower protection on raw materials and intermediate goods. Finally, protection evidenced considerable variation both across sectors and among commodities in a single sector (Levy, 1986, p. 3).

With such extensive protection, how did the KMT regime encourage domestic producers to climb out of their comfortable infant industry cribs? In some cases, programs were applied to reduce tariff protection by an agreed per cent per year, provided producers reduced their prices as their efficiency increased. The government used the instrument of liberalization with precision, at times down to the level of individual factories, enforcing requirements that industries become able to compete internationally within an agreed time frame. In other cases, it appeared to be enough to level the playing field between locally produced and imported goods, allowing exporters to expand and sell their surpluses abroad.

Simon points out that in its first several decades on Taiwan, the KMT was 'reluctant to open the Taiwanese economy to outside forces and was adament in its belief that the local economy would be destabilized by allowing greater economic openness' (Simon, 1988, p. 143). Taiwan's resistance to lowering protection is reflected in many African countries. Even Mauritius, which enjoyed manufactured exports growth averaging 30 per cent a year between 1983 and 1988, was 'not ready' in 1986 'to agree to (the World Bank's proposed) schedule for phased rationalization of the overall tariff structure' (Gulhati and Nallari, 1990, p. 55).

Protection can be effective in the support of infant industries, but the risk is high that entrenched interests will resist being 'weaned'. Export promotion may offer the missing discipline. Taiwan had a strong and autonomous state that was able to enforce requirements that industries increase their competitiveness or face lowered protection. When the structure of protection is set deliberately and regularly adjusted to encourage the performance of targeted domestic industries, as it was in Taiwan, resistance to wholesale liberalization is probably well-placed. When the structure of protection is established primarily to encourage multinational investment with few backward links to the domestic economy, or to protect uncompetitive state-owned industries for long periods of time, as seemed to be the case in many African countries, carefully phased liberalization, coupled with export promotion mechanisms, may be necessary to stimulate more productive use of resources. Countries without Taiwan's capacity to finely tune the tariff structure, or without the autonomy of the Taiwan government and its ability to enforce scheduled reductions in protection, domestic content requirements, and other industrial policies despite entrenched interests, may find that the theoretical 'level playing field' of a low, even tariff structure to be best for stimulating efficient investment.

However, if it is true that intelligent manipulation of tariffs accelerated Taiwan's industrial performance, foreign aid resources could also be invested in building the capacity of government officials to more finely tune the tariff structure to encourage efficient import substitution, and export diversification. In addition, as one advisor to the World Bank argued recently, 'since the effects of import liberalization on export performance can be weak and delayed, policy ought to concentrate on exports directly' (Rodrik 1990, p. 941). Concentrating on exports directly would also better reflect the experience of Taiwan.

Export Promotion

Export promotion instruments were intended both to remove positive discrimination against production for export, and to provide direct incentives for exporters. Among the direct incentives were lower interest, short-term loans as export finance credits, with nominal rates of less than 12 percent, compared with ordinary business loans, with bank rates of approximately 20 per cent and private moneylender rates of 36 per cent (Scott, 1979, p. 340).[22] Export sales were exempt from business taxes; duty-drawbacks were extensively used. Taiwan also provided export insurance at reasonable rates, export quality inspections, beginning in 1953, and assisted companies to market exports through branch offices of the Central Trust of China (*Industry of Free China*, 1968, p. 36).

Exemptions from duty or duty drawbacks applied both to direct and indirect exporters. By 1955, early in the country's efforts to expand exports, the executive branch had established regulations allowing exporters to import or purchase inputs without paying duties or taxes by posting a bond that pledged to pay duty or tax if the materials were not in fact exported.[23] This simplified the rebate process, allowing export manufacturers much better control over these funds. The government sacrificed substantial revenue in order to implement the rebate scheme. In 1972, for example, the value of taxes forgone due to duty drawbacks and duty exemptions would have doubled customs revenues (Levy, 1986, p. 4, citing Westphal, 1978, p. 20).

In general, Taiwan's program contrasted in a number of important ways with similar schemes in Africa. First, the rebates were available to both direct and indirect exporters, meaning that domestic producers who imported inputs to make intermediate goods or produce raw materials and sold them to a factory producing for export would be able to deduct duties on those products. This made sure that domestic producers were not discriminated against by exporters looking to source raw materials and intermediate inputs. In addition, the Taiwanese program provided rebates from duties almost immediately; in the case of posting a bond, the rebate was effective the same day the goods were exported. In Nigeria, by contrast, receiving a rebate can take six months to more than a year, and the process is so cumbersome that many industries do not bother to even apply. In Madagascar, the duty-free import scheme requires that 51 documents be stamped and verified an average of three times each (Nash, n.d., p. 30).[24] Finally, Taiwan was able to remove the discretionary aspect of the rebate by making it a function of fixed input–output coefficients, which by 1968 had been set for 7000 products (Levy, 1986, p. 6).

Once exports were well developed in Taiwan and the country began to run up against import barriers in its chief markets, the government concentrated on upgrading the quality of exports within certain broad categories, providing incentives to firms to increase the value of their products but not the quantity (Gold, 1986, p. 82). When Taiwan was given a quota for exports to a certain country, the government allocated the quota in part to manufacturers based on past performance, and in part to 'those manufacturers whose bids to fulfill export orders are at the highest prices compatible with securing the orders' (Scott, 1979, p. 345).

Neoclassical theory finds it difficult to explain why the export promotion bias in the East Asian NICs has worked so well. As noted by Ron Findlay: 'In terms of the standard theory of trade and welfare, a bias in favor of exports is no better in principle than a bias against them. . . . It is therefore hard to see why an export-promotion strategy should produce such successful results . . . it is clear that an answer must be sought outside the conventional bounds of the standard model, in the murky but relevant waters of such concepts as X-efficiency and "learning by doing"' (quoted in Fransman, 1984, p. 53).

Export Processing Zones

Taiwan established one of the world's first export processing zones (EPZ) in Kaosiung in 1965 expressly to encourage technological advance and expand exports. The EPZ combined the attraction of an industrial estate (and associated infrastructure) with the ease of 'one stop' administrative approval processing. Although widely regarded as successful, the zones never accounted for a large percentage of Taiwan's exports – generally less than ten per cent. A different model of export processing zones adopted by Mauritius in 1970 has been highly successful in promoting exports. Nigeria is about to open its first EPZ, and other African countries are now looking to take advantage of their new situation as low-cost suppliers of labor.[25]

Taiwan's EPZ experience suggests several lessons. The zones were successful at drawing foreign investment and providing employment, mainly of unskilled labor (trained on the job), but also of local managers and technicians. Wages were higher and working conditions in the zones were widely regarded as more attractive than outside (Scott, 1979, p. 340). Finally, and perhaps most importantly, the zones were not the only area of export promotion and were regarded by the government as a transition mechanism, intended to lower transaction costs connected with investment for export during a period that combined import substitution and associated protection, with export promotion.[26] The government, both through bonded factories outside the zones, and through numerous other export incentives, promoted export activity throughout the country.

Liberalization

Liberalization of trade and other economic policies in Taiwan has been incremental, gradual, with important sequencing, a strategy that maintained stability. Only in the early 1970s, when the nation had a trade surplus of US$474 million, did the government embark on a major liberalization program (CEPD, 1989). Between 1970 and 1974, the share of items under import control dropped from 41 per cent to 2.3 per cent (Wade, 1990, p. 123). A floating exchange rate was introduced only in 1978, interest rates were liberalized in 1981, and the capital market was liberalized in 1983. In fact, the entire period of this study (1952–1972) was characterized by a strictly controlled trade and financial system. Taiwan's government emphasized stability, and its control of two key parameters – the exchange rate, and the interest rate – backed up by a conservative fiscal and monetary policy, ensured stability, enhanced predictability, and encouraged investment.

Nigeria, by contrast, implemented a liberalization program very quickly. In 1986, the exchange rate system was liberalized, price controls removed, import licenses abolished, and agricultural market-ing boards eliminated. One result has been an inability of the government to maintain stability in key economic parameters. Interest rates in Nigeria have been set by the market in recent years, with wide swings in the *real* interest rate from −39 per cent to 16.5 per cent over the 1988–1990 period (World Bank). Nigeria's rapid liberalization experience, and the instability and backtracking that have marked it, are repeated in any number of other African countries. Though in part they reflect the lack of domestic consensus and weak elite commitment to structural adjustment reforms, a different analysis might suggest that more careful attention to the sequencing of reforms may have resulted in a program with greater political sustainability. Both Taiwan and South Korea liberalized their trade regimes over a long period of time, with substantial liberalization occurring only in the 1970s and 1980s. In contrast, many African countries are undergoing trade liberalization precisely when their economies are at their weakest, rather than once they have built up the ability to compete. The severity of the balance of payments crises faced by these countries magnifies the necessity of policy reform, but it is clearly an open question as to whether rapid liberalization has been best for restoring financial health, or whether support for a more gradual liberalization would have been a more sustainable strategy in Africa.

Science and Technology

During the 1960s and 1970s, Taiwan was able to expand production by following the technology curve and product cycle established by Japan, often purchasing second-hand technology directly from Japan. Technology policy in this period promoted diffusion and adaptation, rather than outright invention. In fact, Taiwan became so adept at imitation that in the early 1980s, the US Trade Representative's office accused Taiwan of producing 60 per cent of the counterfeit and pirated items in the world markets (Simon, 1988, p. 216). Taiwan had loose or nonexistent laws protecting international patents or copyrights, and had failed to sign international conventions on copyrights. It is impossible to calculate how much of Taiwan's early growth was fueled by the learning that went on while trying to reproduce products protected elsewhere in the world.

In the early 1970s, toward the end of the period under study, when Taiwan's competitive advantage in low cost labor was ending, the government supported a transition to growth led by technological innovation and increased automation. The Industrial Technology Research Institute (ITRI) was established in 1973 to enhance R & D efforts. Policies explicitly to develop 'high caliber manpower in natural science and engineering' were designed in this period (Li, 1988). This suggests that in the earlier period of industrialization, a broadly educated workforce, and sufficient engineering skills to adapt imported processes for local conditions may be the most efficient strategy. Governments and international agencies could assist African entrepreneurs to make connections with the producers at the previous level of the international product cycle, through joint ventures, or even assisted business trips and study tours. For Taiwan, this model was Japan; for some African countries, it could be Taiwan. Indeed, in one area of Nigeria, where education has long been valued, local entrepreneurs have been importing and adapting used machinery from Taiwan, to produce locally the products they formerly imported from Taiwanese companies (Brautigam, 1992; Forrest, 1992).

Foreign Investment in Industry

Although opening up the economy to foreign trade and foreign investment is a cornerstone of structural adjustment policies, Taiwan's experience only partially fits the model of liberalization. Foreign investments with 100 per cent foreign ownership were allowed, and Taiwan did not limit repatriation of profits or restrict foreign firms from bringing in their own nationals in technical or management positions. Unlike the liberal model, Taiwan restricted the entry and activities of multinational companies in many ways, tightening controls as goals of technological upgrading and foreign equity investments were reached.

Foreign investment was low to negligible in the 1950s, but policy changes in the late 1950s and early 1960s encouraged investment.[27] While most proposals of all types were approved in the 1960s, by the 1970s the government was more selective, welcoming foreign investors primarily in production for export in areas where Taiwan did not yet have critical technologies or capacity.[28] Foreign investment was thus welcomed in electronics (33 per cent of approvals, 1952–1974), metal products and machinery (18 per cent), and chemicals (11 per cent), but not in labor-intensive industries, e.g. agriculture and forestry (1 per cent), paper and paper products (1 per cent), food processing (2 per cent), in services such as construction, transport, and banking (EPC, 1975). The export requirements ensured that industries established by foreigners in Taiwan would be internationally competitive, while local content requirements have pushed foreign investors to help upgrade Taiwanese suppliers to international quality standards. By 1976, the minimum percentages of domestic content required for local manufacture of motorcycles was 90 per cent; of switch exchangers, 80 per cent; and of color television sets, 50 per cent (Scott, 1979, p. 333).

Many of the foreign firms that have invested in African countries have taken advantage of generous protection granted by governments interested in employment and other economic benefits of foreign investment. Producing for the domestic market, behind high tariff walls, these firms have had little incentive to maintain a sharp competitive edge. Orienting foreign investment toward exports was a critical component of Taiwan's strategy, that enabled greater economies of scale through increased production, ensured continual upgrading of the technologies used, and maintained the international competitiveness of the country's production.

The state in Taiwan took an active role in creating backward and forward linkages between foreign and local capital. Local sourcing, subcontracting, and worker training targets were mandated and frequently revised, and the government monitored and enforced them, threatening (and carrying out its threats) to remove protections and incentives for firms that failed to meet their targets.[29] In Nigeria, by contrast, although the same targets are frequently part of the investment package, the government fails to monitor and take action early when targets are clearly not being met. In the motor vehicle assembly industry, for example, foreign firms agreed to progress in stages toward 100 per cent local content but failed to develop programs to implement this strategy. After 30 years of assembly, less than 30 per cent of components are locally procured.

Did Taiwan follow its static comparative advantage in industrial policy (at the heart of the theorizing behind structural adjustment in Africa), as most neoclassical economists suggest? In the period under discussion, the answer is not really. Taiwan provides much more of an example of dynamic comparative advantage. Taiwan's comparative advantage at the start of this period was in its unprocessed agricultural products and its low cost, abundant, educated labor force. During the 1950s and 1960s, however, the Taiwan government used a variety of tools to encourage the development of first, agricultural processing and second, targeted light industries. It introduced measures to speed the economy's adjustment to a predicted rise in real wages once the labor market reached its absorption point. At no point during this period did the country simply liberalize its markets to allow it to seek its static comparative advantage in any neo-classical sense. The approach was multifaceted.

Taiwan stressed both industrial deepening through import substitution for the domestic market, and, simultaneously, supported labor-intensive consumer goods industries producing for export. Recall that the Japanese began the period of primary import substitution in the 1930s, export promotion began in earnest around 1961, and significant liberalization was not imposed until the early 1970s. After World War II, Taiwan had more than twenty-five years of recovery and growth before being subject to significant competition domestically. However, Taiwan avoided the growth of large, protected and rent-seeking industrial sectors by providing incentives for exporting, assisting exporters to become competitive and rewarding them for export performance. When African economies at the early stage of industrialization are faced with full liberalization, the outcome may be efficiency-enhancing for some industries, but fatal for many. The alternative of domestic protection coupled with strong incentives for export allowed Taiwan's industries a protected base from which to reach out to international markets.

THE STATE AS AGENT

In the past decade, the economics literature has rediscovered the state. While much of this literature focuses on the rent-seeking role of the state, others have pointed to the state's critical role as an agent of development. Douglass North (1990) has charted the state's role in establishing institutions – the contracts and property rights that reduce transaction costs and structure an economy's activities. Robert Wade (1990) and Alice Amsden (1989) have pioneered detailed studies of developmental state intervention in East Asia.

The state in Taiwan took an active role as the agent of the country's industrial transformation. Taiwan's industrial development depended heavily on strategic interventions by a government marked by stability, strength (capacity and autonomy) and elite ideological commitment to economic performance. Both by supplying public goods such as agricultural research, paved roads and electricity, and through purposive intervention in the economy, the Taiwan government acted to reduce many of the high transaction and production costs common in developing countries. The role of the state in Taiwan was formed in part by elite values formed in response to the KMT's defeat on the mainland. It was also shaped by a high degree of capacity, and of autonomy.

Stability and economic performance became critical political values in Taiwan following the forced retreat of the Nationalist Chinese leadership to Taiwan after their humiliating exodus from mainland China and exile on an underdeveloped island. The value placed on stability was reflected over and over again in policy choices made by Taiwanese officials. Economic performance became both a goal and a means of legitimization for an authoritarian, nondemocratic government. The broad elite consensus on these values was importantly conditioned by the perceived threat of communist takeover.

Furthermore, the strategy followed by the KMT government reflected the high level of state capacity on the island. The concentration of trained personnel that shifted from China's mainland to the island of Taiwan after 1949 meant that capacity levels in the bureaucracy were unusually high, compared with any African country in its post-colonial period. Thus by 1968, Taiwan had the skilled manpower to establish input–output coefficients for 7000 products, something that would be difficult for most African countries today. US aid helped, as Steve Chan points out: US aid 'was instrumental in promoting the rise of a foreign-educated techno-bureaucratic elite . . . over the opposition of the party old guards and military stalwarts' (Chan, 1990, p. 143). In addition, economic planning was centered in semi-independent agencies, with higher salaries (sometimes double other comparable levels in the government) and other incentives to attract the cream of the graduating classes.

Government planning in Taiwan during early industrialization was done primarily by scientists and engineers. For example, the Industrial Development Bureau received its first economist in 1981, out of a staff of 180 (Wade, 1990, p. 203). K. Y. Yin, an electrical engineer, was the architect of Taiwan's economic reforms in the early 1960s. K. T. Li, Minister of Economic Affairs from 1965–69, and Minister of Finance from 1969–76 was a physicist. In fact, eleven of the country's fourteen previous ministers of economic affairs have been scientists or engineers (Wade, 1990, p. 219). While comparative figures are not available for Africa, it is clear that engineers are a distinct minority in the agencies that provide many African countries with economic advice.[30] Engineers tend to be less bound than economists by the abstractions of economic theory, and, as Ian Little points out, they are more focused on 'the efficacy of forward and backward linkages . . . They are more familiar with what is basically engineering than with rates of return' (Little, 1979, p. 504).[31] This indicates that in developing capacity to support industrial development, it might behoove African governments to invest more in training engineers than neoclassical economists!

Two aspects of state autonomy distinguish Taiwan from most African countries. First, the state in Taiwan gained its autonomy through its origins as an outside power. In part, Taiwan's ability to implement its decisions was due to the origins of KMT political control in a classic 'revolution from above' that removed an entire generation (some 10,000 to 20,000 people) of intelligentia and educated elites and potential opponents in the massacres of 1947. The massacres of 1947 eliminated much of the native intelligentia, while the land reforms of 1949 and the early 1950s eliminated rural elites as an opposition group.

Second, there is little evidence that the state in Taiwan was 'captured' by patronage networks and used to promote their short term interests. Relations between industry (largely dominated by native Taiwanese) and the state (largely dominated by mainland Chinese) have not been particularly close. Business associations in Taiwan have had little influence on the direction of state policy, aside from a consultative role; labor organizations are sharply restricted, and the predominance of small, decentralized industries makes organization difficult in any case. Although state planners encouraged the development of an indigenous capitalist class, the state has remained separate from the capitalist class, steering investment and rewarding performance without the constraint of political indebtedness.

The distinct differences between state capacity and state autonomy in Taiwan compared with Africa may have critical implications, limiting the relevance of some of Taiwan's experience to most African states, which tend, Migdal (1988) argues, to be the opposite of Taiwan's strong state, weak society. This blanket criticism aside, there are many examples of purposive and developmental state actions across the subcontinent, with the experiences of Mauritius – as highlighted among the four African states in this chapter – as only one example. In addition, the entrenched interests formed by the relatively brief import substitution era in Sub-Saharan African may not be as difficult to dislodge as those in place since the 1930s in Latin America. Finally, efforts to build up the capacity – through higher level technical training, graduate education, and other means – of governments and elites in other parts of the world has sometimes resulted in value and ideology shifts; the 'Chicago Boys' of Chile are one example of how this has worked in practice.

CONCLUSIONS: LESSONS FROM TAIWAN'S INDUSTRIALIZATION, 1952–1972

Taiwan in 1952 and Sub-Saharan Africa today are different in many important respects, both in areas that this chapter has been able to address such as colonial history, experience of foreign aid, infrastructure, and agricultural foundations, and in areas outside the scope of this chapter, such as cultural heritage and international economic conditions. Despite these differences, however, this chapter has argued that some elements of Taiwan's industrialization policies bear further study by African policy-makers, both because some elements seem to confirm recommendations that are commonly part of stabilization efforts but often rejected by African governments (deficit reduction, positive real interest rates, devaluation), and because others conflict with the liberalization conditions frequently attached to structural adjustment programs.

As this review has pointed out, there are quite different preconditions for industrialization in Taiwan and in Sub-Saharan Africa. Japanese colonial investments produced a stronger agricultural sector, more extensive infrastructure, and more educated citizens than anything the European colonial powers left behind in Africa. An extensive, government-imposed land reform preceded the export push, providing industrial development with a base of equitable asset (land) distribution, and spreading the benefits of growth quite evenly. The state made considerable investments in agriculture, raising productivity and supporting diversification while simultaneously relying on agriculture as an important source of tax revenues in support of industrial development. United States foreign aid was more extensive, more oriented toward infrastructure and balance of payments support, than aid received by African countries, much of which was spent on well-meant but ineffective integrated rural development and social sector programs. Public investment in roads and railways reduced distances between town and village, enabling farm families to keep pace with urban dwellers, supplementing their incomes through factory employment.

As the decade of the 1990s moves to its midpoint, African countries remain mired in a vicious circle of debt, low productivity, low skill levels, crumbling infrastructure, and poverty. The gap between Africa and Asia continues to widen, and critics both inside and outside the Bretton Woods institutions are calling for revisions of standard structural adjustment strategies. What might Africa 'learn' from Taiwan's experience?

First, while African countries are called on to liberalize 'in the *midst* of macroeconomic instability' (Rodrik, 1990, p. 933), Taiwan followed a different strategy. The sequencing of policy reforms in Taiwan emphasized the gradual, but sustainable, achievement of stability before trade or financial system liberalization, price deregulation, or privatization. The government concentrated on reducing inflation (1949–1952) and government fiscal deficits (1952–1962), and implemented repeated, gradual devaluations through the 1950s (from NT\$5 to NT\$40 to the US\$) before maintaining a fixed rate at NT\$40 after 1960. Macroeconomic stability including managed exchange rates and tight control over government spending and money supply throughout the twenty years under discussion.

Second, Taiwan's industrial support policies involved an extensive government role, while structural adjustment programs are predicated on reducing the role of the state. The government maintained a monopoly of foreign exchange and banking, and set fixed interest rates and exchange rates. The government also maintained extensive public ownership of strategic industries, although it concentrated on increasing their efficiency. Taiwan did not cleave solely to its static comparative advantage in cheap labor and agriculture, but rather followed the model of Japan by investing in the creation of a new, dynamic comparative advantage in skilled labor, manufacturing and electronics technology.

Third, Taiwan's export-oriented regime was not 'liberal' but highly protected, with a variety of tariff and non-tariff barriers, quantitative restrictions and outright bans that rewarded performance, enhanced market stability for producers, and lowered start-up risks. Given the inability of neoclassical theory to establish a link between liberalization and the rate of growth, as opposed to the level of allocative efficiency (Rodrik, 1990), it may be that an illiberal regime such as Taiwan's actually supports growth, perhaps in the 'murky' area of X-efficiency and 'learning by doing', as suggested by Ron Findlay.

Fourth, because of the generous levels of aid provided by the US during Taiwan's period of stabilization and deficit reduction, public investment levels did not have to be curtailed, but were in fact enhanced. Education, transport infrastructure, and power supply all improved during stabilization. Levels of aid available to current adjusters are generally much lower, and are unable to cushion the forced reduction in government spending. However, other aspects of Taiwan's reforms are similar to structural adjustment programs in Africa.

Fifth, as structural adjustment often recommends, Taiwan did devalue the NT$ as part of an effort to shift from import substitution with overvalued exchange rates to import substitution with export promotion. However, the nominal exchange rate was tightly controlled by the government, which kept it at realistic levels, although at times, it was allowed to become slightly undervalued.

Sixth, interest rates in Taiwan were high in real terms, similar to recommendations in structural reform packages that interest rates be set at positive real levels. Positive and high rates undoubtedly assisted the high savings rate and local resource mobilization, while not subsidizing capital and assisting industry to develop in a labor-intensive manner.

Seventh, assisted by generous aid from the U.S., and driven by the fear of hyperinflation, the government in Taiwan rejected deficit spending strategies and made efforts to 'balance the budget' through direct and indirect taxation, bringing about a budget surplus from 1964 onward.

Taiwan has the advantage of proximity to Japan, a model frequently visited and closely studied by government planners and business people alike. Sub-Saharan Africa has no such model, with the possible exception of post-apartheid South Africa. African countries will lack the advantage Taiwan had when its export push began in the friendlier international environment of the 1960s and 1970s. The international economy remains in recession, and demand for Africa's commodity exports is poor. Finally, the state in Taiwan is one of considerable capacity and a high degree of autonomy. All of these factors are ones that make Taiwan's path a difficult one to emulate, and this chapter does not propose such emulation, but rather encourages reflection.

Notes

1. An earlier version of this paper was presented at the 1991 Annual Meeting of the African Studies Association, St. Louis, MO. This paper was originally drafted while the author held an International Affairs Fellowship from the Council on Foreign Relations. Howard Stein and Tyler Biggs made helpful comments on an earlier draft of this article. Alemayehu Mengistu Wondim and Nikolaos Makris provided research

assistance. The author is to blame for any errors or misinterpretations that remain.

2. Figures for Côte d'Ivoire are for 1986–87; for Ghana 1988–89; for Botswana 1985–86 (World Bank, 1992a, pp. 276–7).
3. Although the spoken Japanese and Chinese languages are not related, Japanese is written using Chinese characters, as well as an additional set of phonetic letters. This eased the transition from literacy in Japanese to literacy in Chinese.
4. Economic aid commitments ended in 1965; disbursements in 1968. Military aid continued until the break in official relations in 1979.
5. The US provided an additional $2.5 billion in military supplies and equipment, almost entirely financed by grants.
6. Although an independent study commissioned in 1966 by the US aid agency calculated that aid had 'doubled the annual rate of growth of Taiwan's GNP, quadrupled the annual growth of per capita GNP and cut thirty years from the time needed to attain 1964 living standards' (Jacoby, 1966, p. 152), others are more skeptical as to the utility of the model used to project these results, saying that 'the causal mechanism is not at all clear' (Ranis, 1979, p. 246). We can safely assume, however, that the net effect of this aid was positive, although Taiwan's later success is not a direct function of the aid (other countries receiving similar magnitudes have not performed nearly as strongly).
7. The amount varied depending on the quality of the land. The ceiling for medium quality paddy land was 2.9 hectares.
8. Amsden (1979) argues that 'Widespread emphasis on risk-reduction is evident in Taiwan's agricultural policies and seems to be one of its important lessons' (p. 357).
9. At the same time, however, rice consumption was also decreasing as higher incomes underwrote a shift from cereals to higher food value foods as a larger share of diet.
10. In absolute terms, the value of unprocessed agricultural exports like mushrooms and asparagus rose from NT$324 million in 1952 to NT$8145 million in 1972, but their relative value fell from 22.1 per cent of total exports to only 6.8 per cent of total exports (EPC, 1975). Processed agricultural product exports also rose in value from NT$1025 in 1952 to NT$ 11822 in 1972, but fell from 69.8 per cent of all exports to 9.9 per cent, illustrating the shift from natural resource-based to labor-based light industrialization.
11. According to Gustav Ranis, 'government policy in the 1950s, supported by US project aid allocations, was to maintain capacity well ahead of demand, to distribute it throughout the island, and perhaps most importantly, to aim for realistic (that is, no profit, no subsidy) overall pricing levels while maintaining a uniform set of rates as between rural and urban areas' (Ranis, 1979, p. 215).
12. According to the World Bank, 1991 tariffs for electricity in 'developing countries', average US$0.04/kwh, and only cover some two-fifths of the cost of supply (World Bank, 1992a, p. 117).
13. In a number of countries with active adjustment programs there has been significant declines in enrollment. In Tanzania, for example, the

percentage of school age children enrolled in primary schools dropped from 72 to 63 per cent between 1985 and 1989 (World Bank, 1992a, p. 117).

14. Although overtime pay was stipulated in the labor code, it was not always enforced. Likewise, in 1973, a requirement of one day off every seven days was not being observed by 37 per cent of inspected factories. A minimum wage law was on the books, but the level was lower than the average daily rate for manufacturing (Galenson, 1979, p. 407).

15. Most firms provided subsidized meals and free or subsidized dorms; many provided free transport and uniforms.

16. At the time of independence, government workers in French West Africa were being paid at the same levels as in France, and much higher than the local private sector was able to pay.

17. This may vary by government unit. For example, the tobacco monopoly offered its employees subsidized loans at four per cent covering up to 40 per cent of a house purchase. In 1975, beyond the period under discussion, the national government started a housing program for workers (Galenson 1979, pp. 421–40).

18. According to Robert Wade (1990), until 1980, the 'powerful and autonomous central bank. . .was not even legally accountable to anyone other than the president, including the cabinet and legislature' (p. 209).

19. According to the World Bank, which advocates outward orientation, an inward-oriented trade regime is characterized by 'controls, high and variable tariff protection and quantitative restrictions and administrative allocation', while an outward-oriented regime 'emphasizes linkages to the world economy through exports and enhanced import capacity' (Bhattacharya and Linn, 1988, p. xi).

20. Scott (1979) notes that as of July 1972, half of the 'controlled' commodities were shifted to 'permissible' status (p. 331).

21. R. H. Erzan et al. (n.d.) calculate that countries in sub-Saharan Africa in the 1980s had the highest rate of import license requirements, advanced import deposits and Central Bank authorization requirements, leading to the highest overall rate of nontariff barriers among developing country groups.

22. These lower rates, it must be emphasized, are still high in real terms compared with other industrialized countries.

23. However, manufacturers had to pay a fee for a bank guarantee to cover the duty (Scott, 1979, p. 326).

24. Nash (n.d.) comments that 'exporters must employ special firms or a great deal of staff time to process each request' (p. 30).

25. Free trade zones have also been established in Togo and Cameroon.

26. For example, investors inside the EPZ could use imports duty free in manufacturing export products. Outside the zone, or the bonded factories, manufacturers had to pay duty on imported materials, then apply for a tax rebate after exporting.

27. Private foreign investment between 1952 and 1961 averaged only US$3 million a year, compared with foreign aid of some US$67 million a year. In the period from 1962 to 1972, foreign investment averaged US$59

million yearly, or, with overseas Chinese investment included, US$134 million a year (CEPD, 1989).

28. Interestingly, most of the technical cooperation projects approved in Taiwan (73 per cent) were between Japanese firms and Taiwanese companies, while US firms tended to 'remain relatively insulated from domestic firms' (Ranis 1979, p. 251) indicating that the nationality of the foreign investor may make a difference in African countries.

29. As a reflection of this, the import content in Taiwan's exports rose consistently over the period under discussion (from 22.9 per cent in 1961 to 63 per cent in 1976), a finding that is probably also true for Japan and Korea (Kuo, Ranis and Fei, 1981, p. 118).

30. While I have no figures to support this, I am confident that to the extent that African countries rely on the World Bank for industrial strategy, they are relying on economists, who far outnumber the engineers at 1818 H Street.

31. For a similar finding in Japan, see G. Allen (1981.) 'Industrial Policy and Innovation in Japan,' in C. Carter (ed.) *Industrial Policy and Innovation.* (London: Heinemann), cited in Wade, 1990, p. 220.

6 Colonialism and Entrepreneurship in Africa and Hong Kong: A Comparative Perspective[1]

S. Gordon Redding and Simon Tam

INTRODUCTION

The contrast in rates of economic growth between post-colonial African states in general and a number of their equivalents in Asia is dramatic. Between 1980 and 1989 economies grew by 10.4 per cent per year in East and Southeast Asia with GNP per capita increasing annually by 6.3 per cent. Over the same period the sub-Sahara African states recorded −1.2 per cent as an average (World Bank, 1990b; 1991).

Apart from China, which was growing from a low base, the fastest Asian growths during the 1980s were recorded by South Korea, Hong Kong, Taiwan and Singapore, countries which depend heavily on indigenous entrepreneurship as a stimulus. The variation in the degree to which societies display a proclivity to foster entrepreneurship is the issue addressed by this chapter and it begins by taking the case of colonial Hong Kong, and its contrast with traditional China. Implications for other post-colonial societies are then considered. African comparisons are treated only briefly in this paper which concentrates mainly on analysing Chinese economic behaviour.

That the Overseas Chinese, especially in Hong Kong and Taiwan, have achieved economic success at the societal level, on the basis of family business, is undeniable (Redding, 1990; Steinhoff, 1980). That the success has reached high levels is equally obvious from the 1990 per capita GDP data of $US13000 and 8000 respectively. These are thus success stories of societies, fundamentally Chinese in nature, which have transformed themselves into significant industrial powers starting

183

from unpromising initial conditions, and affected by colonial experience, one under British governance and the other under Japanese.

The initial conditions include a legacy of Chinese history in which the entrepreneurial drive had been continually suppressed, occasionally crushed, and for centuries denied legitimacy as a basis for claiming respect and position in society. The colonial context, to be considered here for Hong Kong, introduced changes which effected a transformation. This paper is about those changes, the African equivalent, and the nature of the transformation.

In the background lie two major fields of academic debate. Firstly, is the question of the long-term stagnation of Chinese society (Weber, 1951; Needham, 1956; Jones, 1990; Elvin, 1973; etc.) in which an emerging consensus attributes the relative decline to a set of institutions designed to perpetuate central control, although many other supplementary causes are brought into the account. Secondly, is the question of the success of the Overseas Chinese and the puzzle of their capacities being seemingly released when away from their homeland (Redding, 1990; Limlingan, 1986; Wu and Wu, 1980; Clad, 1989). The case of Hong Kong's development and transformation provides an opportunity to illuminate both of these major fields of debate, and to reflect on lessons relevant elsewhere.

In the analysis it will be apparent that certain continuities exist in the way Chinese culture and tradition carry through into the present day entrepreneurial firm (Redding 1990). On the other hand, certain key adjustments have also taken place in the surrounding structures and institutions of society which have produced a new totality. We are reminded here of Eisenstadt's (1968) critique of the Weberian argument connecting values and development when he proposed the notion of the transformative capacities which certain elements may have in releasing the potential for development.

In studying the transformation of Hong Kong society, and the role of colonialism in that process, we shall define the configuration of forces which has conserved the stability of Chinese society historically and observe the dismantling of that structure and its replacement with a dynamic alternative. The period over which this transformation occurred is the last 150 years, although the full release of the potential has been visible only in the last thirty as Hong Kong absorbed many of the traditional functions of Shanghai. A study of the structures of entrepreneurship and the role of the colonial state is directly relevant to Africa for both understanding the different colonial legacy and in considering models of entrepreneurship that can possibly be emulated.

THE TRADITIONAL CONTEXT OF BUSINESS IN CHINA

China is the world's oldest state with a traceable history as an integrated society going back over 3000 years. The basic principles of design for the state superstructure are ancient and they have changed little for around two thousand years. In 1842, when Hong Kong was taken over by Britain, the two societies followed different paths of development. In simple terms what the design of the traditional Chinese state has always entailed is:

(a) a powerful central figure embodying the state as emperor or functional equivalent;
(b) a state superstructure, originally the mandarinate and now the party, which maintains its legitimacy by seizing a monopoly on the interpretation of the state ideology, and which is heavily concerned with the maintenance of order and status quo;
(c) a concern with control and hierarchy;
(d) centralization of power;
(e) disenfranchisement of the major part of the population and separation between them and government;
(f) widespread patrimonialism;
(g) widespread resort to interpersonal linkages as a means of co-ordinating trust in a society which lacks the mechanisms of a civil society based on authoritative self-governing institutions to foster co-operation. (Such as the councils of free cities or professional bodies.)

The main body of society was traditionally divided into four categories in a hierarchy, descending through scholar, farmer, artisan and lastly merchant. Above these the mandarinate, aloof from contact with the minutiae of the daily life of the people, expressed the will of the emperor. The maintenance of order operated through three main forces. Firstly, the precepts of Confucianism left each family as a self-governing unit, and the father in that family as responsible for the conformity of members to the Confucian rules for behaviour. Secondly, the processes of socialization led to each person adopting the behaviours prescribed for specific societal roles (e.g. the filial son, the dutiful wife, etc.) and led also to the sublimation of individual interest. Thirdly, the state was prepared to use terror in the form of severe exemplary punishments, to keep people in line.

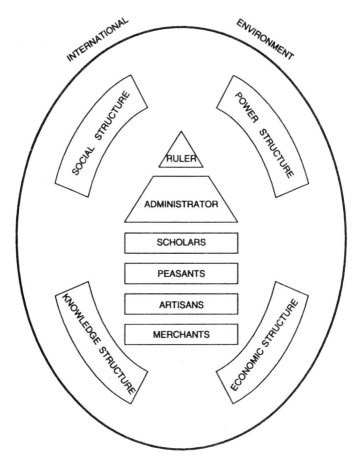

Source: Tam, 1992.

Figure 6.1 A Framework for Exploring the Contextual Structure of Chinese Business

The end product has been relative stability at the cost of relative stagnation, and the forces at work may be seen in Figure 6.1. This proposes a set of four surrounding structures which traditionally maintained the society in equilibrium, a set of forces whose interaction also depended on sealing off the state from external influence.

The four forces are identified as:

1. The **power** structure and in particular the traditions of the centralization and personalization of authority.
2. The **economic** structure and in particular the role of the state bureaucracy.
3. The **social** structure, especially the Confucian design of roles and relationships.
4. The **knowledge** structure, in particular the exclusivity and conformist nature of knowledge.

These forces reciprocated and reinforced one another and were thus able to perpetuate their dominance and their control over the basic components of the social system. A consideration of this equilibrating process will be preceded by a brief description of each of the forces.

The Power Structure

Chinese historical experience, and consequent political philosophy confirmed the need for strong central control as a means of counteracting the disintegration of the state, an ever-present concern in such a huge empire. A logical extension of this central concern with control was the privatization of absolute power (Tsui, 1988) and the perfection of methods for its perpetuation by acting forcefully to prevent the emergence of alternatives.

In these circumstances it became virtually impossible for decentralization to occur, and the mandarin bureaucracy held power only as an agency of the emperor. Outcomes of this were that accountability for 'performance' was a matter of upwards reporting and not downwards accountability to society at large; also disloyalty was severely punished.

The dysfunctions of extreme centralization inevitably followed, one of which was the perpetuation of the rigidities required to maintain order in the social system, and the conformities required in the knowledge system.

The Economic Structure

China's traditional economic structure gradually developed from its early base in the local marketing of farm produce, via the gradual emergence of a national economy for exchange, into a stable but premodern economic system in which the following features were paramount.

1. The atomization of civilian economic power and the high concentration of imperial power in key industries.
2. Intervention by government firms and other agencies in the workings of the system.
3. Subduing of the social status of merchants.
4. Creation of an atmosphere of uncertainty due to unpredictable taxation and occasional confiscation.
5. Coupling of ownership and family structures (in a context of mistrust of alternative forms of bonding).
6. Vertical division of labour following the elaborate hierarchical order of society.
7. Tight boundary restrictions on various economic functions.

The outcome of this set of forces was a series of inhibitions to co-ordination. Commercial and industrial activities could not be integrated to produce organizations of any significant size outside the state sector. Small scale business remained the private sector norm, and small scale trading its usual means of expression. Integration took place in the process of making commerce work for the national market but only on a very limited scale, and the integration and management of the production function never occurred indigenously (Elvin, 1973).

It is no accident that the typical economic unit was the family, as the family's central place in society was also strongly emphasized by the Confucian precepts of the ideological structure, the related social structure, and the divide-and-rule motivations which lay behind the power structure.

The Social Structure

From an early date the state ideology in China was Confucianism, a social doctrine which legitimizes the retention of a hierarchy of power relations on the basis that proper role compliance by each incumbent will result in a stable society moderated with ideals about benevolence and tolerance. The structure rests on extensive socialization, and subsequent conformity, by individuals in families. It is noteworthy that in such a context, expressions of what in the Western world is recognized as individualism were not encouraged. Nor did there exist a system of ideals which provided the individual person with an ethical background against which he was encouraged to reach his or her personal interpretation of appropriate behavior. Appropriateness of behavior was judged by those monopolizing the interpretation of the Confucian doctrine and such judges were always hierarchically superior, whether head of household, mandarin, or eventually emperor.

The perpetuation of Confucianism as the dominating ideology was maintained via the state examination system which controlled entry to the ruling elite. The rewards for membership were then such as to turn all mandarins into guardians of the ideology and in turn of the social structure to which it gave rise. Conservatism was strongly built and constantly reinforced in China.

The Knowledge Structure

The ideological or knowledge base of Chinese society was traditionally a possession and an instrument of the state. In the population at large, scholars were few. Only in periods where central power declined did knowledge become more widely dispersed, but such periods were rare, the more normal position being one where official state doctrine on most matters reigned supreme. This inevitably narrowed the focus of knowledge development and kept out all but the most powerful new perspectives, examples of the latter, for instance, being Buddhism from the sixth century onwards, Western cosmological science in the seventeenth century and Western technology in the nineteenth century.

This is not to say that the official Confucian ideology was unable to adapt. It did, in fact, respond to a number of forces for change and it succeeded in absorbing a number of competing ideologies such as Taoism, Buddhism and even (although less successfully) Western organizational skills (Feuerwerker, 1984). It was nevertheless characterized by an insistence on monopoly over thinking and expression for most of Chinese history, deviation from which usually entailed harsh punishment from the state for those involved. Such a unitary form of thinking inevitably reduced the diversity of knowledge and limited the realm of discourse.

The Confucian ideological system thus provided an all-embracing set of interpretive principles and critical standards and in doing so served to smooth the transitions between dynasties which might otherwise have been revolutionary. Its impact on society was both wide and deep. It designed the key relationships, the right behaviours, the law, academic standards, teaching, policies in many fields, and at base the interpretation of reality. Its effect was to politicize intellectual life, and in doing so to deny it full freedom. It served the power structure, it legitimized the social structure, and it constrained the economic structure.

THE CONTEXTUAL CONFIGURATION OF TRADITIONAL CHINESE SOCIETY

These four main elements of traditional Chinese society, the power, knowledge, social and economic structures, interacted constantly to reinforce one another. They served to reduce variety within the state and thus permitted control. Their capacity to create conformity resulted in the rigid stability of the role structures (depicted at the centre of Figure 6.1) and the extremely long survival of that design.

Each element cross-validated the others. The power structure lived off the ideology which, in turn, it worked to maintain and vice versa. The social structure extended the state power structure and interpreted the ideology at a lower level, thus serving to support both. The economic structure and the state were influenced by the ideology and meshed naturally with the familistic social structure.

The overall theme was one of concentration of power, whether political, economic or ideological, and homogenization of structure to reduce deviance and variety. Every sphere was characterized by vertical domination and by elaborate vertical differentiation (Fei, 1939). Even morality was politicized (Pye, 1985) and inevitably so, too, was law.

As the most completely political construction of social reality, the Chinese state succeeded in driving out alternative possibilities, and in stabilizing to a remarkable degree its social division of labour. Part of this stabilizing rested on the safety device of internal vertical mobility via the examination process into the elite.

In this context the world of the merchant had very limited horizons. Confined to the base of society in terms of the status hierarchy, there were no upwards channels to encourage mobility. The mercantile world was closed off to the most intelligent members and society channelled its best talent into the world of conformist scholarship. The reward system did not encourage entrepreneurship, and the state superstructure, designed to prevent the accumulation of influence by any bodies not within its control, would soon find means of commandeering any undue accumulation of wealth which it might see as threatening (Lau and Kwan, 1988; Zeng, 1983). The ultimate aim of the thinking merchant was to escape from his caste (Godley, 1981).

It would take a massive force to uncouple and dismantle this rigid configuration and to supplant it with an alternative modern form of society. That force in Hong Kong was British colonialism and the process of de-configuration and transformation is now considered.

THE DE-CONFIGURATION OF CHINESE SOCIETY'S CONTEXTUAL STRUCTURE IN HONG KONG: THE IMPACT OF BRITISH COLONIALISM

The argument to be made here is that the injection of an alternative form of governance from Britain to Hong Kong triggered off a de-configuration effect in the contextual environment of this ceded territory, thereby altering the context of entrepreneurship in Hong Kong. In this process, the Chinese power structure was replaced, ideological monopoly was broken, state domination over economic structure subdued and the social structure no longer subjected to the same set of moulding influences. In the contextual structure as a whole, the chain of mutual reinforcement and collective support between the various components was destroyed. The society was thus unfrozen and was made ready to change (Lewin, 1951). In many ways, the historical momentum still carries itself, but to survive, various fragments of these components would have to meet with the test of environmental selection (Aldrich, 1979). While the details of this selection process still await further research, it is now quite apparent that certain legacies of the traditional structure survived. The Chinese members of the society have presumably found them functional and found that they could build an alternative mercantile system around them. The process was not necessarily conscious or deliberate, but by trial and error certain traditional methods of social and economic organization were carried forward into the modern world and, although subject to constant modification and challenge, have tended to remain representative of the Hong Kong version of Overseas Chinese capitalist society. These main legacies are as follows:

1. The tight coupling of ownership and control, and the consequent paternalistic power structure with the resulting dependence of subordinates, insecurity, and required loyalty.
2. The central role of family in determining allegiances, network structures, and organizational boundaries.
3. The use of personalism in facilitating transactions.

4.   A didactic, moral, character of leadership (Pye, 1985; Silin, 1976).
5.   The vertical differentiation of the social order (Hofstede, 1980).

Much was therefore brought forward from Chinese social history. Many instincts were preserved and it could thus be argued that the resulting success of what finally emerged as a design for society was due to the peculiar combination of British and Chinese social philosophies, and the capacity of that combination to release forces to an extent which neither system on its own could sponsor. Arguably the key driving force for societal improvement was a quite remarkable and widely distributed entrepreneurial impetus which the new structures were able to channel, encourage, and assist.

What then were these new structures and how did they supplant the powerful and rigid traditions of the Chinese social order? And how do such structures compare with those adopted by British regimes in Africa?

In 1841 when a group of merchants persuaded the British government somewhat reluctantly to act on their behalf and establish a new colony, a set of forces began to penetrate the originally ceded small territory which in 1898 were extended into the hinterland of the 'New Territories'. These forces were a local interpretation of Victorian principles of public administration and social order and they were coloured by nineteenth century philosophies of free trade and laissez-faire capitalism. They introduced a new form of order into an essentially Chinese territory, and were underpinned by a new set of ethics and ideals. They were also backed by an occasionally demonstrated military and technical superiority capable of inspiring in its victims both awe and resentment, the implications of which are still being played out.

Over the nineteenth century, the following changes slowly took shape and were institutionalized:

1.   The wishes of the people were brought more into account, as the colonial government sought to exercise a benevolent and consultative form of autocracy.
2.   State intervention was replaced by a government policy which limited intervention in the world of business.
3.   In place of state policies which harnessed and disparaged merchants, the new ideals of mercantilism provided respect for the businessman.

4. The state control of upwards mobility via the examination system was eliminated.
5. Merchants previously deprived of many rights in Chinese law were given full equality before the law.
6. State monopolies in major commodities no longer applied.
7. The traditional controls over artisan sub-group membership, exercised by state registration, were replaced by freedom of employment choice and social mobility.
8. Market regulation by local administration was replaced by market regulation via universal law.
9. Expropriation and confiscation were eliminated by the introduction of property rights.
10. Confucianism lost its monopoly influence as Western philosophies made their inroads into the Chinese world.

The result of these changes in institutional structure, and their interaction with traditional elements selected for continuity, was a long term fundamental shift in the structure of society. The traditional Chinese role categories were dismantled and replaced by a society with three interconnected and mutually supportive elements. These were: (a) the British merchants; (b) the new class of Chinese merchants; and (c) the labourers and artisans who slowly created new collectivities for themselves (Chan, 1991).

The principal change of interest here is the emergence of the new Chinese merchant class. This took advantage of the alternative definitions of status accorded by the mercantilist ethic and by the demise or irrelevance of the scholar–gentry class structure. The pursuit of wealth became respectable. The pursuit of bureaucratic office via scholarship became not just irrelevant but actually impossible as British officials monopolized the heights of the civil service. The contest for status shifted to a new battleground.

THE AFRICAN COLONIAL EXPERIENCE

British colonialism in Africa was, as elsewhere, an act of domination, in which the political process served that end (Worsley, 1984, p. 285). An important corollary was that national identity was subjugated and the ensuing political entities were neither states nor nations, but rather political dependencies and aggregations of varied ethnic sub-groups. The sharing of heritage was rare, and so too the sharing of interests and the sharing of agreement on the indigenous source of authority. The typical colonial state was thus highly segmented, especially ethnically. Tanzania had for instance three hundred pre-colonial tribes. Reducing the mosaic to broader categories would normally still yield major divisions, as with the three broad ethnic categories within Nigeria.

It must also be acknowledged that the majority of Sub-Saharan colonial African states were essentially agricultural. Industry did not develop in them except that of primary extraction. Commerce was not highly elaborated and a strong business culture did not exist indigenously.

British colonial administration operated via an elite class of administrators. They were socialized through public school education and upper middle class upbringing. They were remarkably homogeneous in terms of values and attitudes, and these may be summarized as

1. A sense of innate superiority and paternalism.
2. A strong and ethical sense of duty and loyalty to the system they represented.
3. A capacity for high levels of independence and reliability.
4. A snobbish concern with status which included a disdain for the world of business, especially trading and manufacturing.
5. Often a moralistic or religious anti-materialism.

They are well described in James Morris's study of the British Empire:

> They were the children of a unique culture, that of the English public school, with its celibate discipline, its classical loyalties, its emphasis on self-reliance, team spirit, delegated responsibility, Christian duty and stoic control . . . If [the public school system] was intellectually narrowing and chauvinist, well, this was an Empire that survived by the separateness of its rulers, their conviction that what they did was right . . . His inability to grasp the aspirations of Indians, Africans or Malays stemmed from his absolute certainty that their whole manner of thought or way of life was, through no real fault of their own, misguided. (Morris, 1968, p. 220)

A common theme of British colonial administration was the achievement of self-sufficiency at low budget levels (Ehrlich, 1973). The resulting parsimony precluded the kinds of infrastructure investment which would encourage commerce and industry. Common also was a paternalistic concern to protect native landowners from invasion by outside capitalists and anti- capitalist intervention was not uncommon.

In some cases, such as Kenya, settlers could band together in sufficient numbers to challenge the administrative hegemony, but the more usual pattern was one of petty bureaucratic controls which choked initiative (McCarthy, 1982). These combined with the parsimony to discourage the emergence of an articulated economy, and the same factors could be said to have some bearing on the failure of an indigenous entrepreneurial class to appear. In 1962, for instance, Tanganyika had only 137 local companies registered in manufacturing (Tanzania Government, 1968, p. 61). Hong Kong, with less than a third of the population had at the same date 7,500.

COMPARING AFRICAN AND HONG KONG COLONIALISM

Three questions arise from the facts outlined so far. Firstly, was the colonial administrative behaviour fundamentally different in the two contexts? Secondly, were the contexts themselves the main determinants of the difference in outcomes? Thirdly, are there factors independent of the colonial experience which make for variations in the production of entrepreneurs? In order to consider these issues we must now examine in more detail the workings of the Hong Kong system. In particular this requires an understanding of the nature of aspiration in Chinese society and the peculiarly high significance of ownership.

The Hong Kong economy rests almost exclusively on family business and a vast number of tiny firms. In the Chinese sector virtually all firms remain under family control even at large size and they display the predictable features of nepotism, restricted use of professionals, and personalism in decision making. This is not to say that they are inefficient for they have devised ways of surmounting their scale limitations by elaborate processes of network co-ordination between clusters of firms (Redding and Tam, 1985; Tam, 1990).

What is of interest in the context of this paper is the extent to which ownership remains the central guiding principle, and the question is whether there is a particular Chinese view of it which means that their path of development is not one of separating ownership and control, as occurred in the West and in Japan. If the urge to ownership is especially potent, it also has clear implications for entrepreneurial behaviour.

It can be argued in this case that a residual of Chinese tradition is at work and that the ownership of a firm became, in the colonial context, the predominant route to power and status in society. There were virtually no other means of vertical mobility. A related outcome is that the retention of the ownership role, and the power connected to it, requires the holder to fend off aspirants from lower levels by severely restricting their access to sources of authority within the firm. This leaves such aspirants with only one route to status, which is to leave the subordinate position, create their own firm, and then behave to protect the status gained, by guarding it.

The residual which is at work here is the tradition of unequal power relations, a feature of society taken to exquisite points of refinement in China, and still a matter of deeply inbred sensitivity. Connected with this are norms which sanction the self-actualization and fulfillment of the superior while denying the parallel needs of the subordinate. The non-assertiveness and self-denial of the subordinate is also part of the same value system.

The view of power is thus traditional and derives from the configuration noted earlier, and so too is the view of status as bringing with it special rights. The basis for status acquisition shifted from scholarship to commerce but the meanings surrounding the idea of status did not change.

The resulting special nature of ownership in the Hong Kong Chinese case is a composite of characteristics which appear essentially to exaggerate the power discrepancies found elsewhere. In practice this means:

(a)   the owner works in wide opportunity space denied to others;
(b)   the owner monopolizes resource allocation;
(c)   the owner's opinion is disproportionally weighty in decision-making;
(d)   it is the owner's definition of reality which dominates;
(e)   the owner makes tacit claim to superior knowledge by using a didactic style of interaction with subordinates;
(f)   resource allocation is conducted in a context of the dependence of subordinates and the bondage of strong reciprocity norms.

In such a context, the driving out of talent from subordinate positions into the acquiring of parallel ownership status is a fundamental and normal process in the social system. Hence the constant bubbling up of entrepreneurial resources from the base of the economy, one of the world's most dynamic societies.

Our argument so far has been that the institutional changes introduced in the nineteenth century to Hong Kong broke the stranglehold of traditional Chinese social structures by permitting and encouraging a new basis for the allocation of status and then providing infrastructure support which fostered a mercantile climate in which the pursuit of that status could be encouraged. This does not however fully explain the unusual dynamism and constant renewal which the entrepreneurial world of business in Hong Kong displays, or the sense of an expanding universe of entrepreneurs.

To understand this, a more detailed analysis of its current dynamics is required, and these are illustrated in Figure 6.2.

This model proposes four analytical components, the flows of influence between which explain the nature and the intensity of the entrepreneurial phenomenon in Hong Kong.

The creation of a firm by an individual is an act of upward mobility by the rules of this society. It is also perhaps even more significantly a search for wealth and security, often in the face of uncertainty and threat and it is pursued thus with ingenuity and determination. Under the normal conditions of Hong Kong Chinese society, the firm will grow to a point where it becomes socially a store of unbalanced energy and suppressed talent. Power distance will be maintained, and paradoxically will serve as a model for later emulation.

This relative expansion of power at the top and its compression at the base will intensify the urge to upward mobility by highlighting the essential truth that the only route to power is via ownership. (It is of course now possible to escape into the professions, the government, or multinationals but they are outside the scope of this analysis, and in any case have high entry barriers especially educational.)

The pressure on the individual to join the elite stratum of owners then triggers off a fission and refusion cycle. The fission is of two kinds: that where partners break from each other to form individual firms, an impetus which might stem from inequity of ownership, but which could also be attributable to inter-personal tensions; secondly is the breaking out of employees to form new firms, and this source forms the majority of cases.

In the former case the sharing of power seems especially problematic and hard to perpetuate. The idea of one boss is deeply ingrained and usually eventually reached in practice.

198

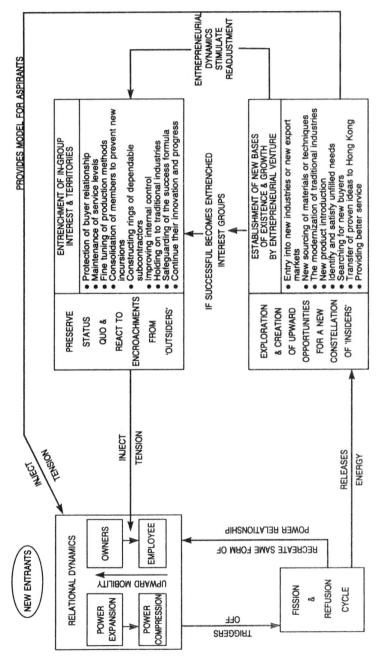

Figure 6.2 The Link between Social and Entrepreneurial Dynamics

In the Chinese business context, firms are found to be associated in network form (Redding and Tam, 1985). A newly fissioned firm, in isolation, therefore leads an uncertain and precarious existence. It would be very difficult for it to inch its way into the core of existing networks, because each is composed of firms having exclusive ties and prioritized commitments. A new firm stays at the periphery. Such a state of affairs is seen as highly undesirable. In order to bring in some measure of external control and reliability, there is found to be a tendency for a new firm to actively promote the formation of newer firms which depend on it, thereby in the long run enabling itself to be surrounded by a ring of dependable units. Hence the refusion process ensures the recreation of new networks. But this process produces system effects, because most of these newer firms will be formed by fission, that is, by facilitating employees to become employers.

This is where the society's main creativity is exercised as new entrants find opportunities in the economy which they can exploit and search for new bases of existence. The routes they follow include

- entry into new industries, or new export markets
- new sourcing of materials or techniques
- the modernization of traditional industries
- new product introduction
- providing better service
- searching for new buyers.

In this process they are competing with the firms and networks already in existence as well as the new starters, and the tensions implicit in this will raise the level of their competitiveness to a point where it puts pressure on the set of firms already entrenched in an industry. The defence of the status quo by these entrenched firms will cause them to defend their positions vigorously and to protect their networks from incursion. They will attempt to prevent encroachment by the new-comers and the techniques adopted include

- protection of buyer relationships
- maintenance of service levels
- fine-tuning of production methods
- consolidation of members to prevent new incursions
- constructing rings of dependable subcontractors
- improving internal control
- holding on to traditional industries

- safeguarding of the success formula
- continue to innovate and progress.

Such response patterns invite further entrepreneurial advances which ensure the competitive spirit remains alive, and entrenched firms find it difficult to remain idle. Ongoing fission from and refusion of networks perennially create and recreate space for entrants to the entrepreneurial strata (Tam, 1992). Over time, the formation of a typical reasonably open, industry takes on the shape of vertical layers, with the newcomers continually emerging from the bottom, while the layers on the top are not given that much chance to cool themselves down. The simple basic realities of this status allocation system, the heroes of which are the mega-rich owners, then impress themselves on the relational dynamics at the base by emphasizing the salience of ownership for success and status in Hong Kong. Thus the cycle is complete.

The real legacy of the colonial transformation of traditional Chinese society was that of assistance at the creation of a machine for growth. That machine produces talent, but with a sense of perpetual motion and the spontaneous multiplication of that talent. It has been fostered by its colonial context.

The model we have described is that machine and that is the Chinese contribution. The context of its creation is the institutional fabric of a hybrid society and that is the colonial legacy. We have noted the significance of the alternative definition of status which mercantilism ushered in. We have observed the de-structuring induced by egalitarianism, and we have seen the stimulating power of such features as law and property rights in encouraging the growth of commerce and industry.

Note must finally be taken of the self-multiplying nature of the process under review, and the way in which entrepreneurs beget more entrepreneurs in a growing stream. The key here is the way in which the constant forming of new small enterprises keeps on creating the seedbeds for aspiration and thus more fission. A newly born entrepreneur will, because of his or her need for external control, create opportunities for aspiring employees, both from within or outside his/her firm to become independent owners. The fission and refusion cycle thus ensures that each entrepreneur will multiple him or herself several times over by creating upward opportunity space for others.

In traditional China, the expression of individuality was severely limited, even in the elite layers of society. Hong Kong by contrast has provided a vast space for the exercise of aspiration. In using this space the traditional tendency to rely on personalistic networks has subtly changed the function of such networks from one which was primarily defensive and supportive, to one which now includes co-operation for gain and the exploitation of opportunity.

The standardizing and homogenizing of society has also been replaced by plurality, diversity and innovation.

Was Colonial Administrative Behaviour Different?

A comparison of this Hong Kong colonial administration with that in Africa shows the same parsimony but suggests one difference which is revealing. The African mode has been characterized as anti-capitalist largely on the grounds of the prevailing value system within the colonial hierarchy. This must be seen against the African context of societies which had limited indigenous traditions of commerce, and which were predominantly agricultural. In Hong Kong, by contrast, the colonial administrators were dealing with extremely sophisticated Chinese business magnates, capable of earning knighthoods for business success and philanthropy. The Chinese were in a position to resist any anti-entrepreneurial behavior by any state officials. It appears that mutual respect was the tone of dealings and in such circumstances an overtly anti-capitalist view would have left any colonial administrator unsuited to work in Hong Kong.

In contrast, the colonial state in Africa, with little overt opposition was able to translate their ideology into a variety of measures which were used to suppress indigenous entrepreneurial activities. The main route to upward mobility for the local population, like the Confucian State, was via state or quasi-state insitutions. In many African countries the background of the elites, who inherited the reins of power at independence, ensured the continuity of the anti-capitalist sentiments that prevailed during the colonial period.[2]

Contexts and Outcomes

The second question posed was whether the differences in contexts are the main determinants of different outcomes. Can Hong Kong's $10,320 per capita and Tanzania's $120 be explained in any significant sense by their colonial experiences, or were other elements more crucial?

The contextual differences of relevance to Hong Kong business success historically are: (a) regional business growth in Asia; (b) long established trading and banking companies; (c) the systems making capital and technology available. In the Hong Kong case these all rest upon a commercial and industrial tradition with deep historical roots. Although China was clearly not as successful as Japan in the last 150 years of modernization, it was nevertheless a country with a strong legacy of complex economic behaviour.

The regional growth, especially in the past forty years has made Hong Kong an important regional headquarters as well as a manufacturing and services base in its own right. This regional success has been helped by political stability, low-cost skilled-labour, trade agreements providing access to Western markets, and the stimulus of Japanese success.

The major trading and banking companies in Hong Kong have also led the way in fostering Hong Kong industry and the largest of them – Swire, Jardines and Hongkong Bank – are clearly colonial in origin. The later arrival of American and European multinationals served to enhance the established structures for business but certainly not to replace them or even seriously challenge them until recently.

Systems for the spreading of capital and technology into an economy operate at one level through the institutions of banking and education, but they also operate at another level. Informal systems of capital formation such as internal family borrowing and small partnership alliances can proliferate where strong norms exist to influence trust, as they do in the Chinese case. Technical information can also be absorbed through trade connections and here the extensive business networking of the Chinese yields advantages.

The Production of Entrepreneurs

As was argued earlier the production of entrepreneurs in Hong Kong has been due to the felicitous combination of two forces. Firstly, are the proclivities in Chinese society to pursue family-based wealth and status. Secondly, was the destructuring by the colonial regime of the more traditional Chinese institutions which had previously kept the society more or less static. Putting this new combination of forces together has yielded the success observed.

In African post-colonial regimes, it is possible to argue that two negative factors have been at work in producing less than impressive economic results. In the first place the colonial administrators were not able to be influenced by a strong local mercantilist ethic. Local businessmen were not comparable with the patrician business leaders of Chinese culture, and the impact of large colonial firms was less in most British African colonies as the government discouraged their presence.

The second key difference is the lack of a strongly developed indigenous commercial and industrial tradition in Africa comparable with that of China. This in turn relates to the diffracted nature of indigenous society and the resulting barriers to economic integration and institutionalization. What this suggests is the enormous challenge ahead for Africa to build the institutions that will help foster a network of commerical and industrial entrepreneurship.

Notes

1. An earlier version of this paper was presented at the Second Global Entrepreneurship Conference, Imperial College, London, 1992. The support of the Institute for the Study of Economic Culture, Boston University, and of its Director, Peter L. Berger, is gratefully acknowledged.
2. For a discussion of the Tanzanian case see Stein (1985).

7 Foreign Investment, the State and Industrial Policy in Singapore

Linda Lim

INTRODUCTION

As one of the world's most successful developing economies, Singapore's economic development has been extensively chronicled (e.g. You and C.Y. Lim (ed.), 1971, 1984; Chen, ed., 1983; Pang and L. Lim, 1985; Krause, Koh and Lee (Tsao), 1987; C.Y. Lim et al., 1988; Sandhu and Wheatley, eds, 1989). Table 7.1 presents some aggregate statistics that document this success. They show a nation that, over a period of roughly twenty years, transformed itself from a state of economic underdevelopment into, by 1991, a 'high-income' country by the World Bank's classification, and is widely regarded today as fully-industrialized.

All countries, and their development experiences, are unique and historically specific, but there are several features of Singapore's development which make it appear to deviate from the norm even more so than other countries. In terms of initial economic conditions, Singapore was (and still is) a small city-state, lacking the rural hinterland that characterizes most other developing countries. At the end of the colonial period in 1963, the city already had an income level and infrastructure far surpassing that of any other ex-colonial territory, and a relatively efficient British-style government bureaucracy. As a long-established world trading port in an excellent geographical location, it had an experienced merchant community, and was well-linked into world trading and financial networks.

Politically, Singapore was even more unique. It has had only one post-colonial governing party, the People's Action Party (PAP), founded and led by a most remarkable leader, Lee Kuan Yew, who relinquished his post as Prime Minister in 1989. Though clearly authoritarian, Lee and the PAP are universally regarded as incorruptible, and the party has been consistently returned to power in general

205

Table 7.1 Singapore's Economic Performance (1960–1990)

	1960	1970	1980	1990
Population (millions)	1.6	2.1	2.4	3.0
Per capita GNP				
(current US$)	443	914	4,645	11,950
Real GDP growth % p.a.				
by decade, eg. 1960–69;	8.7	9.4	7.2	6.9
1990–92				
Inflation (CPI) % p.a.				
by decade	1.2	5.6	2.7	3.0
Unemployment %				
decade average	—	6.0	3.0	2.1
Investment/GDP %	9.5	32.5	40.7	38.0
Domestic Savings/GNP %	−2.6	18.2	38.9	43.8
Exchange rate per US$	—	3.1	2.1	1.8
Domestic exports, US$m	72	593	12,059	34,670
Official foreign reserves				
US$billion	—	1.0	6.4	28.5
Manufacturing				
Output, US$m	155	1,259	14,793	41,961
% GDP	12	20	29	29
Employment (000s)	27	121	285	352
% Total Employment	14	22	30	29
Direct Exports, US$m	56	493	8,960	27,647
Value-added/worker				
US$	1,728	2,937	13,960	36,141
Remuneration/worker				
US$	812	1,068	4,139	11,462

Source: Department of Statistics, Singapore, 1983; MTI, 1986; MTI, 1992;
EDB, 1990c.

elections every four years by an electorate evidently satisfied with the economic prosperity and social goods that its rule has provided.

Why, then, consider possible lessons from Singapore's development for Africa? The answer is that some elements of its success might have relevance for countries which are, like Singapore was at independence, small, open economies, with a poor natural resource base, negligible domestic market, high domestic unemployment, and internal political unrest in an ethnically-diverse population. This chapter will focus particularly on Singapore's use of external resources and markets, especially foreign investment by export-manufacturing multinationals, to propel its growth and industrialization, transforming it from a stagnant colonial port-city into a high-tech industrial center for the world. Its premise is that some of the policies which the Singapore government used to attract foreign capital and extract from it the maximum benefits for the national economy in its quest for industrialization might be instructive for and replicable in African countries now seeking to follow the same path of development.

HISTORICAL BACKGROUND AND INITIAL CONDITIONS

Modern Singapore was founded in 1819 by the British colonial entrepreneur Stamford Raffles, who established a free port on this jungle-covered island at the southern tip of the Malay peninsula, encouraging ships and merchants from all over the world to stop in the deep-water harbor here for trade. The British eventually went on to colonize the whole Malay peninsula, for which Singapore served as the administrative and commercial center, handling the import-export trade for commodity-exporting Malaya and neighboring territories. Immigrants came to Malaya from China, British India and the Dutch East Indies (now Indonesia) to work in the colonial economy, and their descendants make up nearly all of the present-day population of Singapore. From 1941–45, Singapore, together with the rest of Malaya, was under Japanese military occupation, which interrupted its trade with the West.

The British colonial administration returned after the war to encounter a communist insurgency that was essentially defeated by the time the Malay peninsula achieved independence in 1957. Singapore, however, was not granted independence until 1963, when it joined the Federation of Malaysia together with the remaining British North Borneo territories of Sabah and Sarawak; in 1965, Singapore separated from the Federation of Malaysia to become an independent republic (Turnbull, 1977, pp. 281–93). At the time it had a population of under two million people, of whom 75 per cent were ethnic Chinese, 15 per cent Malay, and the rest Indians and other South Asians.

Even before sovereignty in 1965, the PAP government, which was first elected in 1959, had embarked on policies of social and economic development in line with its social-democratic ideology of the time. These included a massive urban resettlement and public housing program, infrastructure development, and broad public investments in health and education, all undertaken by the public sector through new or expanded state agencies (e.g. You and C. Y. Lim (eds), 1971, 1984; Chen (ed.), 1983; Sandhu and Wheatley (eds), 1989; L. Lim,

1989). Although initially undertaken to fulfil social consumption and party-political needs (for re-election), these social expenditures had a strong investment impact as well, and were shaped to serve economic efficiency as well as social and political goals.

In the economic realm, it was recognized early on that Singapore had to diversify its economy away from reliance on the stagnant regional entrepot trade, to create new sources of income as well as employment for a rapidly expanding labor force. Given the island's lack of land and natural resources, industrialization was seen as the only alternative. A UN Industrial Survey Mission led by the Dutch economist Dr. A. Winsemius visited Singapore in 1960, and in 1961 its report was adopted as the blueprint for the island's industrialization.[1] At the time, Singapore's limited industrial base consisted of industries processing raw materials such as rubber, timber, tropical oils and petroleum which were imported from neighboring countries for re-export; industries manufacturing bulky, low-value goods for local consumption such as food and beverages, basic metals, garments and footwear; and printing and publishing for the local market.

Despite Singapore's intrinsic advantages of a strategic geographical location, efficient port facilities and well-developed commercial and financial infrastructure,[2] it was considered that **rapid industrialization could not be induced without active government support**. Certainly the free trade and free capital flows which have all along characterized the Singapore economy had not attracted sufficient industry. On the contrary,

> labour cost was comparatively high by regional standards . . . capital derived from commercial activities lacked structural mobility due to the continued profitability of commercial activities, differences in time horizons, and lack of industrial know-how and management skills among commercial entrepreneurs . . . the free port had led to the entrenchment of brand names and distribution channels which acted as barriers to the development of domestic industries. . .The most serious problem was the limited size of the domestic market. (Chia, 1971, pp. 191–2)

IMPORT-SUBSTITUTING INDUSTRIALIZATION: 1961–1967

The Economic Development Board (EDB) was created in 1961 'to spearhead the industrialization drive through industrial investment promotion, development of industrial infrastructure and facilities, participation in industrial financing, and administering tax incentives' (Chia, 1971, p. 192). The EDB served as the government's executive agency for industrial development, coordinating the functions of different branches of government that related to industry, and providing comprehensive services to both foreign and local investors (Hughes et al., 1993).

Anticipating the merger of Singapore into a larger Malaysian common market, industrialization in Singapore was initially intended to be import-substituting (e.g. Goh, 1969; Hughes and You, 1969, pp. 19–33; Chia, 1971, pp. 89–93; Lee, 1973). The first protective tariffs were introduced in 1960, and tariff protection was extended and accelerated during Singapore's 1963–65 tenure in Malaysia, continuing even after separation. Between 1960 and 1967, real value-added in manufacturing doubled, growing at about 10 per cent a year, and rising from 13.2 per cent of GDP in 1960 to 16.3 per cent in 1967; exports fell from 36 per cent to 30.5 per cent of total manufacturing sales (Chia, 1989, pp. 253, 256). But with separation from Malaysia, the prospects for import-substituting industrialization withered, and a new industrial strategy was required that would both allow sustained growth and absorb surplus labor. Unemployment remained high and was expected to increase with the planned withdrawal of British military forces in 1968.

The import substituting industrial phase in Singapore did contribute to relatively high economic growth in the 1960s, when other sectors of the economy were stagnating. But because it was cut off by Singapore's separation from the rest of Malaysia, which had formed part of the domestic market for import substituting industry, it is not possible to evaluate what the longer-term outcome of this strategy might have been had it been sustained. Import substitution clearly was not sufficient to sustain manufacturing growth in Singapore's small domestic market of the 1960s, nor does it appear to have been a necessary foundation for the subsequent export manufacturing take-off. Rather, in both Singapore and Malaysia, export-oriented industrialization was undertaken by different investors in different industries and under different rules than the earlier import substituting regime. In the Singapore case, the main continuity between these two phases of industrialization was provided by government institutions and policies (like the EDB and tax incentives) which were set up originally to promote import substitution, but were readily turned to focus on export manufacturing instead, which was made easier by the earlier experience.

LABOR INTENSIVE EXPORT MANUFACTURING: 1967–1979

The strategy of labor-intensive export manufacturing was chosen in large part because Singapore's policy-makers did not see any viable alternative – lacking land for agriculture, natural resources for extraction, a domestic market for import-substituting industrialization, and with exportable commercial services well-established but stagnant and expected to decline.[3] Producing for the world market was the only solution, since exporting was necessary to pay for the imports on which the city-state depended for its survival, while the need for mass employment creation dictated a labor-intensive strategy. Hong Kong and Puerto Rico provided ready examples of other resource-poor island states that were already successfully developing labor-intensive export industries. Because of the absence of a potential domestic industrial entrepreneurial class, and the state sector's lack of access to industrial technology and foreign markets, a strong role in the industrialization process was assigned to foreign corporations.[4]

To a considerable extent, Singapore's manufacturing sector in the mid-1960s was already significantly export-oriented, including as it did the processing of raw materials for export, as well as an increasing amount of textile and garment assembly undertaken by MFA-quota-hopping Hong Kong and Taiwan companies. But much more foreign investment was needed than was attracted simply by Singapore's free trade and 'open-door' policies and abundant labor force. An activist government industrial policy systematically and comprehensively served to fill the gaps in Singapore's attractiveness to foreign capital.

Industrial Development Policies of the Late 1960s

One set of policies sought to reduce the capital costs and increase the financial return on private industrial investment. In 1967, the Economic Expansion Incentives (Relief from Income Tax) Act granted profit tax concessions to new 'pioneer industries' as well as to expansions of established industries, and to export-oriented industries. Fiscal incentives were also available for royalties and technical assistance fees, for 'market development expenditures', accelerated depreciation, etc.. Export industries were exempt from tariff and quota restrictions imposed during the earlier import-substitution phase, and there were no restrictions or duty on the importation of equipment and materials, or on the repatriation of profits and capital. The EDB provided assistance with industrial financing, including equity participation and medium- and long-term loans at favorable interest rates for plant equipment and machinery; in 1968 these functions were spun off and taken over by the newly-created Development Bank of Singapore (DBS).

A second set of policies sought to ensure labor peace and productivity in an environment which had hitherto been characterized by high levels of labor unrest,[5] and to augment the industrial skills of the labor force. An Employment Act passed in 1968 standardized terms and conditions of employment and set limits on negotiable fringe benefits. The Industrial Relations (Amendment) Act of the same year excluded issues such as recruitment, retrenchment, promotion and dismissal from collective bargaining, and detailed new procedures for labor negotiation and conflict resolution, including severe limitations on the right to strike. The ruling party also restructured the union movement, capturing control of it through the PAP-controlled umbrella organization, the National Trades Union Congress (NTUC), which was subsequently transformed into a welfarist organization operating various business cooperatives (supermarkets, childcare centers, insurance and taxi services) for the benefit of workers.

Labor productivity was to be enhanced through training and technical education. In 1968, the EDB's technical division was spun off into an Engineering Industries Development Agency (EIDA) that operated industry-specific (metals, electro-mechanical, woodworking, etc.) training centers providing 'Crash training programmes and in plant training facilities . . . for school-leavers to alleviate the . . . shortage of skilled workers in Singapore, and upgrade skilled workers and technicians' (Huan, 1971, p. 228).

A National Productivity Centre (NPC) was also set up that year to increase the level of productivity in local industries and encourage good labor-management relations by providing advisory services and organizing training courses and seminars for lower and middle management and union officials. The Ministry of Education also embarked on various technical education and training programs: technical courses were introduced into the secondary school curriculum; vocational institutes, industrial training centers, technical colleges and polytechnics were established or expanded; and the engineering faculty at the University of Singapore was greatly expanded. In addition, government schemes contributed to companies' costs of overseas training for their workers and made available government scholarship students for jobs in industry. The immigration of persons with technical and professional skills was liberalized.

A third set of policies involved the development of industrial infrastructure and facilities. The EDB's task of developing and operating fully-serviced industrial estates around the island was farmed out in 1968 to the new Jurong Town Corporation (JTC), named after the large and comprehensive Jurong Industrial Complex which was built out of uninhabited jungle hills and swampland in the western part of the island. JTC's industrial estates, together with estates operated by the Housing Development Board (HDB), another government statutory agency, provided ready-built and fully-serviced standard factories for sale or rental, to minimize both the capital outlay and the time required to establish a new industrial venture.

A fourth set of policies involved the provision of information, technical and consultant services. The EDB mounted an aggressive overseas investment promotion campaign, establishing offices in many foreign countries to promote Singapore and provide information and assistance to potential foreign investors. It also undertook project evaluation and feasibility studies for both foreign and local investors, and processed their applications for tax incentives. The EDB's industrial research unit was established as a separate Singapore Institute for Standards and Industrial Research (SISIR) in 1969. Its export promotion center which assisted local industries in their efforts to export was absorbed into INTRACO, a new government international trading company, in 1968.

A word should be mentioned here about Singapore's financial system. In 1967, the Singapore dollar was pegged to gold, and this rate was maintained through devaluations of sterling in 1967 and of the US dollar in 1971 and 1973. The currency remains 100 per cent backed by gold and foreign exchange reserves, but was floated in 1973. The Monetary Authority of Singapore (MAS), which was established in 1970, manages the currency's float against a trade-weighted basket of currencies of Singapore's major trading partners. In this small, extremely open economy, exchange-rate policy substitutes for domestic monetary policy (Lee (Tsao), 1987, pp. 129–36; Grubel, 1989, pp. 378–83).

Several points should be noted about Singapore's industrial development policies during this period. First, the state took the leading role in industrialization, expanding its functions through the proliferation of specialized state agencies which handled different aspects of the industrialization process, from land development to education and training. The EDB served as the lead state agency, developing overall strategy and coordinating the functions of the other agencies. Second, most of the actual industrialization was to be undertaken by private industry; government policies did not discriminate between foreign and local investors, though some tax provisions were more important to foreign than to local investors, and the former required aggressive overseas promotion efforts.

Third, the industrial promotion policies were permissive (unrestricted imports and exports of goods and capital, enhancement of employer prerogatives, etc.) rather than restrictive, and involved implicit subsidization of the costs of investment (tax concessions, training subsidies, low-rent premises, infrastructural facilities, etc.) rather than protection. Fourth, there was sectoral targeting but it was broad and relatively mild, involving mainly targeted promotion activities, and support for labor-intensive and export-oriented activities. Fifth, the state did engage directly in some industrial activities itself, most notably the conversion to commercial use of the naval facilities vacated by British military forces in 1968, which led to the establishment of a major labor-intensive export industry, shipbuilding and repair.

Sixth, state social expenditures on public housing, health (including population control) and education also contributed positively to the industrialization effort: by winning the government popular public support that contributed to labor peace and political stability; by vastly increasing the labor force participation of women (Lim, 1982b) (of particular importance to female-labor-intensive export industries like electronics and garments); by increasing labor productivity and human capital; by implicitly subsidizing the wage (especially through subsidized public housing for the lowest-income workers); and by improving efficiency (e.g. the location of industrial estates in the midst of new public housing estates assisted labor recruitment and minimized transportation costs).

The Results of Industrial Policy 1967–1973

Between 1967 and 1973, value-added in the Singapore manufacturing sector tripled in real terms, doubling its real growth rate over the 1960–7 period to just under 20 per cent a year, and rising from 16.3 per cent of GDP in 1967 to 22.6 per cent in 1973, about the same ratio as manufacturing's share of total employment; exports increased from 30.5 per cent of total manufacturing sales in 1967 to 53.6 per cent in

1973 (Chia, 1989, p. 253). The three new leading export-oriented industries were petroleum refining, transport equipment and oil rigs, and electronic products and components, which by 1971 accounted for a combined share of 43.6 per cent of total manufacturing value-added. The growth in petroleum refining and shipbuilding and repair reflected both Singapore's traditional commodity processing and seaport and naval-base functions based on its strategic geographical location, and new external circumstances which favored these activities, specifically an oil exploration boom in surrounding Southeast Asian waters by Indonesia and Malaysia, and the United States Vietnam War military activity – though it should be noted that, without state enterprise development of the shipbuilding industry, the country would not have been as able to take advantage of these opportunities.

While the two other industries were location-specific, the electronics products and components industry was more of a classical labor-intensive export industry undertaken by 'footloose' offshore sourcing multinationals, attracted to Singapore by the industrial policy changes of 1967 and 1968 and aggressive EDB promotion and recruitment efforts especially in Silicon Valley, California. By 1973, 16 US, 13 European, 11 Japanese and 6 Hong Kong semiconductor, electronics component and consumer product companies had set up operations in Singapore; the industry as a whole (which also included twenty local firms) exported 93 per cent of its total sales and accounted for 24 per cent of manufacturing exports and 20 per cent of the manufacturing workforce (Pang and Lim, 1977, p. 14, 16; Lim, 1978).

Industrial Policy and Performance 1973–79

The rapid growth of manufacturing contributed to the achievement of full employment of the Singapore labor force by 1972. In that year, the government formed a tripartite National Wages Council (NWC) whose role was to ensure 'orderly wage increases' under conditions of full employment. The NWC issued national wage guidelines which tended to be followed throughout most of the economy. In addition, the government could affect labor costs by varying the proportion of wages contributed by employers and employees to the Central Provident Fund (CPF), a compulsory national savings and pension scheme.

During the period 1973–79, NWC recommendations in effect held real wage and labor cost increases below what would have occurred under free market forces, and below real productivity growth (Lim and Pang, 1986, p. 63; Pang and Lim, 1989, pp. 83–8, 94–5; Lim, 1990,

p. 83). This policy together with liberalized controls on the importation
of foreign labor (Pang and Lim, 1982) enabled labor-intensive
industries to maintain their export competitiveness longer than they
would have under free market forces, thereby prolonging and promoting the 'excessive use of labor' in manufacturing. Despite this,
Singapore's industrial growth 'slowed' to an annual average of 8.2
per cent between 1973 and 1979 in the wake of the 1973 OPEC oil crisis
and the ensuing 1974/75 global recession, which adversely affected
foreign investment and exports, resulting in massive if temporary
layoffs in export manufacturing industries.

CAPITAL-INTENSIVE HIGH-TECH MANUFACTURING: 1979–PRESENT

The 1974–5 recession caused Singapore's policy-makers to postpone
economic restructuring in the direction of higher-value-added, less
labor-intensive manufacturing and service activities. This new strategy
was not embarked on until 1979, when the government announced the
launching of a 'Second Industrial Revolution' that would upgrade
established industries and develop new ones to employ more capital,
high technology and skilled labor in the production of high-value
manufactures and services for export (e.g. Chng, Low and Toh, 1988,
pp. 16–34). The goal was to use Singapore's scarce resources, especially
labor, more effectively to ensure high and rising incomes. The key
instrument to achieve this was a 'wage correction policy' aimed at
'restoring wages to market levels' and improving labor productivity by
forcing employers to economize on the use of labor.

For three years, between 1979 and 1981, the NWC recommended
large wage increases, and CPF contributions were also progressively
raised, adding further to labor costs. A 4 per cent Skills Development
Fund (SDF) levy was imposed on employee payrolls to provide funds
for worker training, and other public and public-private sector training
and educational programs and facilities were expanded. In addition,
industrial investment incentives were modified to encourage automation, technological upgrading, research and development, etc. and
targeted selectively at more technologically sophisticated, capital- and
skill-intensive industries identified for 'priority' development.[6]

Labor productivity and capital-intensive investments did increase in
the wake of these policies, but they were arguably as much the result of

market forces (at least in this period) – including the changing technological composition of new export products (given the concentration of Singapore's export industry in the technologically dynamic electronics and computer sectors), and the tight domestic labor market – as of the policies themselves (which did, however, enable or at least facilitate adjustment to the changing market forces). For example, after the official conclusion of the high-wage policy in 1981, wage increases continued to be high, reflecting the underlying shortage of labor.

Another recession, however, intervened in 1985–86, reflecting not only adverse external circumstances – namely global and regional sectoral slumps in commodity prices and in the electronics industry – but also a loss in Singapore's cost competitiveness in export industries relative to its newly-industrializing Asian competitors. The high-wage policy was partly blamed for this since wage costs had risen twice as fast as productivity in the preceding five years. Part of the rest of the blame was assigned to 'high operating costs' which included high charges for government services. A high-level public-private sector Economic Committee was constituted to study the problem; the recommendations of its 1986 Report (MTI, 1986) which were implemented included a two-year wage restraint policy and introduction of a more flexible wage determination system, a reduction in CPF contributions, lower tax rates and more investment allowances.

Industrial investment and growth rebounded after 1986 due not only to the cost-cutting effect of these policies, but also to sectoral recovery, the worldwide currency realignment that improved Singapore's international cost competitiveness, and the resulting surge of foreign investment into its ASEAN neighbors which caused a spurt in regional growth and industrialization. Since then, Singapore's economy and industry have continued to grow rapidly, with only a modest and temporary reduction of growth occurring during the industrial country recession of the early 1990s. By then Singapore had catapulted into the ranks of the World Bank's 'high-income' countries, as well as of the top fifteen trading nations of the world. Despite this the government is not letting up on its strategic industrial policy efforts.

A Strategic Economic Plan (SEP) drawn up in 1991 through a collaborative effort with labor and the business community emphasizes innovation, internationalization, the development of 'core capabilities' and integrated manufacturing and service 'clusters' in industrial sectors such as electronics, precision engineering, information technology and petroleum and petrochemicals, and 'redevelopment' of the domestic economy (MTI, 1991). Though the SEP mentions close collaboration with the private sector, it is the government which will provide the 'lead agencies' for the various 'strategic thrusts' that are called for.

THE ROLE OF FOREIGN INVESTMENT IN INDUSTRIALIZATION

Many developing and newly-industrializing economies have, like Singapore, assigned the state a leading role in industrial development. None, however, has relied on foreign investment to quite the extent that Singapore has (Hughes and You, 1969; Lee, 1977; Tan, 1976, 1984; Yoshihara, 1976; Chia, 1985; Mirza, 1986; C. Y. Lim et al., 1988, pp. 247–74; L. Lim and Pang, 1991, pp. 51–62, 123–34). Tables 7.2, 7.3 and 7.4 show the growth of foreign direct investment in manufacturing, and the distribution of that investment by industrial sector and country of origin.

Table 7.2   Foreign Direct Investment Stock in Manufacturing, Singapore (1970–89)

Year	Millions of Singapore $
1970	778
1971	987
1972	1,260
1973	1,807
1974	2,398
1975	2,584
1976	3,663
1977	4,071
1978	4,586
1979	5,713
1980	7,090
1981	8,382
1982	9,618
1983	10,777
1984	12,651
1985	13,160
1986	14,120
1987	15,893
1988	18,823
1989	21,490

Source: UNCTC, 1992, p. 263.

Table 7.3   Foreign Direct Investment Stock in Manufacturing by Industrial Sector, Singapore (1980 and 1989) (%)

	1980	1989
Food, beverages and tobacco	3.3	3.3
Textiles, leather and clothing	4.2	1.1
Paper	1.3	2.0
Chemicals	3.9	14.1
Coal and petroleum products	43.6	25.0
Rubber products	1.0	1.4
Non-metallic mineral products	1.4	2.0
Metals	5.2	5.8
Mechanical equipment	6.9	5.0
Electrical equipment	18.4	33.1
Other transport equipment	4.8	3.1
Other manufacturing	6.1	3.1
Total (Singapore $ millions)	7,090	21,490

Source: UNCTC, 1992, p. 266.

Table 7.4   Foreign Direct Investment Stock in Manufacturing by Country of Origin, Singapore (1980 and 1989) (%)

	1980	1989
USA	29.6	33.2
Japan	16.7	30.7
Europe	42.2	30.6
EC	39.6	28.7
France	0.8	1.9
Germany	3.4	2.1
Netherlands	18.2	12.0
Spain	0.7	1.4
UK	16.5	11.3
Sweden	0.6	0.8
Switzerland	1.6	0.7
Other	0.3	0.4
Other	11.5	5.4
Total (Singapore $ millions)	7,090	21,490

Source: UNCTC, 1992, p. 267.

From Table 7.2 we can see that, in nominal terms, investment has expanded almost thirty fold between 1970 and 1990. In real terms, the number in 1990 is nearly 15 times the 1970 figure (calculated using inflation figures for Singapore from World Bank, 1983 and World Bank, 1992a). Table 7.3 indicates how closely investment in manufacturing mirrors the restructuring of industry from refining and more labor intensive industries like textiles to higher value added, more capital intensive manufacturing, like electrical equipment and chemicals. Table 7.4 shows the diversity of country origins of investment in manufacturing (more on this below). While the U.S has been the dominant player, Japan's investment in Singapore and other Southeast Asian countries like Thailand significantly increased in the 1980s.

Foreign capital has clearly dominated industry in Singapore. In 1960, less than 30 per cent of total equity capital invested in manufacturing was foreign-owned. By 1990, wholly- or majority-owned foreign firms accounted for 60 per cent of all employment, 76 per cent of all output, and 86 per cent of all exports in the manufacturing sector (EDB, 1990c, p. 4).

As shown in Tables 7.5 and 7.6, foreign manufacturing firms are on average larger, more capital-intensive, more productive and more heavily export-oriented than local Singapore firms, and pay higher wages. Including minority-foreign-owned firms, and considering that most locally-owned firms are involved in supplying foreign firms, Singapore manufacturing is overwhelmingly foreign dominated. From the beginning, foreign investment was welcomed not so much for the cash itself but for the technical know-how, management expertise, and marketing connections which it brings (Huan, 1971, p. 238).

As a small country, and a latecomer to industrialization, Singapore needed the brand names, distribution channels, marketing expertise and intra-company linkages of established multinationals to penetrate world markets with its manufactures. A Texas Instruments semiconductor or a Hitachi television was infinitely more readily (and cheaply) sold on the world market than any equivalents that could be made by local companies, even under foreign licence. Foreign investors also possessed the industrial technology and management expertise lacking in Singapore's merchant trading community. To acquire these scarce and valuable assets, and to use foreign investors to leapfrog up the industrial technology ladder, the Singapore government was willing to forego potential tax revenues, contribute cheap loan or equity capital, and pay for required infrastructure and worker training. Capital was not in short supply in Singapore, but industrial entrepreneurship,

Table 7.5 Principal Statistics of Manufacturing[1] by Major Source of Capital, Singapore 1990

Country	No. of Firms	No. of Workers	Output S$m	Direct[2] Exports S$m	Value Added S$m	Wages[3] S$m	Capital Expend. S$m
Singapore[4]	2,846	145,034	17,304	6,719	5,930	2,666	1,234
Australia	37	2,349	464	211	170	52	25
Hong Kong	50	6,979	451	323	175	101	27
Japan	294	68,956	14,454	9,589	4,191	1,341	1,046
Malaysia	55	2,568	601	246	124	52	22
Switzerland	20	2,844	335	184	146	55	22
Taiwan	20	1,858	276	143	87	32	31
UK	75	8,145	2,680	2,079	1,416	241	98
USA	170	81,131	24,192	19,342	7,116	1,592	1,127
Germany	28	7,768	1,123	1,024	401	147	71
Other Europe	72	21,233	9,140	6,954	1,761	520	429
Others	36	2,809	313	186	89	52	54
Total Foreign	857	206,640	54,029	40,281	15,677	4,186	2,950
Total	3,703	351,674	71,333	47,000	21,607	6,852	4,184

Source: EDB, 1990, p. 6.
[1] Rubber processing & granite quarrying are excluded.
[2] A high proportion of local sales are supplies to export-oriented firms.
[3] 'Wages' includes all employees' remuneration.
[4] Singapore figures include permanent residents (mostly from Malaysia, Hong Kong, Taiwan and Indonesia).

221

Table 7.6 Selected Ratios of Manufacturing Statistics[1] By Capital Ownership, 1990

Ownership	Worker/ Firm	Value-Added/ Firm	Value-Added/ Worker	Wages[2]/ Worker	Wages/ Value-Added (Output)	Direct[3] Exports/ Sales
	No.	S$m	S$	S$	%	%
Wholly Local[4]	41	1.4	34,630	16,711	48.2 (15.8)	33.5
Majority Local	129	7.2	55,811	22,388	40.1 (14.7)	47.5
Majority Foreign	145	8.2	56,748	20,129	35.4 (7.2)	59.2
Wholly Foreign	277	22.1	79,719	20,303	25.5 (7.9)	77.5
Total	95	5.8	61,440	19,485	31.7 (9.6)	65.6

Source: EDB, 1990, pp. 4,9.
[1]Rubber processing and granite quarrying are excluded.
[2]'Wages' includes all employees' remuneration.
[3]A high proportion of local sales are supplies to export-oriented firms.
[4]Singapore figures include permanent residents (mostly from Malaysia, Hong Kong, Taiwan and Indonesia).

technological expertise, and international marketing assets and dis-tribution channels were, and these multinationals were tapped to supply.

As noted above, Singapore's industrial policies did not technically discriminate between local and foreign investors, though certain policies might be expected to be more important to foreign compa-nies, such as free repatriation of profits and capital, double taxation agreements with their home countries, and the EDB's overseas promotion efforts. Singapore's free trade environment benefitted both foreign and local manufacturing companies, which could thus access imported inputs at world prices; the maintenance of free trade was also essential for the survival of the merchant-based local business community. Because of Singapore's small size and history as a free port, there was no economic rationale or domestic political constitu-ency in favor of protecting the domestic market; on the contrary, exporting was readily accepted as the key to industrial development. I have discussed elsewhere (Lim, 1987; Lim and Pang, 1991, pp. 51–3) the particular features of Singapore's political economy which explain the lack of domestic objection to foreign capital:

As a free port and entrepot centre, the city, though full of merchants, had not developed a class of indigenous entrepreneurs who could lead its industrialisation efforts, or who would press the government for protection from imports . . . As industrialisation proceeded, more local entrepreneurs were attracted into manufacturing, but mostly as suppliers to multinational subsidiaries, and many local entrepreneurs in fact came from the ranks of former multinational employees. . . . The export orientation of the foreign manufacturing firms, and their concentration in electronics where there is consider-able proprietary technology and intra-firm trade, meant that there was little market competition between foreign and local firms. (Lim and Pang, 1991, pp. 51–2)

The faster growth and higher wages which result from reliance on multinationals increases the popularity of the government and the market for and assets of state agencies and corporations which service . . . the private sector through the provision of various facilities and essential services which generate surplus revenues for the state. Thus the success and power of the state is closely tied to foreign capital, not local capital from which the state bureaucracy is divided by origins, composition and orientation. Similarly, the fortunes of the working class and even the salaried professional class are also closely tied to foreign capital, which can pay higher wages and guarantee more secure employment and better promotional prospects than most local businesses. (Lim and Pang, 1991, p. 53)

During the first, labor-intensive, phase of export-oriented industrialization, foreign investors were attracted to Singapore largely by its abundant low-wage labor force compared with the investors' industrialized home countries. Thus as the available labor surplus was quickly absorbed and wages rose, the country became vulnerable to possible 'footloose' behavior by multinationals, which had invested relatively little capital in low-skill, labor-intensive activities that could presumably be relocated elsewhere, especially as Singapore's neighbors, Malaysia and the Philippines, had by the early 1970s also embarked on a similar strategy of labor-intensive export manufacturing. But footloose migration out of Singapore was forestalled by the government's 1970s wage restraint policy and by the compensatory attractions provided by other government policies.

In addition, rapid growth in demand and technological shifts in Singapore's prime export industry, electronics, made expansion rather than relocation into neighboring countries more attractive, increased the value-added from skilled and experienced labor, and facilitated if not required capital-labor substitution and technological upgrading; this 'market trend' was reinforced by the government's 'Second Industrial Revolution' policies of 1979 and after. In Singapore's other labor-intensive export industry, textiles and garments, large early MFA quotas, protected Singapore's higher-cost producers (mostly of Hong Kong origin) from would-be lower-wage later entrants, and encouraged them to shift into higher-value product lines, rather than relocate to cheaper locations.

In the 1980s and 1990s, Singapore has continued to maintain itself as a multinational paradise, not only holding on to, but also vastly increasing, foreign investment in its export-oriented manufacturing sector, even as labor costs have soared almost to industrial country levels and labor shortages have become extreme. It has done this by constantly fine-tuning government industrial policy to become a haven for capital-intensive new-technology enterprises and operations in high-tech sectors. State enterprises and agencies may, through 'strategic alliances' with multinationals, share the risks and capital costs of research, development and automated production in areas such as customized (ASIC) semiconductor wafer fabrication. Excellent education, continuous training, and constantly improving human resource management practices have resulted in the Singapore workforce being voted the best in the world for the past eight years in a row by the Geneva-based World Competitiveness Report.

In high-tech industry, human skills and patent capital are the most important ingredients along with state-of-the-art publicly-provided infrastructure. Singapore is able to provide these elements in a framework of strategic industrial policy devised and constantly revised in consultation with business, including the multinational sector itself. The surrounding region which provides a friendly environment for foreign investment and low-costs has allowed Singapore to develop as a complementary regional high-tech manufacturing, design, technical services, training and support center for increasingly regionally-integrated multinational production and marketing networks (Lim and Pang, 1991, pp. 123–34; Lim, 1993; Lim and Siddall, 1993).

The Singapore philosophy vis-à-vis foreign investment in the industrial sector is that multinationals are to be exploited ('tapped' is the favorite word) for the competitive assets that they can bring to the country which will contribute to its particular stage of industrial development. The government's goal is always to maximize learning, technological acquisition, rapid movement up the industrial ladder, and the skills and incomes of its working population. To this end it is willing to contribute capital, tax concessions, infrastructure, education and skills training, and a stable and friendly business environment.

While the country is well-integrated into international production networks in particular sectors, its fortunes are not tied to those of particular multinational companies, which (like local companies) the government refuses to help if they are unable to compete in the rapidly changing local environment and world market. Thus over time many multinational factories in Singapore have closed their doors – particularly in low-value, labor-intensive product lines and processes like simply electronic components and consumer goods – and shut down completely or relocated to neighboring countries, with the Singapore government's blessing. The same is true of local companies, which receive more assistance in relocation. Companies, whether local or foreign, which leave the country, release scarce labor resources which can then be more profitably and securely hired by new, more competitive and high-value companies – for example, the 1980s' shift into computer hard disk drives, in which Singapore now has a 60 per cent share of the world market.

In short, with persistent full employment of the labor force and little equity stake in the foreign capital invested in manufacturing in Singapore, the country minimizes its exposure to the fortunes of particular multinationals in the volatile, high-risk high-tech industrial sector, while maintaining Singapore itself as an attractive investment location for firms from this sector. This strategy maintains a state of chronic excess demand for labor, which maximizes national incomes and labor welfare and concentrates domestic capital in the form of the world's highest per capita savings rate (at $12,000 in foreign reserves per person, about triple that of Taiwan, which is in second place), in the hands of the already high-consuming local populace.[7]

The criticism of the Singapore strategy is that it has neglected the development and even fostered the 'crowding out' of a domestic industrial entrepreneurial class which could provide a counterweight to overdependence on foreign corporations. Only since the late 1980s has the government taken an interest in nurturing local entrepreneurs in the manufacturing sector. Much of its current interest is geared to helping them 'internationalize' – i.e. relocate abroad – with the assistance of many of the government agencies which have hitherto concentrated their efforts on attracting and servicing foreign investment in Singapore (e.g. Lim, 1992, 1993).

At the same time, however, it is noteworthy that many local entrepreneurs and enterprises were spawned by multinationals in various ways, developing to supply and service them, or gaining experience and contacts in their previous employ (Lim and Pang, 1982; Lim, 1983b; Lee (Tsao) and Low, 1990). Government policy did not directly seek to effect local managerial transfer or entrepreneurship generation. It contributed to this process by providing high-quality education and training to the population at large, by maintaining a 'good business environment' that encouraged local as well as foreign investment, and by attracting multinationals whose needs generated market opportunities for local entrepreneurs.

. . . multinationals in Singapore have helped nurture local industrial entrepreneurship in three ways. First, they provide a market for the output of local products . . . Second, the multinationals constitute a training ground for local engineers and technicians, some of whom then form their own companies. Third, the multinationals, by providing product specifications to their local component suppliers, also assist in upgrading the quality of local production. Technology transfer has therefore occurred in terms of the accumulation of human capital and backward linkages . . . the government's emphasis on technical training has resulted in an ever-increasing pool of engineers and technicians in the labor force. There is, therefore, a larger pool of potential industrialists than say, a decade ago. (Lee (Tsao) and Low, 1990, p. 31)

Overall, however, and especially in contrast with a country like South Korea, the focus of Singapore's industrial policy on foreign investment has clearly favored the interests of local labor (in full employment, job security and high wages) over those of local capital which has had a difficult time competing with foreign employers in a tight labor market.

EVALUATING SINGAPORE'S INDUSTRIAL POLICY

Singapore's industrialization has clearly been a spectacular success by almost any indicator, delivering rapid and sustained manufacturing output, employment and export growth, continuous technological upgrading, and high and ever-increasing domestic incomes and living standards. There is little question that the credit for this success is largely due to government industrial policy. Both initial conditions in the 1960s and the external market environment since then have had their favorable and unfavorable aspects and periods, and neither the local business community nor foreign investors were propelled by 'market forces', free trade and capital flows, to initiate industrialization in advance of government measures to encourage it in the 1960s.

When the availability of abundant cheap labor for labor-intensive assembly activities was exhausted in the late 1970s, government policies helped established firms adjust to the new situation. They provide incentives for technological upgrading and capital–labor substitution, as well as new industrial investors whose activities fit better with Singapore's changing comparative advantage. Since the late 1980s, government policies have even sought to promote outward investment in its regional neighbors by Singapore-based multinationals and local firms, again in line with changing country comparative advantages. These policies include infrastructure development by Singapore state agencies in neighboring countries (Lim, 1992; 1993).

It seems highly unlikely that Singapore's local business community with its initially negligible expertise and interest in manufacturing, or foreign investors with their lack of knowledge of and commitment to the country and region, would have undertaken the manufacturing investments that they did without the government's policy interventions. At the end of the labor-intensive phase, for example, the temptation might well have been to relocate to lower-wage locations (as, for example, Hong Kong and Taiwan firms have done) rather than to reinvest in technological upgrading in what for the foreign firms was an offshore location. Upgrading itself would have been much more difficult and costly without the government's assistance with financing, training and supportive infrastructure. For local firms, even relocation is difficult given their small size and imperfect information about risky neighboring countries, and here government agencies have recently stepped in to provide assistance.

Whereas in other countries, private sector groups like business associations might have taken the initiative to collectively push for industrial restructuring policies or activities, the domination of the Singapore manufacturing sector by multinational subsidiaries and the relative weakness of domestic firms made this unlikely. The lack of a large local industrial entrepreneurial class with an entrenched interest in a sizeable domestic market, and the long-term global rather than local orientations of multinationals (as indeed of local firms which must of necessity serve a wider market) leaves the government as the only player in the Singapore economy that can and must take a long-term view of the national interest – as reflected, for example, in the Strategic Economic Plan which looks to the year 2030. The need for negotiation with neighboring governments in developing sub-regional cooperation schemes for multinational investments involving a regional division of labor among neighboring countries also requires government to play a leading role (Lim, 1993). Thus in Singapore, at least, there does not appear to have been a credible potential alternative to strong state action in industrial policy at all stages of development.

This does not mean that the industrial policy measures which were undertaken by the government were always uncontroversial or unerring. For example, the low-wage policy of the 1970s is acknowledged to have probably delayed industrial restructuring, while the high-wage policy of the early 1980s has been criticized by the government itself as a 'blunt instrument' which contributed to the loss of cost competitiveness and hence the recession of 1985–6. Government monopoly-provided infrastructural services such as telecommunications, utilities and factory rental charges have also been criticized for being too costly (they have delivered huge surplus revenues to the public sector). Local firms, especially, complain of the high-cost business environment[8] and 'crowding out' by multinationals which constrains their development; both multinationals and local firms periodically complain about the ever-appreciating Singapore dollar. More generally, Singapore has been accused of following an excessively capital-intensive path of development with resultant inefficient use of capital (e.g. Young, 1992). There are also potential ideological objections to the entrenchment of the state bureaucracy and state enterprise in the political as well as economic life of the nation that is justified by the continued need for industrial policy.

Interestingly, labor is one constituency which does not seem to be dissatisfied with its lot, benefitting as it does from full employment, high and rising wages, and a wide range of efficient government-provided social services including public housing, transportation, education and recreational facilities. (Singapore has been called a 'workers' paradise', and for this, as early as the 1970s it won the expressed admiration of the leading Swedish social democrat, the late Gunnar Myrdal.) Recently, however, dissatisfaction among lower-income voters with rising health care costs as a result of the government's efforts to privatize its health services has made itself felt at the ballot-box, resulting in lower popular-vote totals for the ruling PAP and the election of more opposition Members of Parliament.

The motivation and thrust of industrial policy in Singapore since its inception has always been to maximize local benefits in terms of employment, income and technology transfer. For this reason, and because it is more heavily represented in the electorate, the interests of labor – including skilled and managerial labor – have tended to be favored over those of local capital, and foreign capital has been favored because of its greater ability to deliver high incomes, skills and technology to the populace. Industrial policy has focussed on shaping Singapore's competitive advantages (for example augmenting labor skills and providing state-of-the-art world-class infrastructure) in directions that would attract the desired types of investment, and that would in the long run move the country up the ladder of industrial technology and incomes: it has been 'market-anticipating' or 'market-accelerating', rather than merely 'pro-market' or 'market-conforming'. But this visionary, proactive long-term strategy has occasionally been punctuated by short-run policy responses to immediate cyclical problems; it also evolves continuously in response to changing external and internal circumstances. For a small country playing in the big leagues of world-class corporations facing global competition in world markets, this is arguably the most logical strategy. Dependence on multinationals is mitigated by diversifying among them according to company, investor nationality (we can see this above in Table 7.4) and product-line. This is achieved by selective government investment promotion activities targeted at specific companies in different countries and industries. But because of its size, Singapore also has to target specific niches of the industrial spectrum in order to specialize efficiently in them, and some degree of industrial concentration is unavoidable, imposing an inherent limitation on diversification. Investing in locally-based assets such as labor and infrastructure also ensures that the country is left with productive resources even if foreign (or local) employers decide to leave.

The Example of the Electronics Industry

The example of Singapore's major industry, electronics, will serve to illustrate this policy thrust. Initially, in the late 1960s and early 1970s, during its labor-intensive phase, EDB officials literally 'knocked on doors' of promising foreign firms not only in the US' 'Silicon Valley', but also in Europe and Japan, asking them to set up assembly facilities in Singapore and offering them a variety of tax incentives to do so. Companies like Texas Instruments, National Semiconductor, Fairchild, Hewlett-Packard, General Electric (of the USA), Siemens (of Germany), Philips (of the Netherlands), SGS-ATES (of Italy), Thomson (of France), Matsushita and Hitachi (of Japan) did so, bringing semiconductor, other component and consumer electronics production to Singapore.

The government for its part invested in supporting infrastructure (such as fully-serviced industrial estates) and in education and training of electronics engineers and technicians. Further investments along these lines, and additional tax incentives to encourage technological upgrading, were later undertaken to facilitate and accelerate the transition to skill- and capital-intensive industry in the late 1970s and early 1980s. Keeping an ever-watchful eye on global technological and market trends in the industry, as well as on changing local comparative costs, government industrial policy planners in the 1980s successfully sought investments by the expanding US computer disk-drive industry, while encouraging and facilitating the restructuring, downsizing and relocation of the more labor-intensive consumer electronics and even semiconductor sectors.

Consumer product companies like GEUSA and Philips, which were the largest private sector employers in Singapore up to the mid-1980s, shrank their absolute and relative presence in the country while disk-drive and computer companies like Tandon, Seagate, Micropolis, Conner Peripherals, Apple and Compaq took their place. Some of these companies failed on a global level (e.g. GEUSA in consumer electronics, Fairchild in semiconductors, Tandon in disk-drives) and exited Singapore as a result, while others merged (e.g. Thomson-SGS in semiconductors, Siemens-Nixdorf in computers) but remained in Singapore, and still others came for the first time (e.g. Sony Corporation, after resisting the EDB's overtures for over a decade).

Many electronics multinationals also relocated assembly from Singapore to its neighbors, retaining capital-intensive high-tech manufacturing processes and technical and commercial service operations in Singapore. Relocation was both encouraged and facilitated by the Singapore government; for example, through the development by Singapore government corporations of labor-intensive industrial estates in neighboring Indonesia. By the late 1980s, capital-rich Singapore state enterprises like Chartered Semiconductor and Singapore Technologies were entering into equity joint ventures with multinationals like Texas Instruments, National Semiconductor and Canon in strategic segments of the semiconductor industry. Singapore government corporations are also investing in venture capital high-tech start-ups in the US especially, and undertaking strategic outward foreign investments in other sectors like aerospace, in part to ensure a future role for Singapore in globally-integrated high-tech industry.

Throughout these state-led transformations, domestic full employment has been maintained, and Singapore's human capital and infrastructure have been extensively enhanced; they are now considered 'world-class' and constitute the major attraction for new and established multinationals which still continue to locate and expand here, bringing their state-of-the-art technologies. Though it uses tax incentives extensively to attract foreign investors, the government does so only selectively (though generously), does not extend 'subsidies' to loss-making companies, resists compromising its political principles, and avoids engagement in 'beggar-my-neighbor' competition. In the 1970s, for example, it refused to grant Motorola its requested 'no unionization' guarantee and lost the proposed investment (Motorola went to Malaysia instead); it also refused to continue support for Rollei, a German camera manufacturer in which the government had already taken an equity position, when it failed to compete with Japanese makers, allowing Rollei to go out of business.

In the 1980s, the government refused to help GEUSA, then the country's largest private sector employer, when several of the company's divisions lost international competitiveness and were subsequently forced to close, laying off thousands of workers. More recently, in 1992 Intel Corp. closed a semiconductor plant in Singapore because the Singapore government would not match tax breaks the company was offered for its less-efficient competing plants in Puerto Rico and Scotland. It is arguable that dealing with (substitutable) foreign rather than (politically-connected) domestic companies increases the government's industrial policy autonomy, though it should be noted that it has been equally resistant to calls for support from failing locally-owned companies. In general, the government's policy commitment is to maintaining and enhancing the nation's industrial competitiveness under a free-trading regime in a dynamic global marketplace, rather than to guaranteeing the survival of individual firms, whether foreign or local. The overall policy orientation is to anticipate and support advance adjustment to shifting comparative advantages and international market forces, thus ensuring job security and perpetual income growth for Singaporeans.

Macroeconomic Policy and Industry

Government microeconomic management of Singapore's industrialization has been skilful and largely successful. Macroeconomic management is a more complex and controversial subject: though high growth and relative price stability have been maintained for over thirty years, Lee(Tsao) (1987) argues that there is a need for coordination of different government policy variables which affect the macroeconomy and could have, for example, contributed to the recession of 1985/86. As previously mentioned, exchange rate management (a managed float against a trade-weighted basket of currencies) substitutes for monetary policy in this extremely open economy. In the fiscal policy realm, the government runs persistent public-sector surpluses, controls the vast pool of Central Provident Fund (CPF) compulsory savings as well as a Post Office Savings Bank (POSB) system which taps private voluntary savings, and affects the macroeconomy through variations in public-sector construction, wage and foreign labor policies, and taxes.

The overall macroeconomic effect is one of withdrawal of liquidity from the system, resulting in low inflation and a constantly appreciating exchange rate. The manufacturing sector benefits from low real interest rates and cheap imported inputs and materials, but is also constantly challenged by the adverse effect of currency appreciation on its export competitiveness. Currency appreciation adds to chronic excess demand for labor in exerting upward cost pressures which motivate constant adjustment and upgrading in the industrial sector. In the balance of payments, Singapore runs a chronic trade deficit, but this is always offset by a large services account surplus, and by large net positive inflows of foreign direct investment, resulting in a basic balance surplus and accumulating foreign exchange reserves.

POLICY IMPLICATIONS FOR AFRICA

Singapore's experience with foreign investment and industrial policy suggests several possible lessons for African countries which are seeking to industrialize without reasonable prospect of a domestic market; without a local industrial entrepreneurial class possessing the technology, managerial expertise and marketing connections required for export industrialization; and facing structural adjustment policy pressures to liberalize trade and investment and promote exports.

First, labor-intensive export manufacturing by foreign investors does not take place in a policy vacuum or on the basis of free trade and capital flows and the availability of cheap labor alone. Rather, specific state industrial policy interventions are required, most notably tax incentives, infrastructure and labor education and training, all of which augment a country's comparative advantages. In addition, aggressive overseas promotion is required.

Second, countries should not expect to rely on low-wage labor forever, but rather should anticipate and plan for rising wages and labor costs by investing in increasing productivity over time. Government policy can vary and selectively target tax incentives, promotion, infrastructure, and labor education and training, as this process evolves. It means that the role of government will not just wither away after initiating industrialization, but may actually become more interventionist, though its specific policies will change with the country's stage of development.

Third, social investments should be viewed as a contribution to industrial development, and not merely as providing consumption goods. Public housing, education, transportation and health services all improve labor productivity and efficiency, reduce costs, and promote political and social stability, which are necessary to attract foreign investment. In Singapore these 'distributional' investments were begun in the early 1960s in advance of more 'growth-oriented' measures in the late 1960s.

Fourth, it is possible even for small countries to shape and influence foreign investments such that they deliver maximum benefits to the national economy, particular in higher incomes and technology transfer. Most important here is increasing the technological absorptive capacity of the local working population. In addition to providing or subsidizing education and training, the state can exert pressure on or provide incentives to employers to upgrade worker skills and improve human resource management practices.[10] Its bargaining power, and that of workers, is enhanced, the more foreign investors there are.

Fifth, countries should seek in their industrial policy to favor and develop local resources, especially labor and infrastructure, which are internationally immobile and may be utilized by all investors, rather than protect and subsidize foreign or local companies which may later migrate elsewhere.

Sixth, small countries may wish to develop cooperative strategies with their regional neighbors to attract investments that may locate different parts of an integrated production process in neighboring countries according to different national comparative advantages, and perhaps to supply a regional market. That is, they may seek to develop regionally- rather than merely nationally-derived competitive advantages. Here, the state is needed to play an important official intermediary as well as a developmental role.

There are also, of course, aspects of Singapore's industrial policy which African countries should not seek to emulate. Wage policy, in particular, has a mixed record, and shows that fine-tuning of macroeconomic variables is difficult in a small open economy. Also, Singapore's late-1960s' restraining policies on labor organization are likely to be unpopular in the pro-democracy global political environment of the 1990s, and may result in trade policy problems of market access to developed countries on grounds of the violation of labor or human rights.

The strategic role of the state in industrial policy clearly requires a competent, efficient, incorrupt, dedicated and forward-looking bureaucracy and state entrepreneurial class. Contrary to popular belief (e.g. the 'Confucianist' hypothesis), Singapore did not start out with any particular institutional or cultural advantages in this area.[11] Rather, the PAP in Singapore developed its now-formidable administrative machinery not from any Confucianist roots, but by gradually building on the British civil service structure that it had inherited.[12] Today, Singapore remains the only ethnic Chinese city and nation in the world which is clean, orderly, crime-free and incorrupt.[13] In a multi-racial, immigrant society, this transformation was achieved by the enactment of laws and economic penalties for a multitude of transgressions, both large and small, rather than by reliance on Confucian tradition.

Finally, the international economic environment facing African nations today is different from that which Singapore faced during the early period of its industrialization in the 1960s and 1970s. While today there is more competition for international financial capital among the large number of newly-emerging market economies eager for foreign investment to help them penetrate world markets, there are also new sources of such investment, and many new markets – both of them mainly in Asia. Whereas Singapore's early export-oriented industrialization relied heavily on multinationals from industrialized countries manufacturing for export to their home markets, its later-industrializing Southeast Asian neighbors like Thailand and Indonesia have in the last five years relied much more heavily on export-oriented manufacturing investments from the Asian newly-industrializing economies, including Singapore itself. The proportion of exports from these labor-intensive factories going to the Asian regional market itself (including China) has also been increasing rapidly. For African countries today, it is arguable that the investing nations with the required capital surpluses, global marketing expertise and connections, and appropriate labor-intensive technologies that need to be relocated due to comparative advantage shifts, are more likely to be found in Asia than in either Western Europe or North America. For this reason, official delegations from both Africa and Asia have been making mutual visits to promote trade and investment linkages between the two regions. Capital-rich Singapore, like Taiwan, is additionally seen as an attractive source of foreign aid as well as investment. With economic growth apparently set to take off in many emerging markets (as it has already in China) while it slows and becomes more regionally- rather than globally-focussed in the advanced industrial nations, African countries may be better off looking to Asian investors that can help them supply non-industrial country markets, including in Asia itself.

Because of the idiosyncratic nature of Singapore's macroeconomy due to the combination of extreme openness, heavy government participation and intervention in the economy at large (i.e. beyond the industrial sector), and the city-state's role as an international financial center, it is harder to draw policy implications from its experience for macroeconomic management, and in particular for structural adjustment policy, in Africa. Grubel (1989), for example, attributes Singapore's experience of rapid growth with price stability to its managed-float exchange rate system, and to a budgetary policy which has avoided deficit spending; this would appear to support the need for similar policies of fiscal and monetary control in Africa. In Singapore, however, an interventionist savings policy in the form of the compulsory state-run CPF scheme has both raised national savings and provided the government with cheap borrowings to fund public spending projects. This, together with the government policies to attract foreign investment outlined above, has removed the need to resort to external debt for development financing in both the private and public sectors. There may be a lesson here for African countries seeking to simultaneously promote growth (which I have argued requires interventionist government policy including state spending and tax relief) and reduce external indebtedness, but this is beyond the scope of this essay.

CONCLUSIONS

This chapter has argued that government industrial policy has played, and continues to play, the leading role in Singapore's industrial export success, and that elements of this policy can, and should, be followed in African countries. The chief lesson of the Singapore experience is that reliance on private enterprise and market forces alone is inadequate to attract foreign investment and ensure success in export manufacturing. Rather, the state needs to intervene to facilitate the realization of (both static and dynamic) comparative advantage; to promote, enhance and augment such advantages; to anticipate and facilitate adjustments to and even accelerate desired or inevitable shifts in comparative advantage; and to influence and even shape the investment and production decisions of firms, which are not autonomous of the government policy environment.

In short, Singapore's industrial development strategy has been to manage the multinational, both to attract and retain desired investments, while shedding others, and to extract the maximum benefits for its population in terms of employment, incomes, and skill and technology transfer. For small countries unable to industrialize without escaping the restraints of domestic markets, and thus bound to be dependent on supplying world markets, Singapore provides an instructive case-study on how to not only manage external dependence, but in some cases how to reverse it, by making individual multinationals much more dependent on their Singapore manufacturing location than Singapore is on any individual company.[14] While African countries are unlikely to be able to replicate Singapore's success in its entirety, given the latter's advantages in terms of prior development and location especially, the overall lesson of taking an active role in shaping their own economic destiny, while staying open to international competitive pressures and opportunities, remains a useful one.

Notes

1. Dr. Winsemius remained for over twenty years as Singapore's formal and informal economic advisor and, together with Dr. Goh Keng Swee, a London School of Economics economist who served as Minister of Finance until the early 1980s, is credited with being the 'architect of Singapore's economic development'.

2. Singapore inherited a colonial monetary and banking system, which was subsequently greatly enlarged through various government licensing and tax incentive schemes aimed at turning Singapore into an international financial center engaged in a great deal of offshore business. These policies and institutions are not discussed here because they are not directly related to the industrialization process (except for the Development Bank of Singapore, which is discussed). See, for example, S. Y. Lee, 1984; Bryant, 1989.

3. After winning their independence, Singapore's neighbors sought to reduce their dependence on its entrepot trading services by developing competing facilities themselves (i.e. 'cutting out the middleman'). In addition, a territorial dispute with Malaysia since 1963 had caused Indonesia to officially boycott the port of Singapore (though it could not stop the smuggling which then took place).

4. For an analysis of the political complexities underlying the relative roles of the state, foreign and local private capital in Singapore's economic development, see Lim (1987). Unlike Singapore, Hong Kong was able to rely for capital, technology and industrial entrepreneurship on industrialists who relocated from Shanghai and other mainland Chinese cities after the communist revolution of 1949. Like Singapore, Puerto Rico also relied heavily on (mainly US) multinationals for its industrialization. While Singapore did have an active local, predominantly Overseas Chinese, business class, it was almost exclusively involved in the entrepot

trade, and lacked the knowledge and incentive to venture into manufacturing.

5. Many if not most of the numerous work stoppages conducted by unions in the early 1960s were politically motivated, reflecting the political struggle between 'moderate' and 'left-wing' factions of the PAP which split up in 1962. The 'moderate' PAP faction which retained the reins of government thus had a political motivation to curtail the power of unions, with which they had been locked in an 'anti-communist struggle'. (See Devan Nair (1976).)

6. One casualty of the 'industrial restructuring' policy was the local automobile assembly industry, which lost its tariff protection (without which it could not compete with imports) and closed down in 1980. The government's policy was to shift into export-oriented auto parts and components production instead (see Lim (1982a, pp. 210–14).

7. As an example of high living standards, despite the country's small size (now 3 million people), Singaporeans constitute by far the largest group of foreign tourists in neighboring Malaysia and Indonesia; about one in four Singaporeans travels abroad every year.

8. Some of these costs arise from government social policies – e.g. the world's highest taxes on motor vehicles to reduce traffic congestion – while others reflect strong international demand for limited local resources, especially land and labor.

9. It is also arguable that, politically, a weak local capitalist class poses less of a competitive challenge to the state and ruling party, whose role is rather enhanced by the needs of both foreign capital and labor for it to act as a broker between the two. In addition, the PAP argues that government support and leadership of the union movement is necessary to strengthen the bargaining power of local labor vis-à-vis otherwise much more powerful multinational employers, who concur that government backing of unions make them take the latter's demands more seriously.

10. As mentioned above in the text, in Singapore this has been done, variously, by progressively restricting foreign labor (i.e. tightening labor supply), raising wages, providing fiscal incentives for worker training and capital-labor substitution, and providing worker and management training programs in government and government-affiliated institutes and programs.

11. The southern Chinese merchant and laboring classes which formed the bulk of Singapore's population at independence were economically-motivated migrants who did not have particular respect for the corrupt local and central state bureaucracies that they had left behind in a disintegrating feudal China. In the Confucianist social hierarchy, in any case, merchants and bureaucrats despised each other. The Chinese population of Singapore itself was linguistically heterogeneous, and living with a substantial minority of Malays and Indians. The southern Chinese cultural personality and tradition is also one where 'family means everything, but nation means nothing', and the state is generally to be evaded and avoided (even escaped, through emigration) as a corrupt regulator and onerous tax-collector. Since Singapore itself had no pre-colonial history as an independent nation-state, nationalism was absent

among the population. This contrasts vividly with the homogeneous, 2,000-year-old so-called 'Hermit Kingdom' of Korea, which followed Confucianist traditions much more closely.

12. In the early days, the predominantly English-speaking PAP and the civil service which served it were frequently at odds with the local left-leaning Chinese-speaking merchant and intellectual communities, which were subsequently suppressed, in part by the weakening of Chinese-language education.

13. It is noteworthy that in January 1993, former Prime Minister Lee Kuan Yew seemed to voice second thoughts about this achievement when he publicly lamented the fact that Singapore Chinese businesses could not compete in China because they had 'forgotten' how to use 'relationships' (a code word for bribery and corruption) in business transactions.

14. In the computer disk-drive industry, for example, many US companies came to Singapore in the 1980s virtually as start-ups which were subsequently nurtured by Singapore government assistance, and stayed to derive in some cases as much as 90 per cent of their production for world markets from or through Singapore, for whom, however, each company was only a small and replaceable player in its large diversified pool of multinational employers.

8 East Asia and Industrial Policy in Malaysia: Lessons for Africa?

Chris Edwards

INTRODUCTION

In 1981, the Prime Minister, Dr Mahathir, declared a policy of 'Look East' in Malaysia (Jomo, 1985, p. 312). This was geographically odd. The reference points were Japan, South Korea and Taiwan and yet these could be said to be as much north of Malaysia as east. However, what 'Look East' was intended to signify was a reorientation of foreign, trade and industrial policy away from the UK, the old colonial master[1], towards Japan and the rapidly-growing newly industrialised economies of East Asia.

A few years after the declaration of the 'Look East' policy, a major study of industrial policy was carried out by the Malaysian Government and United Nations Industrial Development Organisation (UNIDO). The team of consultants for this Industrial Master Plan (IMP) was headed by a South Korean, Dr Seongjae Yu. In the *Executive Highlights of the IMP*, Dr Yu contrasted what he called three philosophical assumptions for industrial policy. These were:

(i)   the **market rationale** assumption 'which is presented by America' and for which 'the premise is that the market is rationale in allocating resources and motivating innovative decisions and, therefore, it is not necessary to have any explicit industrial development planning';

(ii) the **state rationale** assumption 'which is adopted by the centrally planned economy, and for which the premise is that decisions made by the state are always rational'; and,

(iii) the **plan rationale** assumption which is identified with Japan and many other newly industrialized countries and for which the 'premise is that while the competitive market mechanism is indispensable, rational planning is fundamentally important in

239

achieving industrial development objectives' (quotes are from the *Executive Highlights of the IMP*, 1986).

The rationale chosen by the IMP was the plan rationale on the lines of South Korea, Japan and Taiwan. The image presented by the IMP was of considerable state intervention in these countries' industrial development, but this image was directly contrary to that presented by the World Bank in 1983. In its *World Development Report* of that year, the World Bank had suggested that there was an inverse relationship between 'distortions from the free market' and economic growth. The methodology that it used has been subjected to fierce criticism (Evans and Alizadeh, 1984; Wade, 1990, p. 19) and the equation of growth in certain economies with free market operations has been subjected to attack. For example, South Korea was ranked by the World Bank as the fourth 'least distorted' economy out of the thirty-one countries that were listed and yet most of the detailed research (Amsden, 1989) that has been done on the South Korean economy and covering the period between the 1960s and the 1980s reveals that there was considerable intervention by the South Korean government. In fact, one writer has gone as far as to say 'No state outside the Socialist bloc ever came anywhere near this measure of control over the country's investible resources' (Lee, 1981, p. 56). However, detailed research has shown extensive intervention to be evident not only in South Korea but also in Japan, Singapore and Taiwan.[2]

These states intervened in a number of areas or 'markets', so that to say that their economies 'suffered few distortions from the free market' is highly misleading. However, it is not only misleading because of the considerable intervention by these governments. The term 'distortions' is itself misleading since it implies that a 'perfect market' exists as a standard by which to judge the operations of the economy. This is wrong not only because of the well-known problems posed for the market by the existence of public goods, externalities and natural monopolies but also because of the less well-publicised problems posed by market transactions and coordination costs. The recent development (or rather resurrection) of game theory and 'Institutional Economics'[3] has highlighted these difficulties. A major problem with the uncontrolled free market is that it tends to make a 'bonfire of the certainties' and for the 'free market' to cope at all adequately with uncertainty requires such a multiplicity of contracts that the transactions costs rapidly escalate. Thus it is increasingly recognised that to compare government failure with market perfection is wrong. **Instead it**

is argued that what economists should be doing is to compare market
failure with government failure.

Once the inevitability of 'free market' failure is acknowledged, then
the desirability of government intervention grows. The test for state
intervention then becomes a less stringent one and the case for the
government pursuing an active industrial policy and disciplining as well
as supporting industry becomes much stronger. In her book *Asia's
Next Giant: South Korea and Late Industrialisation*, Alice Amsden
emphasises that this is the mixture that was achieved in South Korea.
She argues that the South Korean state was able to pick winners and to
create comparative advantage. Amsden goes as far as to say that South
Korean **industrial policy was successful not because the state 'got the
prices right' (the rallying call of the free marketeers) but because it got
them wrong** (1989: 139).

When the IMP in Malaysia talked about the 'plan rationale' of the
East Asian NICs this is what it was referring to. This is the 'rationale'
which was being advocated for Malaysia in 1986, but the adoption of
such a rationale implied a change of policy from that followed in
Malaysia from the 1950s through to the end of the 1980s as the next
section explains.

INDUSTRIAL POLICY AND INDUSTRIALIZATION IN
MALAYSIA – PAST AND PRESENT

In Malaysia, the Government's industrial record can be characterised
as one which has granted too much 'support' to the manufacturing
sector but imposed too little 'discipline'. Support has been given in the
form of tariff and quota protection (TQP) and non-protection
incentives (NPI) (mainly tax holidays and investment incentives). The
total subsidy-equivalent of this support has been estimated to be about
M\$2.3 billion[4] in 1979 and about M\$2.6 billion in 1987, but since 1987
is thought to have risen sharply. Research by the Foreign Investment
Advisory Service of the World Bank has reported (in referring to NPI)
that: '. . . Malaysia's incentive policies offer investors greater incentives than those of either Thailand or Indonesia . . . Only Singapore
offers investors more incentives than Malaysia' (quoted in World
Bank, 1992b, p. 143).

These NPI are discussed by the World Bank (1992b) which estimates
that the tax revenue foregone from the three major types of corporate
tax incentive (the 'tax holiday' arising from Pioneer status, the

Investment Tax Allowance and the Income Abatement for Exports) rose from less than M$0.5 billion between the tax years 1984 and 1988 to more than M$2.5 billion for the tax year 1990 (World Bank, 1992b, p. 141). Thus it is probable that by 1990 the total subsidy from NPI was equal to the subsidy from protection (each about M$2 billion). This means that the total subsidy from protection and non-protection incentives in 1990 was about M$4.0 billion, equivalent to about 3.7 per cent of Malaysia's GNP in that year.

Thus considerable support has been given to the Malaysia manu-facturing sector from both protection and non-protection incentives. This support has been accompanied by only limited disciplines. There have been controls requiring the allocation of corporate shares to 'bumiputras' (Malays), on the terms of 'technology transfer' and, to a limited extent, on pollution, but there have been few other controls. Certainly, by comparison with South Korea, there has been little discipline imposed on the manufacturing industry. There have been few restrictions on direct foreign investment (Lim and Pang, 1991), little pressure on companies to train labour and little or no pressure imposed on companies to integrate production for the domestic market with production for export. Instead, the overwhelming emphasis of indus-trial policy in Malaysia has been on support. However, this support has oscillated between periods when the government has encouraged production for the domestic market to ones in which export-orienta-tion has been emphasised. These phases are summarised in Table 8.1.

At the time of Independence in 1957, Malaysia was backward in terms of its industrial development. The British colonial government had been reluctant to encourage import-substituting industrialization: firstly because higher prices for wage goods would have reduced the profits from the rubber plantations and the tin mines in which British interests were strong, and secondly because the replacement of revenue-raising tariffs by protective tariffs would have reduced government revenue (Edwards, 1975, p. 288). As a result, in 1957 the manufacturing sector in Malaysia was backward given its average income and the population. Malaysia was a 'late, late-starter'.

However, since Independence, considerable encouragement has been given to the manufacturing sector in Malaysia. As shown in Table 8.1, in the 1960s an ISI policy was followed and then, in the 1970s, export orientation was emphasised based on the EPZs. In the first half of the 1980s, there was a second round of ISI based on protectionism and public sector investment in heavy industries and then, following a sharp real devaluation of the ringgit in the mid-1980s and an extension

Table 8.1   Phases of Industrial Development in Malaysia

Period	Phase[1]	Form of[2] Incentive	Favourable aspects?			
			High Exports	Labour- Intensive	Strong Linkage	Regionally Dispersed
1960s	ISI	Mostly TQP[3]	No	No	No	No
1970s	EOI	NPI[4]	Yes[5]	Yes	No	No
1980-85	ISI	Both[6]	No	No	No	To some extent
1986- onwards	EOI	NPI[7]	Yes	Yes[8]	No	No

Source: Author.

[1] ISI (import-substituting industrialization) denotes phases in which encouragement has been given to manufacturing which is geared to production for the domestic market. ISI is a common label for this phase but the label is a little misleading in the Malaysian case since, as I point out later, the extent of import substitution in these industries has been limited.

[2] TQP denotes tariff and quota protection and NPI denotes non-protection incentives.

[3] In this period some NPI were given in the form of tax holidays.

[4] Encouragement was given by setting up Export Processing Zones (Free Trade Zones and Licensed Manufacturing Warehouses) and through the widespread provision of tax incentives.

[5] Production from the EPZs has been highly export-intensive in terms of finished products but highly import-intensive in terms of inputs (see Table 8.2).

[6] Encouragement was given both by protection and by the public- sector financing of 'heavy industries' (steel, automobile assembly and cement industries).

[7] Encouragement was given by a sharp devaluation of Malaysia's real effective exchange rate in 1986 and by an extension of tax incentives.

[8] But note that the export-intensive industries have become increasingly capital-intensive in recent years.

of tax incentives, there was a resurgence of manufactured exports from the EPZs.

In 1987 the World Bank categorised Malaysia as a 'moderately outward-oriented economy' (World Bank, 1987, p. 83), but this categorisation makes little sense. By the late 1980s, Malaysian industry had a **dual structure** with two quite separate export-oriented (EO) and domestically-oriented (DO) sectors superimposed on a resource-based sector. The EO sector was and is selling almost exclusively overseas while the DO sector was and is selling almost exclusively in the domestic market. To average these makes about as much sense as saying that a person with one foot in boiling-hot water and the other in ice-cold water is 'moderately comfortable'.

However, although the EO and DO sectors are quite separate, they do have one thing in common, namely their high import dependence. Both the DO and EO industries are enclaves with few linkages and little integration with the rest of the economy. The lack of linkages is particularly evident when Malaysia is compared with South Korea at a similar stage of development (see Table 8.2).

Thus there has been little depth in Malaysia's industrial development. Local linkages are growing, but they are growing in spite of, rather than because of, government policy. And yet, the performance of the Malaysian economy has been impressive particularly when compared with that of Sub-Saharan Africa (SSA). Between 1965 and 1990, GNP per capita in Malaysia grew in real terms at 4.0 per cent per

Table 8.2   The Import Content of Manufactured Goods – Malaysia (1987) and South Korea (1975)

Description	Percentage of Gross Output Exported Malaysia 1987	Percentage of Total Material Inputs Imported Malaysia 1987	Percentage of Total Material Inputs Imported S. Korea 1975
Resource-Based Industries			
Palm-oil processing	67	0–5	n.a
Wood products	92	5–20	60–70
Petroleum products	n.a	0–5	85–95
Rubber remilling off-estates	95	0–5	35–40
Rubber and plastic products	20	60–70	
Domestically-Oriented Industries			
Food, beverage and tobacco			
(exc. palm-oil processing)	14	60–70	15–40
Paper products	14	50–70	25–30
Chemical products	n.a	80–95	30–35
Non-metallic mineral products	19	20–30	0–15
Metals and metal products	22	60–70	30–35
Transport equipment	7	80–90	30–40
Export-Oriented Industries			
Textiles and clothing	75	80–90	15–20
Electronics and electrical			
machinery	95	80–90	35–45
All industries	54	50–60	35–40

Source: Bank Negara, 1990: 27, POLIND, 1990, Table 1.A.1 and Appendices; UN, 1985.

annum compared with an average for SSA of 0.2 per cent per annum (World Bank, 1992a, p. 219) and between 1980 and 1990 the manufacturing sector in Malaysia grew at an annual average of 8.8 per cent compared with SSA's 3.1 per cent (World Bank, 1992a, p. 221). Thus in spite of its industrial dualism, Malaysia's industrial performance has been outstanding relative to that of SSA. Why? What, if any, are the lessons which SSA can draw from the Malaysian experience?

THE LESSONS FOR SSA?

The first point that needs to be made is that there are no easy generalisations that can be made about SSA's relatively weak economic performance over the past twenty five years. There are 45 or so national economies within SSA and they vary considerably in their historical, political and economic structure. They also vary considerably in economic performance, with some having very good long-term growth records. Thus Lesotho and Botswana have both experienced faster growth rates in real GNP per capita between 1965 and 1990 than Malaysia and the annual (real GNP per capita) growth rates in Burundi, Cameroon, and Mauritius have all been 3 per cent or more. Because of this diversity, a 1989 World Bank report is correct in saying; '. . .there are no quick fixes and no simple blueprints' (World Bank, 1989a, p. 185).

Here I do not attempt to advocate any simple blueprints, but one that can be rejected immediately is a simple reliance on free markets. As I have argued earlier, the issue is not whether governments should intervene but how. Both the Malaysian and South Korean governments have intervened extensively in their economies and they have both experienced rapid growth[5], but in South Korea the growth rate has been particularly fast over the past thirty to forty years due in large part to the extraordinarily effective intervention of the South Korean government.

By contrast, state intervention in SSA has been somewhat misdirected. A common thread running through World Bank reports on SSA has been that poor state policy has provided the major, if not the exclusive, explanation for the poor growth record of SSA and in a useful article entitled 'Explaining Africa's Post-Independence Development Experiences', Tony Killick cites the following weaknesses of government policy in SSA (1992, pp. 22–30):

(i)   inappropriate exchange rates, particularly in the 1970s;
(ii) high taxes and marketing margins on exports;
(iii) heavy protection on production for small domestic markets;
(iv) excessive state consumption and weak state enterprises.

However, having cited these weaknesses, Killick argues persuasively that it is too simplistic to say that poor state policies explain the poor growth record of SSA. He argues that the World Bank view of the problem is misplaced. I agree. Broadly, there are two defects in the World Bank's approach.

Firstly the World Bank's approach is too 'idealistic' in the sense that too little attention is paid to the historical and political constraints to free markets in SSA. In general, in Africa the state is less autonomous (and 'weaker') than in South Korea (see Stein in chapter 2) and yet, as Amsden has argued, to impose free markets requires just as 'strong a state' as does extensive and effective intervention (Amsden, 1989, p. 18). It is beyond the scope of this chapter to examine in detail the political characteristics of SSA, but it is important to note that many economists and political scientists agree on the centrality of political explanations for SSA's comparatively poor economic performance, and many have criticised the World Bank for not paying sufficient attention to political characteristics and constraints in making its recommendations for market reforms.

This lack of attention exists even though, in 1989, the World Bank admitted that 'Underlying the litany of Africa's development problems is a crisis of governance. . .' (World Bank, 1989a, p. 60). How is this crisis to be explained? Although I do not have the space to go into a more detailed discussion here,[6] there are a few points which are useful to note. For example, Hyden has argued that low population densities and 'indirect' colonial rule in SSA have enabled 'traditional' social structures to survive; these structures being characterised by vertical (ethnic) rather than horizontal (class) political groupings. Such vertical structures, it is argued, are hostile to 'formal bureaucratic principles' (Hyden, 1986). Connected with this is the idea that capitalism has not sufficiently 'broken open' African society. Geoffrey Kay has argued that merchant capital, which makes its profit not by revolutionizing production but by controlling markets, tends to block the development of productive facilities. Kay argues that in many parts of the South (and especially in Africa) merchant capital has remained powerful, and as a result, 'we have to face the unpalatable fact that capitalism has created underdevelopment not simply because it has exploited the underdeveloped countries but because it has not exploited them enough' (Kay, 1975, p. 55).

Thus the first defect of the World Bank's obsession with free markets is that it fails to treat sufficiently seriously the structural obstacles to market reforms in SSA stemming from 'political' constraints. The second defect of the World Bank's approach is that it ignores the structural 'economic' obstacles to growth in SSA. One of the most important of these is the smallness of the SSA economies which is highlighted in Table 8.3.

Table 8.3 not only shows (in row 3) that the average GDP of the SSA countries is very much smaller than those of Malaysia and South Korea but it also shows (in row 6) that the 'density of income' is very much lower. The low density of income results from a low GNP per capita (row 4) combined with a low density of population (row 5) in SSA compared with those in Malaysia and South Korea. Thus in 1990 the 'density of income' in SSA was only $7,000 per square kilometre compared with densities many times as great in Malaysia and South Korea.[7]

This low density of income is likely to be a barrier to the growth of the manufacturing sector insofar as the latter is characterised by economies of scale. The importance of scale economies in the manufacturing sector is implied in the work of Kuznets, Chenery and

Table 8.3   SSA, Malaysia and South Korea: A Comparison

	SSA	*Malaysia*	*S. Korea*
Growth in real per capita income (GNP) between 1965 and 1990 (% per annum)	0.2	4.0	7.1
GDP ($ bn. – total)[1]	163	42	236
GDP ($ bn. – country average)	4	42	236
GNP per capita ($)	340	2,320	5,400
Density of population (people per sq. km.)	21	54	432
'Density of income'[2] ($000 GNP per sq.km.)	7	125	2,333

Source: World Bank, 1992a: 219,223
[1]figures in rows 2 to 6 inclusive are for 1990.
[2]derived from multiplying row 4 by row 5.

others who have shown (see Figure 8.1) that not only does the manufacturing sector acquire increasing importance as GNP per capita increases, but its importance is greater for a given GNP per capita the larger a country's population.

Thus it seems plausible to argue that small domestic markets and low 'densities of income' in the countries of SSA prevent producers from achieving the necessary economies of scale to be competitive in the world market. It seems that industry is necessary to development, but that industry thrives on economies of scale which may not be achievable in the small national markets of SSA.

However, in response to this, there is a counter-argument or question that needs to be considered: namely, have recent changes in technology made economies of scale less important? Since the beginning of the 1980s, a number of researchers such as Kaplinsky (1991), Piore and Sabel (1984) and Schmitz (1989) have highlighted the growth of new forms of technology and organisation (usually bracketed under the heading of 'flexible specialisation') which may provide new openings for small-scale production. In opposition others like Harvey (1989, pp. 141–200) and Pollert (1988) have argued that the so-called flexible specialisation is by no means new and that 'Economies of scale still matter, and not just in production' (Sayer, 1989, p. 675). It is argued that economies of scale remain significant not only in manufacturing production but also in marketing (especially export marketing[8]) and in research and development.

If we assume that, in spite of the new technologies, economies of scale are still significant in the manufacturing sector, then the small markets of SSA would seem to continue to be an obstacle to the development of the manufacturing sector. However, another counter-argument or question then arises, namely – surely producers in countries with thin domestic markets may achieve economies of scale by exporting to the larger world market? Yes they may, but the risks may be considerable. Indeed the risks may be so great as to deter small domestic companies from setting up factories big enough to achieve the necessary economies of scale.

How can these risks be reduced? One obvious way is to provide protection in the national market so that the profits from the domestic sales can provide a launching-pad for exports. Thus in South Korea an import-substituting (IS) phase of the 1950s was followed by an export-oriented (EO) phase since the 1960s. The IS phase helped domestic capital to build its competitive strength for the later entry into the world market while the later entry into the world market during the EO

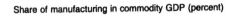

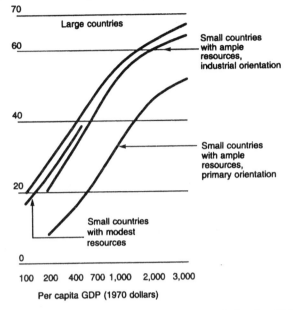

Note: A country was classified as large if its population in 1970 was 20 million or more; otherwise, it was classified as small. A small country was classified as having modest resources if its average per capita production of primaries (defined as GDP less services and manufacturing) in 1960–73 was less than $84 (in 1970 prices); otherwise it was classified as having ample resources. A small country with ample resources was classified as having an industrial orientation if in most years during the period 1969–73 its value added in manufacturing was above the regression plane that predicts manufacturing value added using per capita GDP and population (for smaller countries with ample resources); if in most years the actual manufacturing value added was below the regression plane, the country was classified as having a primary orientation.

The horizontal axis is in log scale. The curves are plots of a logistic function with the population variable held constant at the average value of each group. The number of observations at higher income levels was insufficent to extend the curve for smaller countries with modest resources beyond $400 per capita income.

Commodity GDP is GDP minus the value of services.

Source: UNIDO 1979, figure VI, p. 47, and Annex I and World Bank, 1987, 52.

Figure 8.1 Industrialization and GDP

phase was assisted by the continuing protection on domestic sales. Manufacturers were commonly given protection on their sales in the domestic market on condition that they achieved export targets (Westphal, 1990, p. 47), so that the high profits in the domestic market offset the low profits or even losses in the export market.

Unfortunately for many SSA countries the South Korean route is unlikely to be feasible since the domestic market is too small to provide a profitable platform for exporting. The major source of manufacturing growth in SSA has been from domestic demand (Riddell, 1990, p. 34)[9] but the growth in domestic demand has been too small to provide sufficient back-up for the development of the manufacturing sector. The growth of domestic demand in SSA has been slow because of the slow growth of the primary sector. Between 1980 and 1990 the average annual growth rate of the agricultural sector was 2.0 per cent in SSA compared to 3.8 per cent in Malaysia (World Bank, 1992a, p. 221).

Thus, in SSA, growth in the manufacturing sector has been based on the domestic market but growth in the domestic market has been slow because of the slow growth of the primary sector. Furthermore, the foreign exchange earnings of the primary sector have been too sluggish to finance investment in the manufacturing sector. With about 90 per cent of SSA's exports consisting of primary products in 1989 (Killick, 1992, table 2), the annual growth in the value of exports between 1980 and 1990 was only 0.2 per cent (World Bank, 1992a, p. 245). Can this slow growth be explained by declining prices of primary products in the world market? The answer is 'partly but not entirely', with the conclusion depending on which group of countries within SSA is being examined. For example, if we examine the low-income countries of SSA, the slow growth in primary exports can be explained by a sharp deterioration in prices. For this group of countries the worsening terms of trade reduced real Gross Domestic Product by more than 4 per cent **per annum** over the whole of the 1975–87 period (World Bank, 1989a, p. 24). However for SSA as a whole (and over the same period), this 'income effect' of changes in the terms of trade was mostly positive. Even if we exclude the oil-exporting countries and look only at the oil-importing countries in SSA, the income effect of changes in the terms of trade over the 1975–87 period was neither significantly positive nor negative (World Bank, 1989a, p. 24).

As a result, for SSA in general, declining prices do not provide an 'excuse' for the poor performance of primary exports.[10] The poor performance of exports from SSA over the period 1973–1990 was not just in value but also in volume terms with the volume[11] of exports actually falling slightly (Killick, 1992, table 1).

Thus the growth in primary exports production in SSA has not provided the foreign exchange earnings to finance investment in the manufacturing sector. Nor has the primary sector provided the domestic income base for the expansion of the manufacturing sector. This means that the South Korean route to manufactured exports (launching them from a platform of domestic demand) is not open to the countries of SSA.

However if the South Korean route is not viable, is there an alternative exporting route available? Possibly there is, with Malaysia providing the model. As I have argued earlier in this chapter, the rapidly-growing export-oriented (EO) part of the manufacturing sector in Malaysia has been quite separate from production for the domestic market. The most rapid growth in production for export has been from 'enclave-like' export processing zones. If this is so, it is reasonable to ask why the exporters were prepared to take the risk of exporting on such a scale and without the back-up of a protected domestic market. Were they provided with large direct export subsidies? The answer is 'no'. Direct subsidies pose two problems. One is that such subsidies are likely to contravene the regulations of the General Agreement of Tariffs and Trade (GATT) and lead to countervailing duties in the importing countries. The other is that direct subsidies are likely to be a major drain on public sector revenue. Thus direct export subsidies pose major problems for any Less Developed Country wanting to expand manufactured exports.

Why then were exporters from Malaysia prepared to take the risks? The answer is that the EO sector has been dominated by direct foreign investment (DFI). By far the most important exporting sub-sector of Malaysian manufacturing is electronics and electrical machinery and foreign companies own almost the whole of this sub-sector. Electronic components from Malaysia are exported by transnational companies (TNCs) which are large and invariably vertically-integrated. These TNCs have had an advantage over domestic capital in exporting by their ability to spread risks although it has also been alleged that, for political reasons, foreign capital was given preferential treatment in Malaysia over domestic, mostly Chinese, capital (Jesudason, 1990).

The 'Malaysian model' of exporting manufactures is, then, one based on foreign companies producing in 'enclave' EPZs without grants.[12] Is this model a viable one for SSA to copy? The answer is 'possibly', but the route is not an easy one. For foreign companies to find it profitable to use SSA as a base for manufactured exports, there needs to be a good supply of cheap labour and a good physical infrastructure.

Cheap labour means not low wage **rates** but low wage **costs** after allowing for differences in productivity. At the beginning of the 1970s, when Malaysia started its export drive from Export Processing Zones (EPZs), it had such a labour force available. The rice-producing and primary exporting (rubber, tin and oil palm) sectors provided a 'reserve army' of under-employed which, combined with anti-Trades Union action by the government and the widespread recruitment of women in the EPZs, ensured low real wage rates. At the same time, the education levels of the Malaysian labour force were high so that levels of labour productivity were sufficiently high to ensure low production costs. By comparison, the education levels in SSA are low. For example, in 1989, 59 per cent of the relevant age group were enroled in secondary schools in Malaysia, while the corresponding percentage in SSA was only 18 per cent (World Bank, 1992a, p. 275). Thus, the education level in SSA, which was extremely low at the time of Independence in the 1960s (Fransman, 1982, p. 33; Killick, 1992, p. 43), remains relatively low, whereas even as much as a quarter of a century ago (in 1965) the education level in Malaysia was high with the percentage enroled at the secondary level being 28 per cent.[13]

Not only are education levels in SSA low when compared to other Less Developed Countries, but the physical infrastructure is also weak. The exporting of manufactures requires the sort of infrastructure (seaports, roads, telecommunications, airports, housing for workers) which had been developed prior to Independence in Malaysia. The infrastructure had been developed on the west coast of Peninsular Malaysia to serve the primary (rubber and tin) sectors. In addition to providing the basis for the development of a good infrastructure, primary commodities provided a steady flow of foreign exchange into Malaysia. In 1965 all but about 10 to 15 per cent of Malaysia's exports consisted of primary products (Jomo, 1990, p. 56) – about the same proportion as in SSA in 1965 and 1989 (Killick, 1992, table 2). However, Malaysia has been a more open economy with its exports being a greater proportion of GDP – in Malaysia, 42 and 79 per cent in 1965 and 1990 respectively compared with 22 and 29 per cent in 1965 and 1990 respectively (World Bank, 1992a, p. 235).[14]

The primary sector has also provided Malaysia with a good public sector revenue basis. In 1960 export duties on rubber and tin provided about a quarter of Federal Government revenue, equivalent to about 3 per cent of GNP (Jomo, 1990, p. 176). In turn, this revenue provided the basis for further public sector rural development programmes (most notably under the Federal Land Development Authority), producing primary commodities for export – especially palm oil and rubber – so that even as recently as 1980, export duties provided 18 per cent of Federal Government revenue – equivalent to almost 5 per cent of GNP.

By contrast with Malaysia, the infrastructure in much of SSA has been weak. The low density of population and the low (relative to Malaysia) ratio of exports to GNP in SSA has meant that the development of the infrastructure has been poor. In particular, the road network was poor at the time of Independence in the 1960s and remained so into the 1970s and 1980s (Killick, 1992, p. 43). As a result of the weak infrastructure and of what Riddell (1990, p. 36) calls a weak 'climate' of exporting in SSA, export expansion from SSA has been slow in spite of declining real effective exchange rates, especially since the early 1980s (Killick, 1992, pp. 23–5).

As a result of the relatively cheap and productive labour force and the developed physical infrastructure in Malaysia, the rates of profit achieved by foreign capital investing in Malaysia have been attractive. Data given by the Malaysian Government (DOS, 1987) suggests that the before-tax rate of profit achieved in Malaysia by foreign-controlled companies was 19 per cent. This seems to be higher than the average of between 15 and 19 per cent achieved on capital invested in the major industrial economies (UNDP, 1992, p. 53). In the light of this, it is perhaps not surprising that foreign investors have been so willing to invest in Malaysia and by 1985, the stock of DFI in Malaysia was 29 per cent of GDP. The corresponding figure in Africa was only 13 per cent, although it should be noted that the African percentage was well above the 6 per cent of Asia and almost equal to the 14 per cent of Latin America (UNCTC, 1988, p. 129).

However, although the level of DFI in Africa as measured by the percentage of GDP is high relative to the rest of the South, the stock of DFI per capita is relatively low. In the 1980s, Africa received only about 2 per cent of the world's DFI (UNDP, 1992, p. 52), even though the continent contained over 10 per cent of the world's population.

SUMMARY AND SOME CONCLUSIONS

It would seem, then, that the prospects for industrial development in SSA are weak. The national markets are too small and too slowly-growing to generate the economies of scale necessary for efficient production. Furthermore the national markets are even too small to enable SSA to copy South Korea – namely to launch into export markets from a 'subsidised' protected domestic market.

At the same time, most of the countries of SSA are likely to find it difficult to copy the alternative Malaysian 'model' of exporting manufactures from 'enclave' Export Processing Zones. Such exporting from Malaysia has been carried out by foreign companies which have been able to bear the risks of exporting because of their size and their vertical integration. These foreign manufacturing companies have been attracted to Malaysia by relatively high rates of profit, which in turn have been facilitated by the existence of a cheap but educated labour force and an efficient physical infrastructure which had been put in place to serve the primary exporting sectors of rubber, tin and later, palm oil.

Relatively speaking, SSA has a poor physical and human infrastructure so that its ability to attract foreign investment has been limited. Yet it is hard to envisage domestic capitalists in SSA taking the risk to invest on a sufficient scale to export competitively unless they have the support of direct export subsidies. At the same time such subsidies are not only expensive in terms of public sector finance but also run the risk of violating GATT regulations.

Thus the prospects for industrialisation in SSA are poor and there are no simple blueprints which will guarantee success. It is doubtful whether the free market blueprint commonly advocated by the World Bank and International Monetary Fund is likely to be successful. These international institutions have argued that once free markets are introduced and the 'playing fields are levelled', then economies are likely to take off. In opposition to this, it has been argued that the 'free market playing field' is not an even one and that 'late industrialisers' such as South Korea and Taiwan have managed to achieve rapid industrialisation not only because of pervasive and efficient state intervention but also because of land reforms and massive US aid at least in the 1950s and into the 1960s.

However, industrialisation is necessary for the development of SSA since the prospects of the primary sector are weak because of the probability of declining terms of trade. Furthermore, much of this industrialisation needs to be export-oriented to efficiently take advantage of economies of scale. The development of export-oriented industries requires industrial targeting, the development of an improved physical and human infrastructure and investment in other supply-side policies (Fransman, 1982, p. 31; Riddell, 1990, p. 58).

By contrast, state intervention in SSA has been pervasive but not efficient. In addition, other conditions for manufacturing expansion have been unfavourable. The level of education of the labour force is low and the physical infrastructure is poor. Thus, some of the elements of the 'Malaysian model' (of foreign investors exporting manufactures from 'enclave' Export Processing Zones) are missing.

Thus the prospects for development in SSA led by the primary sector are not good because of the likelihood of declining terms of trade. At the same time, industrialization is necessary but is subject to economies of scale which might only be achievable by exporting to the world market. However, the physical and human infrastructure for such exporting has to be developed. This is likely to require not only industrial targeting by the state but also substantial investment in supply-side policies (Fransman, 1982, p. 31; Riddell, 1990, p. 58). However, this in turn will require not only an increase in the present level of aid to SSA (currently running at about $30 per capita per annum according to the UNDP (1992, p. 41) but also a re-direction towards the manufacturing sector of such aid that is given.

Notes

1. Malaysia (or rather West, or Peninsular Malaysia) gained its political independence in 1957. In 1963, the North Bornean states of Sarawak and Sabah joined the Federation as did Singapore. Two years later, Singapore left the Federation to become a separate Republic and since then, Malaysia has consisted of the eleven states of Peninsular Malaysia and the two East Malaysian states of Sabah and Sarawak.
2. See, for example, Rodan, 1989; Van Liemt, 1988; Wade, 1990; and White, 1988.
3. See, for example, Aoki et al., 1990; Chang, 1991; and Williamson, 1985.
4. The exchange rate of the Malaysian ringgit ($M) to the US dollar was 2.30 in 1976–80, 2.35 from 1981–85 and 2.64 from 1986–90 (see table 5.4 in Ministry of Finance, 1989/90; 1990/91).
5. This is true not only of Malaysia and South Korea but also of many other middle-income countries. As Chenery put it in a recent book; '. . ..(An) examination of the experiences of countries which have successfully pursued export-led growth shows that their governments followed active interventionist policies, albeit with heavy reliance on market incentives' (Chenery et al., 1986, p. 358)
6. See Killick (1992, pp. 34–40) for more on this.

7. There are two problems associated with the data in table 8.3. One is that the 1990 data compare Malaysia and South Korea which were both highly developed in that year with a much less developed sub-Saharan Africa. The second objection is that average densities of income hide concentrations of population (and purchasing power) in the cities of SSA (such as Abidjan, Dakar, Nairobi, and Lagos). However, on the first point, it should be noted that, even as long ago as 1965, the 'density of income' (in terms of GNP per sq. km. in 1990 prices) was $26,000 in Malaysia which was almost four times as large at the 1990 figure of $7000 for SSA countries (shown in table 8.3). Note that South Korea's density of income in 1965–at about $283,000– was about 40 times as great as the 1990 figure for the SSA countries. Thus the density of income for SSA countries in 1990 is low even when compared to the 1965 densities of Malaysia and South Korea. However, I recognize that average density figures are only a crude indication of the ease with which a country can exploit economies of scale.

8. In a study of 'Small Manufacturing Enterprises in Developing Countries', Ian Little argued that: 'Big firms have economies of scales in export marketing, and it is generally true that most small units export little or nothing' (Little, 1987, p. 230). Little also argued that, in terms of the most efficient use of resources, small is not beautiful. As Little put it: 'If anything, medium-size firms come out best' (Little, 1987, p. 230).

9. Riddell analyzed the sources of growth in seven countries in SSA. These were Botswana, Cameroon, Côte d'Ivoire, Kenya, Nigeria, Zambia and Zimbabwe. He found that across all these economies up to the late 1980s the predominant source of growth of the manufacturing sector was domestic demand – as opposed to import substitution or exporting (Riddell, 1990, pp. 33–4).

10. However, as stated above, the 'income effect' of declining terms of trade for low income countries (notably Mauritania, Zaire and Zambia) was particularly serious (Killick, 1992, p. 18).

11. However it should be noted that the data on changes in export volume from SSA are conflicting. For example, for the period between 1983 and 1987, the IMF estimated that the annual growth rate for export volume from SSA was 2.2 per cent while the Worls Bank's estimate was **minus** 1.8 per cent per annum (Killick, 1992, p. 24).

12. However, although no direct grants have been given to exporting companies, most companies in the Malaysian EPZs have been encouraged by being given considerable tax holidays and incentives.

13. However, it should be noted that, even as long ago as 1965, the GNP per capita in Malaysia (in 1990 prices) was well above that of SSA in 1990. GNP per capita in Malaysia in 1965 (in 1990 prices) was US$869 compared with US$340 in SSA in 1990 (calculated from World Bank, 1992a, p. 219.

14. Malaysia's flow of foreign exchange earnings from primary products has been steady but not destabilising. Between 1960 and 1990, there have been no sharp rises in Malaysia's real effective exchange rate arising from sharp improvements in the external terms of trade, except in 1973.

Bibliography

Abbey, Joe (1991) 'Lessons of Experience and the Future of Adjustment Lending', in Thomas Vinod et al., *Restructuring Economies in Distress, Policy Reform and the World Bank* (Oxford: Oxford University Press for the World Bank) pp. 523–526.

Adams, F. G., and L. R. Klein (eds) 1982) *Industrial Policies for Growth and Competitiveness: An Economic Perspective* (Lexington, Mass.: Lexington Books).

Adelman, Irma (1974) 'South Korea', in H. Chenery et al. (eds), *Redistribution with Growth* (London: Oxford University Press for the World Bank).

Africa Watch (1991) *Academic Freedom and Human Rights Abuses in Africa* (New York: Human Rights Watch).

Aldrich, H. E. (1979) *Organizations and Environments* (New Jersey: Prentice-Hall).

Allen, G. C. (1964). *A Short Economic History of Modern Japan* (London: Macmillan).

Amsden, Alice (1979) 'Taiwan's Economic History: A Case of Etatisme and a Challenge to Dependency Theory', *Modern China* 5(3)(July) 3, pp. 341–80.

Amsden, Alice (1989). *Asia's Next Giant: South Korea and Late Industrialization* (New York: Oxford University Press).

Amsden, Alice (1994) 'Why isn't the Whole World Experimenting with the East Asian Model to Develop?: Review of the World Bank's *The East Asian Miracle: Economic Growth and Public Policy*'. The Graduate Faculty, Political Economy, New School for Social Reseach, Working Paper No. 47, presented at the Allied Social Science Meeting, January.

Aoki, M. et al. (eds) (1990) *The Firm as a Nexus of Treaties* (London: Sage Publications).

Ariff, Mohamed and Hal Hill (1985) *Export-Oriented Industrialization: The Asean Experience* (Sydney: Allen & Unwin).

Arrow, Kenneth (1962). 'The Economic Implications of Learning by Doing', *Review of Economic Studies* 29 (June) pp. 154–94.

Balassa, B. (1971). 'Industrial Policies in Taiwan and Korea', *Welwirtschaftliches Archiv*, 106(1), pp. 55–77.

Balassa, B. (1981). *The Newly Industrialized Countries in the World Economy*. (New York: Pergamon Press).

Balassa, B. (1984). 'Adjustment Policies in Developing Countries: A Reassessment', *World Development*, 12(9), pp. 955–72.

Balassa, B. (1985). *Change and Challenge in the World Economy* (London: Macmillan).

Balassa, B. et al. (1982) *Development Strategies in Semi-industrial Economies*. (Baltimore, MD: Johns Hopkins University Press).

Ban, S. H. et al. (1980) *Rural Development*, Harvard East Asian Monograph, 89 Cambridge, Massachusetts: Council on East Asian Studies, Harvard University).

258 Bibliography

Bank Negara (1990). *Annual Report* (Kuala Lumpur: Bank Negara).

Bank of Korea (1973) *Economic Statistic Yearbook* (Seoul: Bank of Korea).

Bank of Korea (1976) *Economic Statistic Yearbook* (Seoul: Bank of Korea).

Barrett, Richard and Chin Soomi 'Export-Oriented Industrializing States in the Capitalist World System; Similarities and Differences' (1987) in F. Deyo (ed.), *The Political Economy of the New Asian Industrialism*, pp. 23–43.

Bates, Robert (1981). *Markets and States in Tropical Africa: The Political Basis of Agricultural Policies* (Berkeley: University of California Press).

Bates, Robert (1987) *Essays on the Political Economy of Rural Africa* (Berkeley: University of California Press).

Bates, Robert (1989) 'The Reality of Structural Adjustment: A Sceptical Appraisal', in S. Commander, *Structural Adjustment and Agriculture: Theory and Practice in Africa and Latin America* (London: Overseas Development Institute).

Bhagwati, J. (1978) *Anatomy and Consequence of Exchange Control Regimes* (Cambridge: Ballinger).

Bhagwati, J. (1985) *Wealth and Poverty* (Oxford: Basil Blackwell).

Bhattacharya, Amarendra and Johannes F. Linn (1988) 'Trade and Industrial Policies in the Developing Countries of East Asia', World Bank Discussion Paper, No. 27 (Washington, DC: The World Bank).

Biggs, Tyler S. and Brian Levy (1988) 'Strategic Interventions and the Political Economy of Industrial Policy in Developing Countries', EEPA Discussion Paper, No. 23, October.

Boone, Catherine. (1994) 'Trade, Taxes and Tribute: Market Liberalization and the New Importers in West Africa', *World Development*, 22(3), pp. 453–69.

Bond, Michael H. and G. Hofstede (1990) 'The cash value of Confusian values'. in S. R. Clegg and S. G. Redding (eds), *Capitalism in Contrasting Cultures* (New York: de Gruyter).

Brautigam, Deborah (1992) 'Regional Industrialization in Eastern Nigeria', Report prepared for Nigeria Country Operations, West Africa Region. (Washington, DC: World Bank).

Brautigam, Deborah (1993) 'Substituting for the State: Explaining Industrial Development in Eastern Nigeria', paper presented at the African Studies Association Annual Meeting, Boston, Mass., December.

Brautigam, Deborah (1994) 'African Industrialization in Comparative Perspective: The Question of Scale', in Bruce J. Berman and Colin Leys (eds), *African Capitalists in African Development* (Boulder: Lynne Rienner Publishers) pp. 139–162.

Bryant, Ralph C. (1989). 'The Evolution of Singapore as a Financial Centre', in Sandhu and Wheatley (eds), *Management of Success: The Moulding of Modern Singapore* (Singapore: Institute of Southeast Asian Studies), pp. 337–72.

Business Korea (1983) *Monthly Economic and Trade Review*. Seoul, various issues.

Bureau of Labor (1978) *Yearbook of Labor* (Seoul: Bureau of Labor).

Cable, Vincent (1991) 'African Trade Policies and Multilateral Negotiations', in J. Frimpong-Ansah et al. (ed.), *Trade and Development in Sub-Saharan Africa* (Manchester: Manchester University Press) pp. 152–87.

Campbell, Horace, and Howard Stein (eds) (1992). *Tanzania and the IMF: The Dynamics of Liberalization* (Boulder, Colo.: Westview Press).

Chan, Steve, (1990) 'State Making and State Breaking: The Origins and Paradoxes of the Contemporary Taiwanese State', in E. Greenberg and T. Mayer (eds), *Changes in the State: Causes and Consequences* (Newbury Park, Ca.: Sage).

Chan, W. K. 1991. *The Making of Hong Kong Society*. Oxford: Clarendon Press.

Chang Ha-Joon (1991) 'The Political Economy of Industrial Policy', unpublished PhD thesis submitted at the Faculty of Economics and Politics, University of Cambridge.

Chen, Peter S. J. (ed.) (1983) *Singapore Development Policies and Trends* (Singapore: Oxford University Press).

Chenery H, Robinson S and Syrquin M. (1986) *Industrialization and Growth: A Comparative Study* (New York: Oxford University Press for the World Bank).

Chhibber, Ajay (1989) 'The Aggregate Supply Response: A Survey', in Commander (ed.), *Structural Adjustment and Agriculture* (London: Overseas Development Institute) pp. 56–68.

Chia Siow Yue (1971) 'Growth and Pattern of Industrialization', in You and Lim (eds), *The Singapore Economy* (Singapore: Eastern Universities Press) pp. 189–223.

Chia Siow Yue (1984) 'Export Processing and Industrialisation: The Case of Singapore', in Eddy Lee (ed.), *Export Processing Zones and Industrial Employment in Asia* (Bangkok: International Labour Organisation/AR-TEP) pp. 95–156.

Chia Siow Yue (1985) 'Singapore', in *Patterns and Impact of Foreign Investment in the ESCAP Region* (Bangkok, Thailand: UN-ESCAP) pp. 193–224.

Chia Siow Yue (1986) 'The Economic Development of Singapore: A Selective Survey of the Literature', in Basant K. Kapur (ed.), *Singapore Studies* (Singapore: Singapore University Press) pp. 183–242.

Chia Siow Yue (1989) 'The Character and Progress of Industrialization', in Sandhu and Wheatley (eds), *Management of Success: The Moulding of Modern Singapore* (Singapore: Institute of Southeast Asian Studies, pp. 250–79.

Chng Meng Kng, Linda Low and Toh Mun Heng (1988) *Industrial Restructuring in Singapore* (Singapore: Chopmen Publishers).

Choo, Hakchung (1987) *Income Distribution and Its Determinants: The Case of Korea* (Seoul: Korean Development Institute).

Choo, Hakchung and Daemo Kim (1978) *Probable Size Distribution of Income in Korea* (Seoul: Korean Development Institute)

Chudnovsky, D., M. Nagao, and S. Jacobson (1984) *Capital Goods Production in the Third World: An Economic Study of Technical Acquisition* (London: Francis Pinter).

Clad, J. (1989) *Behind the Myth: Business, Money and Power in Southeast Asia* (London: Grafton Books).

Clegg, S. R. and S. G. Redding (eds) (1990) *Capitalism in Contrasting Cultures* (New York: de Gruyter).

Clegg, S. et al. (1990) 'Post-confucianism, Social Democracy and Economic Culture', in S. Clegg and S. G. Redding (eds), *Capitalism in Contrasting Cultures* (New York: de Gruyter) pp. 31–78.

Cline, William (1982) 'Can the East Asian Model of Development be Generalized?', *World Development* 10(2), pp. 81–90.

Coase, Ronald (1992) 'The Institutional Structure of Production', *American Economic Review*, (82)4.

Cody, J., H. Hughes, and D. Wall (eds) (1980) *Policies for Industrial Progress in Developing Countries* (London: Oxford University Press).

Commander, Simon (1989a) 'Prices, Markets and Rigidities: African Agriculture, 1979–88', in Commander, *Structural Adjustment and Agriculture* (London: Overseas Development Institute), pp. 228–43.

Commander, Simon, (1989b) *Structural Adjustment and Agriculture: Theory and Practice in Africa and Latin America* (London: Overseas Development Institute).

Commins, Stephen (ed.) (1988) *Africa's Development Challenge and the World Bank* (Boulder: Lynne Rienner Publishers).

Cornia G. et al. (1987) *Adjustment with a Human Face, I, Protecting the Vulnerable and Promoting Growth* (Oxford: Clarendon Press).

Cotter, William R. (1979) 'How Aid Fails to Aid Africa'. *Foreign Policy*, pp. 107–119.

Council for Economic Planning and Development (CEPD) *Taiwan Statistical Data Book*. Taipei, Taiwan (various years).

Cumings, Bruce (1987) 'The Origins and Development of the Northeast Asian Political Economy: Industrial Sectors, Product Cycles and Political Consequences.' in Deyo (ed.), *The Political Economy of the New Asian Industrialism* (Ithaca: Cornell University Press) pp. 44–83.

Davidson, Basil (1983) *Modern Africa* (New York: Longman).

Davies, Rob, and David Saunders (1987) 'Stabilization Policies and the Effect on Child Health in Zimbabwe', *Review of African Political Economy*, 38 (April), pp. 3–23.

Deyo, Frederic (ed.) (1987) *The Political Economy of the New Asian Industrialism* (Ithaca: Cornell University Press).

Devan Nair, C. V. (ed.) (1976) *Socialism That Works: The Singapore Way* (Singapore: Federal Publications).

Dore, Ronald P. (1959) *Land Reform in Japan* (London: Oxford University Press).

Dore, Ronald P. (1965) 'Land Reform and Japan's Economic Development', *Developing Economies*, 3(4) (December), pp. 487–96.

Dornbusch, R. and Reynoso A. (1993) 'Financial Factors in Economic Development,' in R. Dornbusch (ed), *Policy Making in the Open Economy: Concepts and Case Studies in Economic Performance* (Oxford: Oxford University Press), pp. 64–89.

DOS (1987) *Report of the Financial Survey of Limited Companies*. Department of Statistics (DOS), Kuala Lumpur, Malaysia (published in October 1989).

Dower, John W. (ed.) (1975) *Origins of the Modern Japanese State: Selected Writings of E. H. Norman* (New York: Pantheon).

Eatwell, J. (1982) *Whatever Happened to Britain? The Economics of Decline* (London: Duckworth).

Economic Development Board (EDB) (1990a) *Economic Development Board Annual Report* (Singapore: EDB).

Economic Development Board (EDB) (1990b) *Economic Development of Singapore, 1960–1990* (Singapore: EDB).

Economic Development Board (EDB) (1990c) *Report on the Census of Industrial Production 1990* (Singapore: EDB).

Economic Planning Board (1982) *Economic White Papers, 1979, 1983, Budgetary Summary*.

Economic Planning Council (EPC) *Taiwan Statistical Data Book* (Taipei, Taiwan: Government of the Republic of China) (various years).

Economist, The (1992) 'Survey: Taiwan, Planning Ahead', October 10.

Economist Intelligence Unit (EIU) (1993) *Country Report, Taiwan* (1).

Edwards C. B. (1975) 'Protection, Profits and Policy. An Analysis of Industrialization in Malaysia', PhD thesis, UEA, Norwich.

Ehrlich, Cyril (1973) 'Building and caretaking: economic policy in British tropical Africa 1890–1960', *Economic History Review*, XXVI (4).

Eisenstadt, S. N. ed. (1968) *The Protestant Ethic and Modernization, A Comparative View* (New York: Basic Books).

El-Namaki, M. S. S. (1986) 'The Strategic Positioning of Some Newly Industrialized Countries in the International Market', *Advances in Strategic Management*, 4, pp. 279–301.

Elvin, M. (1973) *The Pattern of the Chinese Past* (Stanford: Stanford University Press).

Engineering Export Promotion Council of India (1981) *Project Export News*, July 15.

Erzan, R. H. et al. (n.d.) 'Profile of Protection in Developing Countries', UNCTAD Discussion paper, No. 21.

Evans, D. and Alizadeh P. (1984) 'Trade, Industrialization and the Visible Hand', in R. Kaplinsky (ed.). *Third World Industrialization in the 1980s* (London: Frank Cass).

Evans, Peter (1987) 'Class, State and Dependence in East Asian Development: Lessons for Latin Americanists', in Deyo (ed.), *The Political Economy of the New Asian Industrialism* (Ithaca: Cornell University Press) pp. 203–26.

Fei, John (1983) 'Evolution of Growth Policies of NICS in a Historical and Typological Perspectives', East-West Center conference paper, Honolulu, Hawaii, April.

Fei, John and Gustav Ranis (1961) 'A Theory of Economic Development', *American Economic Review*, 51 (September), pp. 533–65.

Fei, John, Gustav Ranis, and Shirley Kuo (1979) *Growth with Equity: The Taiwan Case* (New York: Oxford University Press).

Fei, X. T. (1939) *Rural China* (Shanghai: Guancha She).

Feuerwerker, A. (1984) 'The state and the economy in late Imperial China', *Theory and Society*, 13(3), pp. 297–325.

Food and Agriculture Organization of the United Nations (1991) *The State of Food and Agriculture, 1990* (Rome: FAO).

Forrest, Tom (1992) 'The Advance of African Capital: The Growth of Nigerian Private Enterprises', in Frances Stewart, Sanjaya Lall and Samuel Wangwe (eds), *Alternative Development Strategies in Africa* (New York: St. Martin's Press) pp. 368–401.

Frank, C. R. Jr., K. S. Kim, and L. E. Westphal (1975) *Foreign Trade Regimes and Economic Development: South Korea* (New York: National Bureau of Economic Research).

Fransman M. (ed.) (1982) *Industry and Accumulation in Africa* (London: Heinemann).

Fransman, M. (1984) 'Explaining the Success of the Asian NICs: Incentives and Technology', *IDS Bulletin*, 15(2).

Galenson, Walter (ed.) (1979) *Economic Growth and Structural Change in Taiwan: The Postwar Experience of the Republic of China* (Ithaca, NY: Cornell University Press).

Godfrey, Martin (1985) 'Trade and Exchange Rate Policy in Sub-Saharan Africa', *IDS Bulletin*, 16, no. 3, pp. 31–8.

Godley, M. (1981) *The Mandarin-Capitalists from Nanyang* (Cambridge: Cambridge University Press).

Goh Chok Tong (1969) 'Industrial Growth, 1959–66', in Ooi and Chiang, *Modern Singapore*, pp. 127–46.

Gold, Thomas (1986) *State and Society in the Taiwan Miracle* (Armonk, NY: M. E. Sharpe).

Goldsmith, Raymond W. (1983) *The Financial Development of India, Japan, and the United States: A Trilateral Institutional, Statistical, and Analytical Comparison* (New Haven: Yale University Press).

Green, Reginald Herbold (1989) 'Articulating Stabilisation Programmes and Structural Adjustment: Sub-Saharan Africa', in Commander (ed.), *Structural Adjustment and Agriculture* (London: Overseas Development Institute) pp. 35–54.

Griffin, Keith, and Azizur Rahman Khan (eds) (1972) *Growth and Inequality in Pakistan* (London: Macmillan).

Grubel, Herbert G. (1981) *International Economics* (Homewood, Ill.: Irwin).

Grubel, Herbert G. (1989) 'Singapore's Record of Price Stability, 1966–84', in Sandhu and Wheatley (eds), *Management of Success*, pp. 373–98.

Gulhati, Ravi and Raj Nallari (1990) 'Successful Stabilization and Recovery in Mauritius', EDI Development Policy Case Series (Washington, DC: World Bank).

Haggard, Stephan (1988) 'The Politics of Industrialization in the Republic of Korea and Taiwan', in Hughes (ed.), *Achieving Industrialisation in East Asia*, pp. 260–82.

Haggard, Stephan (1990) *Beyond the Periphery: The Politics of Economic Growth in the Newly Industrializing Countries* (Ithaca, NY: Cornell University Press).

Haggard, Stephan and Tun-jen Cheng (1987) 'State and Foreign Capital in the East Asian NICs.' in Deyo (ed.), *The Political Economy of New Asian Industrialism* (Ithaca: Cornell University Press), pp. 84–135.

Halliday, Jon (1975) *A Political History of Japanese Capitalism* (New York: Pantheon).

Harberger, Arnold (1988) 'Growth, Industrialization and Economic Structure: Latin America and East Asia Compared', in Hughes (ed.), *Achieving Industrialisation in East Asia*, pp. 164–94.

Hankook Ilbo, September 27, 1981.

Harris, John R., and Michael P. Todaro (1970) 'Migration, Unemployment, and Development: A Two-sector Analysis', *American Economic Review*, 60 (March), pp. 126–42.

Harvey, D. (1989) *The Condition of Post-Modernity* (Oxford: Basil Blackwell).

Hayami, Yujiro (1975) *A Century of Agricultural Growth in Japan: Its Relevance to Asian Development* (Tokyo: University of Tokyo Press).

Hazlewood, Arthur (1991) 'Foreign Aid and Economic Development in Kenya', in Uma Lele and Ijaz Nabi (ed.), *Transitions in Development: The Role of Aid and Commercial Flows* (San Francisco: International Center for Economic Growth).

Helleiner, Gerald (1990) 'Structural Adjustment and Long Term Development in Sub-Saharan Africa', *Centro Studi Luca D'Agliano-Queen Elizabeth House*, no. 18 (March).

Hirschmeier, Johannes (1964) *The Origins of Entrepreneurship in Meiji Japan* (Cambridge, Mass.: Harvard University Press).

Ho, Samuel (1978) *Economic Development of Taiwan, 1860–1970* (New Haven: Yale University Press).

Ho, Samuel P. S. (1980) 'Small-Scale Enterprises in Korea and Taiwan', World Bank Staff Working Paper, No. 384 (Washington, DC: The World Bank).

Hofstede, G. (1980) *Culture's Consequences: International Differences in Work-Related Values* (London: Sage).

Hong, W. (1979) *Trade Distortions and Employment Growth in Korea* (Seoul: Korea Development Institute).

Hong, W. and L. B. Krause (eds) (1981) *Trade and Growth of the Advanced Developing Countries in the Pacific Basin* (Seoul: Korea Development Institute).

Huan, S. H. (1971) 'Measures to Promote Industrialization', in You and Lim (eds), *The Singapore Economy* (Singapore: Eastern Universities Press), pp. 224–45.

Hughes, Helen (ed.) (1988) *Achieving Industrialization in East Asia* (Cambridge: Cambridge University Press).

Hughes, Helen and You Poh Seng (eds) (1969) *Foreign Investment and Industrialisation in Singapore* (Madison: University of Wisconsin Press).

Hughes, Helen, Linda Low, Toh Mun Heng, Soon Teck Wong and Tan Kong Yam (1993) *Challenge and Response: Thirty Years of the Economic Development Board* (Singapore: Times Academic Press).

Hyden G. (1986) 'African Social Structure and Economic Development', in R. J. Berg and J. S. Whitaker, *Strategies for African Development* (Berkeley: University of California Press).

Hymer, Stephen (1970) 'The Efficiency (Contradictions) of Multinational Corporations', *American Economic Review*, 60 (May), pp. 441–53.

IMP (1986) *Executive Highlights*. Malaysian Industrial Development Authority/UNIDO.

Industry of Free China (1968) 'Export Promotion in the Republic of China', January.

International Development Center of Japan (1982) 'Japan's Historical Development Experience and the Contemporary Developing Countries: Issues for Comparative Analysis', Tokyo, February.

Inukai, Ichirou (1979) 'The Kogyo Iken: Japan's Ten Year Plan, 1884', *Kyoto Sangyo University Economic and Business Review* (May), pp. 1–100.

Inukai, Ichirou (1981) 'Experience in Transfer of Technology from the West: Lessons from False Starts', in Haruo Nagamine (ed.), *Nation-building and Regional Development: The Japanese Experience* (Hong Kong: Maruzen Asia). UN Centre for Regional Development 10, pp. 76–98.

Ishikawa, Shigeru (1981) *Essays on Technology, Employment, and Institutions in Economic Development: Comparative Asian Experience* (Tokyo: Kinokuniya).

Ishikawa, Shigeru (1982) 'Relevance of the Experiences of Japan to Contemporary Economic Development', *The Philippine Review of Economics and Business* 19, pp. 255–79.

Jacoby, Neil (1966) *US Aid to Taiwan: A Study of Foreign Aid, Self-Help and Development* (New York: Praeger).

Jenkins, Rhys (1991) 'The Political Economy of Industrialization: A Comparison of Latin American and East Asian Newly Industrializing Countries', *Development and Change* 22, pp. 197–231.

Jesudason, J. V. (1990) *Ethnicity and the Economy: the State, Chinese Business and Multinationals in Malaysia* (Singapore: OUP).

Johnson, Chalmers (1982) *MITI and the Japanese Miracle* (Stanford, Cal. Stanford University Press).

Johnson, Bruce F. et al. (1992) in Uma Lele (ed.), *Aid to African Agriculture: Lessons from Two Decades of Donors' Experience* (Baltimore: Johns Hopkins University Press).

Jomo, K. S. (ed.) (1985) *The Sun Also Sets. Lessons in Looking East* (Kuala Lumpur: INSAN).

Jomo, K. S. (1990) *Growth and Structural Change in the Malaysian Economy* (Macmillan: London).

Jones, E. L. (1990) 'The real question about China: Why was the Song economic achievement not repeated?', *Australian Economic History Review*, 30(2) (Sep), pp. 5–22.

Jones, J. P. and I. Sakong (1980) *Government Business, and Entrepreneurship in Economic Development: The Korean Case* (Cambridge: Harvard University Press).

Kaplinsky, R. (1991) 'From Mass-Production to Flexible Specialisation; a Case Study from a Semi-Industrialized Economy', IDS Discussion Paper 295, Brighton, Sussex, November.

Kapur, Basant K. (ed.) (1986) *Singapore Studies: Critical Surveys of the Humanities and Social Sciences* (Singapore: Singapore University Press).

Kay, G. (1975) *Development and Underdevelopment: A Marxist Analysis* (London: Macmillan).

Khan, Mohsin S. et al. (1990) 'Adjustment with Growth: Relating the Analytical Approaches of the IMF and the World Bank', *Journal of Development Economics*, 32.

Killick, T. (1992) 'Explaining Africa's Post-Independence Development Experiences', Overseas Development Institute, Working Paper 60, London.

Kim, C. N., H. Kajiwara, and T. Watanabe (1984) 'A Consideration of the Compressed Process of Agricultural Development in the Republic of Korea', *The Developing Economies*, 22(1).

Kim, K. D. (1979) *Man and Society in Korea's Economic Growth: Sociological Studies* (Seoul: Seoul National University Press).

Kim, K. S. (1970) 'The Economic Impact of the Vietnam War in Southeast and East Asia – with special reference to Balance-of-Payments Effects', *Asian Forum*, 2(2), pp. 22–31.

Kim, K. S. (1977) *Planning Model and Macroeconomic Policy Issues* (Seoul: Korean Development Institute).

Kim, K. S. (1981) 'Enterprise Performances in the Public and Private Sectors – Tanzanian Experience (1970–1975)', *Journal of Developing Areas*, 15(3).

Kim, K. S. (1985a) 'Industrial Policy and Development in South Korea', Kellogg Institute Working Paper, University of Notre Dame.

Kim, K. S. (1985b) *Políticas y Desarrollo Industrial en Corea del Sur* (Mexico City: NAFINSA and UNIDO).

Kim, K. S. (1988a) 'The Korean Case: Culturally Dominated Interactions.' in Lee Tavis (ed.) *Multinational Managers and Host Government Interactions*,' (Notre Dame, IN: University of Notre Dame Press) pp. 173–203.

Kim, K. S. (1988b) 'Issues and Perspectives in Tanzanian Industrial Development: with Special Reference to the Role of SADCC', in M. Hodd (ed.), *Tanzania after Nyerere* (London: Francis Pinter Publishers) pp. 92–102.

Kim, K. S. (1992) 'The Political Economy of Statism in the Korean Development', The Kellogg Institute Working Paper, No.166, University of Notre Dame.

Korea Development Bank (1983a) 'Private Equipment Investment Trends in Korea', (Seoul: Korea Development Bank).

Korea Development Bank (1983b) *Annual Report* (Seoul: Korea Development Bank).

Korea International Economic Institute (1980) *Current Status and Major Issues of Korea's Mechanical Engineering Industries* (in Korean) (Seoul: Korea International Economic Institute).

Korea Society for Advancement of Machine Industry (1983) *Statistics on Korean Machinery Industry*.

Krause, Lawrence B. (1987) 'The Government as an Entrepreneur', in Krause, Koh and Lee (Tsao) *The Singapore Economy Reconsidered* (Singapore: Institute of Southeast Asian Studies) pp. 107–27.

Krause, Lawrence B., Koh Ai Tee and Lee (Tsao) Yuan (1987) *The Singapore Economy Reconsidered* (Singapore: Institute of Southeast Asian Studies).

Krueger, Anne O. (1978) *Liberalization Attempts and Consequences* (New York: National Bureau of Economic Research).

Krueger, Anne O. (1980) *The Development Role of the Foreign Sector and Aid – Studies in the Modernization of the Republic of Korea: 1945–1975* (Cambridge, Mass.: Harvard University, Council on East Asian Studies).

Krueger, Anne O., Hal B. Lary, Terry Monson, and Narongchai Akrasenee (eds) (1981) *Trade and Employment in Developing Countries, Vol. I, Individual Studies* (Chicago: University of Chicago Press).

Krugman, P. (ed.) (1986) *Strategic Trade Policy and the New International Economics* (Cambridge, Mass.: MIT).

Kuo, Shirley, Gustav Ranis, and John Fei (1981) *The Taiwan Success Story: Rapid Growth with Improved Distribution in the Republic of China, 1952–1979* (Boulder, Colo.: Westview Press).

Kurian, G. T. (ed.) (1992) *Encyclopedia of the Third World*, 4th edition (NY: Facts on File).

Kuznets, Paul, W. (1977) *Economic Growth and Structure in the Republic of Korea* (New Haven: Yale University Press).

Kuznets, Simon (1966) *Modern Economic Growth: Rate, Structure, and Spread* (New Haven: Yale University Press).

Kwon, Okyu (1988) 'Recent Labor Disputes and Wage Increases in Korea', *Korea's Economy*, 4(3).

Lall, Sanjaya (1992) 'Structural Problems of African Industry' in Frances Stewart, Sanjaya Lall and Samuel Wangwe (eds), *Alternative Development Strategies in Africa*, pp. 103–43.

Lee, E. (ed.) (1981) *Export-Led Industrialization and Development* (Geneva: ILO).

Lee, Kyu Sik and Alex Anas (1989) 'Manufacturers' Responses to Infrastructure Deficiencies in Nigeria', World Bank Policy, Planning and Research Staff, Report INU 50, Washington, DC.

Lee Sheng-Yi (1984) 'Money, Banking and Finance in Singapore', in You and Lim (eds), *Singapore: Twenty-five Years of Development*, pp. 108–38.

Lee Soo Ann (1973) *Industrialization in Singapore* (Melbourne, Australia: Longman).

Lee Soo Ann (1977) *Singapore Goes Transnational* (Singapore: Eastern Universities Press).

Lee, Teng-hui (1971) *Intersectoral Capital Flows in the Economic Development of Taiwan, 1895–1960* (Ithaca: Cornell University Press).

Lee (Tsao) Yuan (1987) 'The Government in Macro-economic Management', in Krause, Koh and Lee (Tsao), *The Singapore Economy Reconsidered*, pp. 128–73.

Lee(Tsao) Yuan and Linda Low (1990) *Local Entrepreneurship in Singapore: Private and State* (Singapore: Institute of Policy Studies/Times Academic Press).

Lele, Uma (1990). 'Structural Adjustment, Agricultural Development and the Poor: Some Lessons from the Malawian Experience', *World Development*, 18 (September), pp. 1207–19.

Levy, Brian (1986) 'Prospects and Perils for Small and Medium Enterprises in Outward-Oriented Industrial Expansion: Lessons from Korea and Taiwan', EEPA Discussion Paper, No. 8, November.

Lewin, K. (1951) *Field Theory in Social Sciences* (New York: Harper & Row).

Lewis, W. Arthur (1964) 'Economic Development with Unlimited Supplies of Labor', *Manchester School* 22 (May), pp. 139–91.

Li, K. T. (1961) 'The Growth of Private Industry in Free China,' *Industry of Free China*, 16 (1) (July 25).

Li, K. T. (1988) *The Evolution of Policy Behind Taiwan's Development Success* (New Haven: Yale University Press).

Lim Chong Yah et al. (1988) *Policy Options for the Singapore Economy* (Singapore: McGraw-Hill).

Lim, Linda Y. C. (1978) 'Multinational Firms and Manufacturing for Export in Less Developed Countries: The Case of the Electronics Industry in Malaysia and Singapore', 2 vols, unpublished PhD dissertation, Department of Economics, University of Michigan, Ann Arbor.

Lim, Linda (1982a) 'The Motor Vehicle Industry in Singapore', in *The Scope for South-East Asian Subregional Co-operation in the Automotive Sector* (Bangkok, Thailand: UN-ESCAP) pp. 201–16.

Lim, Linda Y.C. (1982b) *Women in the Singapore Economy*. Economic Research Centre Occasional Paper Series No. 5 (Singapore: National University of Singapore).

Lim, Linda Y.C. (1983a) 'Singapore's Success, The Myth of the Free Market Economy', *Asian Survey*, 23(6), pp. 752–64.

Lim, Linda Y.C. (1983b) 'Chinese Business, Multinationals and the State: Manufacturing for Export in Malaysia and Singapore', in Linda Y.C. Lim and L.A. Peter Gosling (eds), *The Chinese in Southeast Asia, Volume 1: Ethnicity and Economic Activity* (Singapore: Maruzen Asia) pp. 245–74.

Lim, Linda Y.C. (1987) 'The State and Private Capital in Singapore's Economic Development', *Political Economy, Studies in the Surplus Approach*, 3(2), pp. 201–22.

Lim, Linda Y.C. (1989) 'Social Welfare', in Sandhu and Wheatley (eds), *Management of Success: The Moulding of Modern Singapore* (Singapore: Institute of Southeast Asian Studies), pp. 171–200.

Lim, Linda Y.C. (1990) 'Singapore', in *Labor Standards and Development in the Global Economy*. Washington, DC: US Department of Labor Bureau of International Labor Affairs) pp. 73–96.

Lim, Linda Y.C. (1992) 'Models and Partners: The Economic Development of Singapore and Malaysia and Their Implications for Socialist Economic Reform in Southeast Asia'. Paper presented at the Social Science Research Council (New York) Conference on Marketization in Southeast Asia, Chiang Mai, Thailand, January 15–17, 1993.

Lim, Linda Y.C. (1993) 'The Role of the Private Sector in ASEAN Regional Economic Cooperation', in Lynn Mytelka (ed.), *New Modes of South-South Economic Cooperation* (Paris: OECD Development Centre).

Lim, Linda Y.C. and Pang Eng Fong (1982) 'Vertical Linkages and Multinational Enterprises in Developing Countries', *World Development*, 10(7) (July), pp. 585–95.

Lim, Linda and Pang Eng Fong (1986) *Trade, Employment and Industrialisation in Singapore* (Geneva: International Labour Office).

Lim, Linda Y.C. and Pang Eng Fong (1991) *Foreign Direct Investment and Industrialisation in Malaysia, Singapore, Taiwan and Thailand* (Paris: OECD Development Centre).

Lim, Linda Y.C. and Nathaniel Siddall (1993) 'Foreign Investment, Trade and Technology Linkages in Asian Developing Countries in the 1990s', in John Dunning (ed.), *Globalization and Developing Countries* (London: Routledge & Kegan Paul (for UNCTC)) (forthcoming).

Limlingan, V. (1986) *The Overseas Chinese in ASEAN: Business Strategies and Management Practices* (Manila: Vita Development Corporation).

Lindauer, David and M. Roemer (eds) (1993) 'Development in Asia and Africa: Legacies and Opportunities', Harvard Institute for Economic Development (September).

Lipton, Michael (1977) *Why Poor People Stay Poor: A Study of Urban Bias in World Development* (London: Maurice Temple Smith).

Little, Ian M. D. (1979) 'An Economic Renaissance.' in Walter Galenson (ed.), *Economic Growth and Structural Change in Taiwan* (Ithaca: Cornell University Press) pp. 448–507.

Little, Ian (1981) 'The Experience and Causes of Rapid Labor Intensive Development in Korea, Taiwan Province, Hong Kong, and Singapore and the Possibilities of Emulation', in E. Lee (ed.), *Export-Led Industrialization and Development* (Geneva: International Labor Organization) pp. 23–45.

Little, Ian (1985) 'The Experience and Lessons of Asia's Super Exporters', in V. Corbo et al. *Export Oriented Development Strategies: The Success of the Five Newly Industrialized Countries* (Boulder: Westview Press).

Little, Ian (1987) 'Small Manufacturing Enterprises in Developing Countries', *The World Bank Economic Review*, 1(2).

Little, Ian et al. (1970) *Industry and Trade in Some Developing Countries* (London: Oxford University Press).

Lockwood, William W. (1954) *The Economic Development of Japan: Growth and Structural Change, 1868–1938* (Princeton: Princeton University Press).

Low, Linda (1984) 'Public Enterprises in Singapore', in You and Lim, *Singapore: Twenty-five Years of Development* (Singapore: Nan Ying Xing Zhou Lianhe Zaobao) pp. 253–87.

Loxley, John (1989) 'The Devaluation Debate in Tanzania', in Bonnie K. Campbell and John Loxley (eds), *Structural Adjustment in Africa* (New York: St. Martin's Press) pp. 13–36.

Luedde-Neurath, Richard (1986) *Import Controls and Export-oriented Development: a Reassessment of the South Korea Case* (Boulder: Westview).

Luedde-Neurath, Richard (1988) 'State Intervention and Export-oriented Development in South Korea', in Gordon White (ed.), *Developmental States in East Asia* (London: Macmillan) pp. 68–112.

Lundberg, Erik (1979) 'Fiscal and Monetary Policies', in Walter Galenson (ed.), *Economic Growth and Structural Change in Taiwan* (Ithaca: Cornell University Press) pp. 263–307.

McCarthy, D. M. P. (1982) *Colonial Bureaucracy and Creating Underdevelopment 1919–1940* (Arnes: Iowa State University press).

Mackie, J. (1988) 'Economic Growth in the ASEAN Region: the Political Underpinnings', in Helen Hughes (ed.), *Achieving Industrialisation in East Asia* (Cambridge: Cambridge University Press) pp. 283–326.

Mahajan, V. S. (1976) *Development Planning: Lessons from the Japanese Model* (Calcutta: Minerva Associates).

Mason, E. S. et al. (1980) *The Economic and Social Modernization of the Republic of Korea: 1945–1975* (Cambridge, Mass.: Harvard University, Council on East Asian Studies).

Meier, Gerald and William Steel (eds) (1987) *Industrial Adjustment in Sub-Saharan Africa* (Washington: World Bank).

Migdal, Joel (1988) *Strong Societies and Weak States: State-Society Relations and State Capabilities in the Third World* (Princeton: Princeton University Press).

Mills, Cadman Atta (1989). 'Structural Adjustment in Sub-Saharan Africa', Economic Development Institute Policy Seminar Report No. 18 (Washington, DC: World Bank).

Minami, Ryōshin (1973) *The Turning Point in Economic Development: Japan's Experience* (Tokyo: Kinokuniya).

Minami, Ryōshin (1976) 'The Introduction of Electric Power and its Impact on the Manufacturing Industries: With Special Reference to Smaller Scale Plants', in Hugh Patrick (ed.), *Japanese Industrialisation and its Social Consequences* (Berkeley: University of California Press) pp. 299–325.

Minami, Ryoshin (1985) *The Economic Development of Japan* (London: Macmillan).

Ministry of Finance (1989/90) *Economic Report* (Kuala Lumpur: Ministry of Finance).

Ministry of Finance (1990/91) *Economic Report* (Kuala Lumpur: Ministry of Finance).

Ministry of Trade and Industry (MTI), Singapore (1986) *The Singapore Economy: New Directions.* Report of the Economic Committee, February.

Ministry of Trade and Industry (MTI), Singapore (1991) *The Strategic Economic Plan, Towards A Developed Nation.* Report of the Economic Planning Committee, December.

Minoru, Tachi, and Okazaki Yoichi (1965) 'Economic Development and Population Growth – with Special Reference to Southeast Asia', *Developing Economies*, 3(4), (December) pp. 497–515.

Mirza, Hafiz (1986) *Multinationals and the Growth of the Singapore Economy* (New York: St. Martin's Press).

Mizoguchi, T., D. H. Kim, and Y. I. Chung (1976) 'Overtime Changes of the Size Distribution of Household Income in Korea, 1963–71', *The Developing Economies*, 14(3) (September).

Mody, Ashoka, Sudipto Mundle, and K. N. Raj (1985) 'Resource Flows from Agriculture: Japan and India', in Ohkawa and Ranis, *Japan and the Developing Countries* (Oxford: Basil Blackwell) pp. 272–91.

Moore, Mick (1988) 'Economic Growth and the Rise of Civil Society: Agriculture in Taiwan and South Korea', in White (ed.), *Developmental States in East Asia* (London: Macmillan) pp. 113–52.

Mosley, Paul and John Weeks (1993) 'Has Recovery Begun? Africa's Adustment in the 1980s Revisited', *World Development*, 21(10) (October), pp. 1583–606.

Mosley, Paul et al. (1991) *Aid and Power: The World Bank and Policy Based Lending* (two volumes) (London: Routledge).

Morris, James (1968) *Pax Britannica.* (London: Penguin).

Murakami, Atsushi (1989) 'Japan and United States: Roles in Asian Development', in Naya et al. (eds) *Lessons in Development: Comparative Study of Asia and Latin America* (San Francisco: International Center for Economic Growth).

Nafziger, E. Wayne (1983) *The Economics of Political Instability: The Nigerian–Biafran War* (Boulder, Colo: Westview Press).

Nafziger, E. Wayne (1988) *Inequality in Africa: Political Elites, Proletariat, Peasants, and the Poor* (Cambridge: Cambridge University Press).

Nafziger, E. Wayne (1990) *The Economics of Developing Countries* (Englewood Cliffs, NJ: Prentice-Hall).

Nafziger, E. Wayne (1993) *The Debt Crisis in Africa* (Baltimore: Johns Hopkins University Press).

Nakamara, James (1966) *Agricultural Production and the Economic Development of Japan, 1873–1922* (Princeton: Princeton University Press).

Nakamura, Takafusa (1983) *Economic Growth in Prewar Japan*. Translated by Robert A. Feldman (New Haven: Yale University Press).

Nam, C. H. (1980) '*Import Substitution vs. Export Promotion: Comparison in Korea's Incentive Structure*', Korea Development Research (Winter) (in Korean).

Nash, John (n.d.) (circa 1989) 'An Overview of Trade Policy Reform with Implications for Sub-Saharan Africa,' Trade Policy Divison, The World Bank, Washington, DC.

Naya S. et al. (1989) *Lessons in Development: A Comparative Study of Asia and Latin America* (San Fransisco: International Center for Economic Growth).

Needham, J. (1956) *Science and Civilization in China*, vol. 2 (Cambridge, Mass.: Cambridge University Press).

Nishimuzu, M. and S. Robinson (1984) 'Trade Policies and Productivity Change in Semi-Industrialized Countries', *Journal of Development Economics*, 16(1\2).

North, Douglass (1990), *Institutions, Institutional Change and Economic Performance* (Cambridge: Cambridge University Press).

Nove, Alec (1983) *The Economics of Feasible Socialism* (London: George Unwin).

Okhawa, Kazushi (1983) 'Japan's Development: A Model for Less-Developed Countries?', *Asian Development Review*, 1(2), pp. 45–57.

Ohkawa, Kazushi, and Gustav Ranis (eds) (1985) *Japan and the Developing Countries: A Comparative Analysis* (Oxford: Basil Blackwell).

Ohkawa, Kazushi and Henry Rosovsky (1973) *Japanese Economic Growth: Trend Acceleration in the Twentieth Century* (Stanford: Stanford University Press).

Ohkawa, Kazushi, Yutaka Shimizu, and Nobukiyo Takamatsu (1982) '"Agricultural Surplus" in Japan's Case: Implication for Various Possible Patterns in the Initial Phase of Development', International Development Center of Japan Working Paper, No. 19, March.

Ohkawa, Kazushi and Miyohei Shinohara (eds) (1979) *Patterns of Japanese Economic Development: A Quantitative Appraisal* (New Haven: Yale University Press).

Ohkawa, Kazushi, Miyohei Shinohara, M. Umemura, M. Ito, and T. Noda (1957) *The Growth Rate of the Japanese Economy since 1878* (Tokyo: Kinokuniya).

Ooi Jin-Bee and Chiang Hai Ding (eds) (1969) *Modern Singapore* (Singapore: University of Singapore).

Pack, Howard, and Larry Westphal (1986) 'Industrial Strategy and Technological Change: Theory Versus Reality', *Journal of Development Economics*, 22, pp. 8–128.

Pang Eng Fong and Linda Lim (1977) *The Electronics Industry in Singapore: Structure, Technology and Linkages*, Economic Research Centre, Research Monograph Series No. 7 (Singapore: University of Singapore).

Pang Eng Fong and Linda Lim (1982) 'Foreign Labour and Economic Development in Singapore', *International Migration Review*, 16(4) (Fall), pp. 548–76.

Pang Eng Fong and Linda Lim, (1985) 'Rapid Growth and Relative Price Stability in a Small Open Economy: The Experience of Singapore', in Vittorio Corbo, Anne O. Krueger and Fernando Ossa, *Export-Oriented Development Strategies, The Success of Five Newly Industrializing Countries* (Boulder, Colorado: Westview Press) pp. 79–110.

Pang Eng Fong and Linda Y.C. Lim (1989) 'Wage Policy in Singapore', in *Government Wage Policy Formulation in Developing Countries: Seven Country Studies*, Labour-Management Relations Series No. 73 (Geneva: International Labour Organisation) pp. 75–101.

Parfitt, Trevor W. and Stephen P. Riley (1989) *The African Debt Crisis* (London: Routledge).

Park, C.K. (ed.) (1980) *Macroeconomic and Industrial Development in Korea* (Seoul: KOI Press).

Patrick, Hugh (ed.) (1976) *Japanese Industrialization and its Social Consequences* (Berkeley: University of California Press).

Piore M. and C. Sabel (1984) *The Second Industrial Divide* (New York: Basic Books).

POLIND (1990) 'Policy Assessment of the MIPS and IMP'. Economic Planning Unit/Ministry of International Trade and Industry, Kuala Lumpur (unpublished).

Pollert, A. (1988) 'Dismantling Flexibility', *Capital and Class*, 34 (Spring).

Population Reference Bureau (1991) *1991 World Population Data Sheet* (Washington, DC: Population Reference Bureau).

Putterman, Louis (1993) 'Economic Reform and the Tanzanian Smallholder'. Paper presented at the African Studies Association Annual Meeting, December.

Pye, L.W. (1985) *Asian Power and Politics: The Cultural Dimensions of Authority.* (Cambridge Mass.: Harvard University Press).

Quarco, Philip (1990) 'Structural Adjustment Programmes in Sub-Saharan Africa: Evolution of Approaches', *African Development Review*, 2(2) (December), pp. 1–26.

Ranis, Gustav (1955) 'The Community-centered Entrepreneur in Japanese Development', *Explorations in Entrepreneurial History*, 8(2), pp. 80–98.

Ranis, Gustav (1979) 'Industrial Development', in Walter Galenson (ed.), *Economic Growth and Structural Change in Taiwan, The Postwar Experience of the Republic of China* (Ithaca, NY: Cornell University Press) pp. 206–62.

Ranis, Gustav (1985) 'Can the East Asian Model of Development be Generalized? A Comment,' *World Development* 13(4).

Ranis, Gustav (1989) 'What Latin America Can Learn from the East Asian Development Experience' paper prepared for the Department of State External Research Conference, October 26.

Ranis, Gustav (1990) 'Asian and Latin American Experience: Lessons for Africa', *Centro Studi Luca D'Agliano-Queen Elizabeth House Development Studies*, No. 19, March.

Redding, S.G. (1990) *The Spirit of Chinese Capitalism* (New York: de Gruyter).

Redding, S.G. and Tam, S. (1985) 'Networks and molecular organizations: an exploratory view of Chinese firms in Hong Kong', in K.C. Mun and T.S. Chen (eds), *Proceedings: Inaugural meeting of the Southeast Asian Region*

Academy of International Business (Hong Kong: The Chinese University of Hong Kong) pp. 129–42.

Reiger, H. C. and W. Veit (1990) 'State Intervention, State Involvement and Market Forces-Singapore and South Korea', in Manfred Kulessa (ed.), *The Newly Industrialized Economies of Asia, Prospects of Co-operation* (Berlin: Springer-Verlag) pp. 155–79.

Republic of Korea (1962) *Summary of the First Five Year Economic Development Plan 1962–1967* (Seoul: Government Printer).

The Republic of Korea Government (various years). *The Five-Year Development Planning*, various series (in Korean).

Rhee, Y. W., B. Ross-Larson, and G. Pursell (1984) *Korea's Competitive Edge: Managing the Entry into World Markets* (Baltimore and London: Johns Hopkins University Press).

Riddell, R. (1990) *Manufacturing Africa* (London: James Currey).

Riddell, R. (1993) 'The Future of the Manufacturing Sector in Sub-Saharan Africa', in Thomas Callaghy and John Ravenhill (eds), *Hemmed in: Responses to Africa's Economic Decline* (New York: Columbia University Press) pp. 215–47.

Rodan, Garry (1989) *The Political Economy of Singapore's Industrialization: National State and International Capital* (London: Macmillan).

Rodrik, Dani (1990) 'How Should Structural Adjustment Programs Be Designed?', *World Development*, 18 (7), pp. 933–47.

Rodrik, Dani (1992) 'Conceptual Issues in the Design of Trade Policy for Industrialization', *World Development*, 20(3), pp. 309–20.

Roemer, M. and K. S. Kim, (1979) *Studies in the Modernization of the Republic of Korea 1945–75: Growth and Structural Transformation* (Cambridge, Mass.: Harvard University Press).

Rostow, Walter W. (1971) *The Stages of Economic Growth: A Non-communist Manifesto* (Cambridge: Cambridge University Press).

Ruttan, Vernon (1984) 'Integrated Rural Development Programs: A Historical Perspective', *World Development*, 12(4), pp. 393–401.

Sakong, I. (1983) 'Economic Development and the Role of Government', *Research in Korean Development*, 37 (March), pp. 2–21.

Sandhu, Kernial Singh and Paul Wheatley (eds) (1989) *Management of Success: The Moulding of Modern Singapore* (Singapore: Institute of Southeast Asian Studies).

Sarkar, Prabirjit and H. W. Singer (1991) 'Manufactured Exports of Developing Countries and their Terms of Trade since 1965', *World Development*, 19(4) (April), pp. 333–40.

Sayer A. (1989) 'Post-Fordism in Question', *International Journal of Urban and Regional Research*, 13(4), pp. 666–95.

Schmitz H. (1989) 'Flexible Specialisation – a New Paradigm of Small-Scale Industrialization', IDS Discussion Paper No. 261, Brighton, Sussex, May.

Schumpeter, Joseph A. (1939) *Business Cycles*, 2 vols (New York: McGraw-Hill).

Schumpeter, Joseph A. (1961) *The Theory of Economic Development* (Cambridge, Mass.: Harvard University Press).

Scott, Maurice (1979) 'Foreign Trade', in Walter Galenson (ed.), *Economic Growth and Structural Change in Taiwan*, pp. 308–83.

Seah, Linda (1983) 'Public Enterprise and Economic Development', in Chen (ed.), *Singapore Development Policies and Trends* (Singapore: Oxford University Press) pp. 129–59.

Seiya, Munakata (1965) 'The Course and Problems of National Education', *Developing Economies*, 3 (December), pp. 540–59.

Sen, A. (1983) 'The Profit Motive', *Lloyds Bank Review*, 147 (January).

Seoul Chamber of Commerce (1982) *Retrospect and Reflections of the Korean Economy in the Past Two Decades* Seoul, Korea (in Korean).

Shinohara, Miyohei (1970) *Structural Changes in Japan's Economic Development* (Tokyo: Kinokuniya).

Shinohara, Mihohei (1982) *Industrial Growth, Trade, and Dynamic Patterns in the Japanese Economy* (Tokyo: University of Tokyo Press).

Shishido, Toshio (1983) 'Japanese Industrial Development and Policies for Science and Technology', *Science*, 219 (21 January), pp. 259–64.

Silin, R. H. (1976) *Leadership and Values: the Organization of Large-Scale Taiwanese Enterprises* (Cambridge, Mass.: Harvard University Press).

Simon, Denis (1988) 'Technology Transfer and Technology Policies on Taiwan,' in E. Winkler and S. Greenhalgh (eds) *Contending Approaches to the Political Economy of Taiwan* (Armonk, NY: M. E. Sharpe).

Stein, Howard (1985) 'Theories of the State in Tanzania: A Critical Assessment', *Journal of Modern African Studies*, 23(1), pp. 105–23.

Stein, Howard (1992) 'Deindustrialization, Adjustment, the World Bank and the IMF in Africa', *World Development*, 20(1), pp. 83–95.

Stein, Howard (1993) 'Institutional Theories and Structural Adjustment in Africa'. Paper presented at the Conference on Public Choice Theories and Third World Experiences, Third World Economic History/Development Group, London School of Economics and Political Science, London, England, September.

Stein Howard and E. W. Nafziger (1991) 'Structural Adjustment, Human Needs and the World Bank Agenda', *Journal of Modern African Studies*, 24(1) (March), pp. 173–89.

Steinberg, D., K. S. Kim, J. Jackson, and P. Song (1982) *Korean Agricultural Research – the Integration of Research and Extension* (Washington, DC: Agency for International Development).

Steinhoff, M. (1980) *Prestige and Profit: the Development of Entrepreneurial Abilities in Taiwan 1880–1972.* Development Studies Centre, Monograph No. 20 (Canberra: Australian National University).

Stern, Ernest (1991) 'Evolution and Lessons of Adjustment Lending', in Thomas Vinod et al. *Restructuring Economies in Distress, Policy Reform and the World Bank* (Oxford: Oxford University Press for the World Bank) pp. 1–7.

Stewart, Frances (1974) 'Technology and Employment in LDCs', in Edgar O. Edwards (ed.), *Employment in Developing Nations* (New York: Columbia University Press) pp. 80–93.

Stewart, Frances (1991) 'Are Adjustment Policies in Africa Consistent with Long-Term Development Needs?', *Development Policy Review*, 9(4) (December), pp. 413–36.

Stewart, Frances, Sanjaya Lall, and Samuel Wangwe (eds) (1992) *Alternative Development Strategies in Africa* (London: St. Martin's Press).

Summers, Lawrence (1991) 'Knowledge for Effective Action', Keynote Address prepared for presentation at the third Annual World Bank Conference on Development Economics, Washington, DC, April 25–26, 1991.

Syrquin, Moshe and Hollis B. Chenery (1989) *Patterns of Development, 1950 to 1983*, World Bank Discussion Paper 41 (Washington DC: World Bank).

Tai, Hung-chao (1989) *Confucianism and Economic Development, An Oriental Alternative* (Washington: The Washington Institute Press).

Takeda, Takao (1965) 'The Financial Policy of the Meiji Government.' *Developing Economies* 3 (December), pp. 427–49.

Tam, S. K. W. (1990) 'Centrifugal versus centripetal growth processes: contrasting ideal types for conceptualising the development patterns of Chinese and Japanese firms' in S. R. Clegg and S. G. Redding (eds), *Capitalism in Contrasting Cultures* (New York: de Gruyter).

Tam, S. K. W. (1992) 'The fission and refusion cycle and the formation and reformation of Chinese business networks'. Working Paper (Hong Kong: Mong Kwok Ping Management Data Bank, University of Hong Kong Business School).

Tan, Augustine H. H. (1976) 'Foreign Investment and Multinational Corporations in Developing Countries', in C.V. Devan Nair (ed.), *Socialism That Works: The Singapore Way* (Singapore: Federal Publications) pp. 86–96.

Tan, Augustine H. H. (1984 'Changing Patterns of Singapore's Foreign Trade and Investment since 1960', in You and Lim (eds), *Singapore: Twenty-five Years of Development* pp. 38–77.

Tanzania Government (1968) *Background to the Budget: An Economic Survey* (Dar es Salaam: Government Printer).

Thorbecke, Erik (1979) 'Agricultural Development', in Walter Galenson (ed.). *Economic Growth and Structural Change in Taiwan* (Ithaca: Cornell University Press), pp. 132–205.

Tsui, M. H. (1988) *The Altar of Power* (Beijing: Labour Publishing).

Turnbull, C. M. (1977) *A History of Singapore 1819–1975* (Kuala Lumpur: Oxford University Press).

UNCTC (1988) *Transnational Corporations in World Development; Trends and Prospects* (New York: United Nations Centre on Transnational Corporations).

UNDP (1992) *Human Development Report 1992* (New York: Oxford University Press for the UNDP).

UNESCO (1973) *Statistical Yearbook* (New York: United Nations).

UNESCO (1990) *Statistical Yearbook* (New York: United Nations).

UNIDO (1979) *World Industry Since 1960; Progress and Prospects* (New York: United Nations).

United Nations (1985) *Input-Output Tables for Developing Countries, Volume 1* (New York: United Nations).

United Nations (1987) *National Accounts Statistics: Main Aggregates and Detailed Tables, 1985* (New York: United Nations).

United Nations (1992) *Statistical Yearbook* (New York: United Nations).

United Nations Economic Commission for Africa (UNECA) (1989) *African Alternatives to Structural Adjustment Programmes: A Framework for Transformation and Recovery* (Addis Ababa: United Nations Economic Commission for Africa).

Van Liemt, G. (1988) *Bridging the Gap: Four NICs and the Changing International Divisions of Labour* (Geneva: ILO).

Vernon, Raymond (1966) 'International Investment and International Trade in the Product Cycle', *Quarterly Journal of Economics*, 2 (May), pp. 190–207.

Vogel, E. F. (1979) *Japan as Number 1: Lessons for America.* (Cambridge, Mass.: Harvard University Press).

Wade, Robert. (1984) 'Dirigisme Taiwan Style', *IDS Bulletin*, 15(2), pp. 65–70.

Wade, Robert (1988a) 'The Role of Government in Overcoming Market Failure: Taiwan, Republic of Korea and Japan', in Helen Hughes (ed.), *Achieving Industrialisation in East Asia* (Cambridge: Cambridge University Press) pp. 129–63.

Wade, Robert (1988b) 'State Intervention in 'Outward Looking' Development: Neoclassical Theory and Taiwanese Practice' in White (ed.), *Developmental States in East Asia* (London: Macmillan) pp. 30–67.

Wade, Robert (1990) *Governing the Market: Economic Theory and the Role of Government in East Asian Industrialization* (Princeton: Princeton University Press).

Wall Street Journal January 26, 1994.

Weber, M. (1951) *The Religion of China* (Glencoe, Illinois: The Free Press).

Weiss, John (1988) *Industry in Developing Countries, Theory, Policy and Evidence* (London: Routledge).

Westphal, L. (1981) 'Empirical Justification for Infant Industry Protection', World Bank Staff Paper, No. 445.

Westphal, L. (1990) 'Industrial Policy in an Export-Propelled Economy: Lessons from South Korea's Experience', *Journal of Economic Perspectives*, 4(3) (September), pp. 41–59.

Westphal, L. and I. Adelman (1972) 'Reflections on the Political Economy of Planning: The Case of Korea', in Jo and Park S. Y. (eds) *Basic Documents and Selected Papers of Korea's Third Five Year Economic Development Plan (1972–1976)* (Seoul: Sogang University).

Westphal, L. and K. S. Kim (1977) 'Industrial Policy and Development in Korea.' World Bank Working Paper, No. 263 (August, Washington, DC: World Bank).

Westphal, L. et al. (1984) 'Exports of Technology by Newly Industrializing Countries–the Republic of Korea', *World Development*, 12 (April/June), pp. 505–33.

Whang, I. J. (1987) 'The Role of Government in Economic Development: The Korean Experience', *Asian Development Review* (January), pp. 71–88.

White, Gordon (ed.) (1988) *Developmental States in East Asia* (London: Macmillan).

Williamson, O. (1985) *The Economic Institutions of Capitalism* (New York: The Free Press).

Woo, Jennie Hay (1988) 'Education and Industrial Growth in Taiwan: A Case of Planning', EEPA Discussion Paper, No. 18, August.

World Bank (1977a) *Korea, Appraisal of the Heavy Machinery Project, Vol. I* (Washington, DC: The World Bank).

World Bank (1977b) 'Industrial Policy and Development in Korea', Staff Paper No. 263.

World Bank (1979a) *Korea: Development of the Machinery Industries* (Washington, D.C.: World Bank).

World Bank (1979b) *World Development Report, 1979* (New York: Oxford University Press).

World Bank (1980) 'Fostering the Capital Goods Sector in LDCs: A Survey of Evidence and Requirements', Staff Paper No. 376, March.

World Bank (1981a) *Accelerated Development in Sub-Saharan Africa: An Agenda for Action* (Washington, DC: The World Bank).

World Bank (1981b) 'Korean Industrial Competence', Staff Paper No. 469.

World Bank (1981c) *World Development Report, 1981* (New York: Oxford University Press).

World Bank (1983) *World Development Report, 1983* (New York: Oxford University Press).

World Bank (1984) *World Development Report, 1984* (New York: Oxford University Press).

World Bank (1987) *World Development Report, 1987* (New York: Oxford University Press).

World Bank (1988a) 'Education in Sub-Saharan Africa: Policies for Adjustment, Revitalization, and Expansion', World Bank Policy Study (Washington, DC: The World Bank).

World Bank (1988b) *World Development Report, 1988* (New York: Oxford University Press).

World Bank (1989a) *Sub-Saharan Africa: From Crisis to Sustainable Growth, A Long-Term Perspective Study* (Washington, DC: The World Bank).

World Bank (1989b) *World Development Report, 1989* (New York: Oxford University Press).

World Bank (1990a) *Social Indicators of Development* (Baltimore: Johns Hopkins University Press for the World Bank).

World Bank (1990b) *World Development Report, 1990* (New York: Oxford University Press).

World Bank (1991) *World Development Report, 1991* (New York: Oxford University Press).

World Bank (1992a) *World Development Report, 1992* (New York: Oxford University Press).

World Bank (1992b) *Malaysia: Fiscal Reform for Stable Growth* (Washington DC: World Bank).

World Bank (1993) *The East Asian Miracle, Economic Growth and Public Policy* (New York: Oxford University Press).

World Bank (1994) *Adjustment in Africa, Reforms, Results and the Road Ahead* (New York: Oxford University Press).

World Bank and UNDP (1989) *Africa's Adjustment and Growth in the 1980s* (Washington and New York: World Bank and UNDP).

Worsley, Peter (1984) *The Three Worlds: Culture and World Development* (London: Weidenfeld & Nicolson).

Wu, Y. L. and Wu, C. L. (1980) *Economic Development in Southeast Asia: The Chinese Dimension* (Stanford: Hoover Institution Press).

Wu, Y. L. and Wu, C. L. (1985) *Becoming an Industrialized Nation: ROCs' Development on Taiwan* (New York: Praeger, 1985)

Yamamura, Kozo (1968) 'A Re-examination of Entrepreneurship in Meiji Japan (1868–1912)', *Economic History Review*, 21 (February), pp. 148–58.

Yasuba, Yasukichi (1976) 'The Evolution of Dualistic Wage Structure', in Patrick, *Japanese Industrialisation and its Consequences* (Berkeley: University of California Press) pp. 249–298.

Yeh, Stephen H. K. (ed.) (1975) *Public Housing in Singapore* (Singapore: Singapore University Press).

Yoshihara, Kunio (1976) *Foreign Investment and Domestic Response: A Study of Singapore's Industrialization*, (Singapore: Eastern Universities Press).

You Poh Seng and Lim Chong Yah (eds) (1971) *The Singapore Economy* (Singapore: Eastern Universities Press).

You Poh Seng and Lim Chong Yah (eds) (1984) *Singapore: Twenty-five Years of Development* (Singapore: Nan Yang Xing Zhou Lianhe Zaobao).

Young, Alwyn (1992) 'A Tale of Two Cities: Factor Accumulation and Technical Change in Hong Kong and Singapore', in Olivier Jean Blanchard and Stanley Fischer (eds), *NBER Macreconomies Annual 1992* (Cambridge, Massachussetts: MIT Press) pp. 14–54.

Youngman, A. J. (1982) *Hong Kong, Economic Growth and Policy* (Hong Kong: Oxford University Press).

Zeng, Z. X. (1983) *Philosophies and Policies to Disparage and Harness Merchants in Chinese Feudal Society* (Beijing: People's Publisher).

Zymelman, Manuel (1990) 'Science, Education, and Development in Sub-Saharan Africa', World Bank Technical Paper No. 124 (Washington, DC: The World Bank).

Zysman, J. (1983) *Governments, Markets, and Growth: Financial Systems and the Politics of Industrial Change* (Ithaca and London: Cornell University Press).

Index